*Shakespeare Observed*

SAMUEL CROWL

# Shakespeare Observed

*Studies in Performance
on Stage and Screen*

·

OHIO UNIVERSITY PRESS

ATHENS

Ohio University Press books are printed on acid-free paper ∞

Library of Congress Cataloging-in-Publication Data
Crowl, Samuel.
  Shakespeare observed : studies in performance on stage and screen
/ Samuel Crowl.
      p.     cm.
  Includes index.
  ISBN 0–8214–1034–2
  1. Shakespeare, William, 1564–1616—Film and video adaptations.
  2. Shakespeare, William, 1564–1616—Dramatic production.
  3. Shakespeare, William, 1564–1616—Stage history—1950–   I. Title.
PR3093.C76   1992
792.9'5—dc20                                          92–9364
                                                        CIP

Designed by Laury A. Egan

*For Susan, Miranda, and Samuel*

But all the story of the night told over,
And all their minds transfigur'd so together,
More witnesseth than fancy's images,
And grows to something of great constancy;
But howsoever, strange and admirable.

# Contents

# LIST OF ILLUSTRATIONS

(Following page 80)

1. Malcolm (Stephen Chase) insists on being served by Macbeth (Jon Finch). Polanski's *Macbeth*. (British Film Institute)

2. Macbeth (Jonathan Pryce) stirs both his passion and guilt with Lady Macbeth (Sinead Cusack). Adrian Noble's Royal Shakespeare Company production. (Joe Cocks Studio)

3. Doll Tearsheet (Jeanne Moreau) gently scolds her "whoreson tidy Bartholomew boar-pig," Falstaff (Orson Welles). Welles's *Chimes at Midnight*. (British Film Institute)

4. Othello (Orson Welles) and the Carpaccio mirror. Welles's *Othello*. (British Film Institute)

5. Bottom (James Cagney) and Titania (Anita Louise). Reinhardt/Dieterle's *A Midsummer Night's Dream*. (British Film Institute)

6. Bottom (Paul Rogers) and Titania (Judi Dench). Hall's *A Midsummer Night's Dream*. (British Film Institute)

7. Kenneth Anger as the little changeling boy. Reinhardt/Dieterle's *A Midsummer Night's Dream*. (British Film Institute)

8. Prospero (Heathcote Williams) covering the walls with his mathematical projections. Jarman's *Tempest*. (British Film Institute)

9. John Bury's stage design for Peter Hall's National Theatre production of *Hamlet*.

10. Romeo (Anton Lesser) responding to Juliet's presence on the balcony. Ron Daniels's Royal Shakespeare Company production. (Joe Cocks Studio)

11. Juliet (Judy Buxton). Ron Daniels's Royal Shakespeare Company production. (Joe Cocks Studio)

12. The Fool (Antony Sher) and King Lear (Michael Gambon) in their music hall routine. Adrian Noble's Royal Shakespeare Company production of *King Lear*. (Joe Cocks Studio)

[ ix ]

# ACKNOWLEDGMENTS

THE CHAPTERS of this book have led three lives. All but the final chapter were conceived originally as performance pieces to be read or presented at professional meetings and conferences. I am grateful to the organizers of the Ohio Shakespeare Conference, the Shakespeare Association of America, the World Shakespeare Congress, the Modern Language Association, the Midwest Modern Language Association, the Association for Theatre in Higher Education, the University of Illinois, West Virginia University, and Florida State University for inviting me to present early versions of this material to their audiences. Some of those presentations were subsequently revised and expanded into essays for publication. An early version of chapter 2 was published in *Soundings;* a shorter version of chapter 3 appeared in the *Shakespeare Quarterly;* sections of chapter 5 were published in *Literature/Film Quarterly* and *Shakespeare on Film Newsletter;* and the first section of chapter 6, under the title " 'Hid Indeed within the Centre': The Hall/Finney *Hamlet*," appeared in *Shakespeare Survey.*

My late parents, Lester and Margaret Crowl, provided me with an ideal introduction to Shakespeare observing: Alec Guinness's Richard III directed by Tyrone Guthrie on Tanya Moiseiwitsch's revolutionary thrust stage under the tent at Stratford, Ontario, in the summer of 1953. I was twelve. From that moment on Shakespeare became as much a part of this midwestern boy's summer as baseball and fishing.

That early fascination later was nourished and deepened by two extraordinary Shakespeare professors: Edwin Barrett and C. L. Barber. They taught me how to read and taste the "bitter-sweet of this Shakespearean fruit." Though I am sure he is unaware of its impact, Professor Norman Rabkin's lovely, selfless courtesy to two graduate students struggling through the summer of their comprehensive exams at Indiana University has long been cherished as an example of the academic world at its best.

Many friends and past and current colleagues at Ohio University have provided encouragement and support primarily by participating in an ongoing lively conversation about literature and performance, both as art and life. I want particularly to thank Alan Booth, Ben

Geary, Wayne Dodd, John Hollow, Jack Matthews, Dean McWilliams, Stanley Plumly, Calvin Thayer, Shawn Watson, and Edgar Whan. I owe a special debt to Lewis and Susan Greenstein, Edward and Carolyn Quattrocchi and Duane Schneider for the extravagant generosity of their friendship and their personal interest in the progress of this study.

My work has been strengthened by dialogue with Shakespeareans across the country concerned with performance issues, and I wish to thank John F. Andrews, H. C. Coursen, Peter S. Donaldson, Miriam Gilbert, Barbara Hodgdon, Jack Jorgens, Michael Manheim, Michael Mullin, and especially Kenneth Rothwell for including me in such stimulating critical exchanges.

Maurice Daniels arranged for my observership with the Royal Shakespeare Company back in 1980 and has become a warm friend and wonderful source of knowledge about the company he served so well for over twenty-five years. Sir Peter Hall, Trevor Nunn, and Adrian Noble have been quick to respond to my queries over the years about their work, and Ron Daniels and the cast of his *Romeo and Juliet* deserve special thanks for allowing this intruder to observe their fascinating rehearsal work.

Elizabeth Walsh of the Folger Shakespeare Library and Roger Pringle, Sylvia Morris, and Mary White of the Shakespeare Centre Library have been most kind in making the resources of their fine institutions available to me on many occasions. Jane Byrne was extremely helpful in locating still photographs of Shakespeare films in the archives of the British Film Institute. Helen Gawthrop of the Ohio University Press has been an ideal production manager full of patience and sound advice to a novice seeing his first book into print.

Several generations of Ohio University students have challenged my thinking about Shakespeare and in the process have sharpened my response to his plays on the page and in performance. I will single out several who must stand for many: John Culbert, Susan DeFord, Pat Grean, Tim Holm, Brad Lafferty, Chris Moorman, Jane Perez, Douglas Roberts, Scott Roberts, Lynn Rubin, and David Skal.

I am grateful to Ohio University's Experimental Education Fund for granting the resources which allowed me to first develop and teach a course on Shakespeare on film. A University Professorship in 1975 provided the initial stimulus for creating the London Theater Program, and I wish to thank the many undergraduates who have served on the University Professor Selection Committee over the past twenty-two years for their outstanding efforts in rewarding fine teaching.

# Acknowledgments

My colleagues, during the past ten years, in University College have been gracious and patient in indulging a dean who refused to give up teaching and writing about Shakespeare when he entered administration. Patty Pyle, our office manager, deserves special mention for keeping the College running so efficiently while also giving her careful and intelligent attention to every page of this book as it emerged from many drafts. I owe her a debt only those still trapped in the Age of the Typewriter will fully fathom.

My life as Shakespearean and dean has been made infinitely smoother by the support of two exceptional administrators. Provost James Bruning encouraged my teaching and scholarship by his own example; President Charles Ping has become a valued friend who has given his active support to this project from its inception. It has been a pleasure to participate in the renaissance Ohio University has experienced under his leadership.

Professor Susan Crowl is a passionate fellow observer, who has shared many of the performance pleasures recounted here. She has stolen time away from her own work with Browning and James to clear away the tangled scrub which threatened to obscure many of my ideas and much of my prose. The infelicities which remain were too rough-hewn for even her fine hand to shape or prune.

I have been blessed with a family who have eagerly woven Shakespeare into the fabric of our quotidian routine, lived on the edge of a woods in the midst of another Athens. Making this book has been a mixture of work and playing holiday, and it is a rare treat to dedicate it to those who have enlivened and enriched both the work and the play.

*Athens, Ohio*
*October 1991*

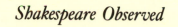

*Shakespeare Observed*

## CHAPTER ONE

# The Art of Observation

•

FOR EXPERIENCED Shakespeare observers all performances are thrice-told tales. The perceiving eye absorbs the performance even as the mind's eye attends to text. Both are augmented by the inner ear buzzing with those other voices, both critical and dramatic, carried by the observer into the theater. This book describes these three tales as they interact in the mind and experience of one Shakespeare observer in the last third of the twentieth century.

In our age Shakespeareans have rediscovered the theater not as a musty museum but as an active site for the exploration of the Shakespearean dynamic as it is rediscovered and reinterpreted by each generation. Although the theatrical and academic worlds rightly continue to regard each other with wary eyes, we are nevertheless living through a period of unprecedented exchange, of spirited dialogue, between literary criticism and production approaches to Shakespeare's plays. Significantly, the path back to the theater as a location for exploring modern and postmodern critical ideas about the nature and meaning of Shakespeare's art has wound through the world of film.

The explosion of campus interest in film in the 1960s and the growing availability of 16mm prints of the major sound Shakespeare films led many professors to begin scheduling several such films to give students some opportunity to experience Shakespeare in one mode of performance. In the process we discovered that many of the available films were far superior to their reputations, often established through dismissive reviews by academic Shakespeareans unknowledgeable about film and unwilling to concede that a performance could ever match or even approximate the vision of the play they carried fixed in their imaginations. Students responded enthusiastically. Ordinarily they were inhibited by Shakespeare's reputation and the reams of critical commentary on the plays and were often reticent to contribute to class discussions. They were, however, eager to talk about how films coupled Shakespeare's words with moving images.

Classes devoted to discussions of Shakespeare's films became a communal enterprise. Because students often had only a single opportunity to see the film, class became a vital moment when everyone's perceptions counted and had to be pooled as a resource for all. This was a fertile moment for such explorations because the period from Akira Kurosawa's *Throne of Blood* (1957) to Roman Polanski's *Macbeth* (1971) proved to be the richest in the history of sound-filmed Shakespeare, giving us, among many, Orson Welles's *Chimes At Midnight* (1966), Franco Zeffirelli's *Romeo and Juliet* (1968), Peter Hall's *A Midsummer Night's Dream* (1969), Grigori Kozintsev's *Hamlet* (1964) and *King Lear* (1970), and Peter Brook's *King Lear* (1970). It was a heady era, and performance criticism became one of the voices beginning to challenge traditional approaches which focused exclusively on Shakespeare's text, as though Shakespeare had written with an audience of eager academic New Critics in mind rather than for the polyglot assemblages who found their way to the liberties—as Steven Mullaney has so brilliantly demonstrated—in search of outlaw pleasure and excitement on any given Elizabethan afternoon.[1]

Film gave us our liberty in thinking and writing about Shakespeare, and that led us and our students back to the theater. Shakespeare has blossomed in a variety of soils and climates around the globe, but a sustained Shakespearean theatrical tradition thrives on its native grounds in London and Stratford. As international airfares lowered, they created a boom in college study-abroad programs. Taking groups of American students to London and Stratford for intensive theater study became as easy and inexpensive as taking them to New York, where the classical diet was generally far less steady or rich. It also became so common that it became the subject of Richard Nelson's witty and acerbic parody of such sojourners, *Some Americans Abroad*, first produced, appropriately, by the Royal Shakespeare Company in 1989.

One of Trevor Nunn's innovations with the Royal Shakespeare Company was making its work and its approach to Shakespeare more available to students and scholars through a variety of programs which took actors from the company out into British schools and communities to discuss their work, brought them to American campuses through the Center for Theatre, Education, and Research at the University of California at Santa Barbara, and brought Shakespeare scholars and theater professionals to Stratford to observe the company in rehearsal and to use the facilities of the Shakespeare

Centre and the Shakespeare Institute. Under the inspired leadership of Maurice Daniels, the RSC's development administrator in the 1970s, Stratford became not just a center for the historical study of Shakespearean performances there but a site where academic scholars and theater professionals could, however uneasily, begin to engage in dialogue. By the 1980s, our own National Endowment for the Humanities was underwriting summer seminars for high school and college teachers held in Stratford-upon-Avon under the tutelage of such distinguished American Shakespeare scholars as Miriam Gilbert and Jay Halio, pioneers in the performance approach to teaching and writing about the plays.

During this time, the leadership of British Shakespeare devolved from the actor-managers to the new breed of university-educated directors. These men, most of whom had read English at Cambridge, felt less estranged from the work of academic Shakespeareans. Though the stories are legion of Tyrone Guthrie's and Laurence Olivier's consultations with Ernest Jones to pluck the heart out of Hamlet's and Iago's mysteries, the interchange between director and literary critic had been the exception not the rule.

Again, the tradition changed when Peter Hall took charge of direction at Stratford. As Hall has repeatedly documented, two critical influences dominated his program at Stratford: his National Service experience in Germany, where he witnessed the fruits of state support for permanent theatrical companies, and his own intellectual experience at Cambridge, particularly in his exposure to F. R. Leavis and his iconoclastic ideas about text and society. Coupled with Hall's attraction to Leavis, and his devoted attention to the moral seriousness of literary texts, came Peter Brook's championing of the work of Jan Kott, whose collection of essays *Shakespeare Our Contemporary* can be seen as a central work in the shift away from the new critical approach to unpacking Shakespeare's art.

Kott and Leavis, admittedly, make an odd couple, but they provided stimulus to Hall and Brook as they struggled to find and consolidate a modern approach to speaking Shakespeare's verse and a modern way of visualizing the look and shape of a Shakespeare production. Their own imaginative synthesis of Kott and Leavis adapted Leavis's cool and ironic approach to the text to the speaking of Shakespeare's verse and produced an anti-rhetorical verbal style that neatly mirrored Kott's chilling middle-European reading of the plays. Such an approach allowed them new avenues into a Shakespeare no longer constrained as a Renaissance apologist for the sanctity of

[ 5 ]

hierarchy as presented in E. M. W. Tillyard's influential *Elizabethan World Picture*.

Hall and Brook were determined to make the repertory system work, and to do so meant a stress on company rather than star. The success of their efforts has led to one of the richest periods in the history of British Shakespeare. It led to a revolution in the critical world as well. RSC productions like the Hall-Barton *The Wars of the Roses*, Brook's *King Lear*, Hall's *Hamlet*, and Brook's *A Midsummer Night's Dream* drew new audiences to Stratford, audiences who came to see heralded productions rather than star actors. These productions were different in look and feel and sound. They represented a radical break with past production traditions. As they have now passed into the realm of theatrical legend it is worth remembering that, like many of the now lauded Shakespeare films, they were often met with initial hostility by both academics and the press.

As mentioned above, the Hall-Brook approach accomplished the transfer of attention from star actor to the developing work of a company of performers. Such an approach allowed the academic Shakespearean access to such productions because interpretative developments could be charted over time within a relatively stable group of actors and directors rather than across the career of a star performer—a Gielgud, Olivier, or Richardson—as he moved through a series of Shakespeare roles in a wide variety of contexts from occasional seasons at the Old Vic or Stratford to West End productions under their own management to productions developed for tours to Europe or America.

This approach also spelled the end of the career of the most brilliant drama reviewer of the post-war period, Kenneth Tynan, although he clearly recognized this development and was an early supporter of the work of both Hall and Brook. Tynan's critical genius had been his ability to describe the galvanizing moments of heroic acting, and his prime subject was, of course, Laurence Olivier. Olivier was the actor who sparked and shaped Tynan's adoration, and the dazzle of Tynan's verbal descriptions of Olivier's studied histrionics often rival the performance itself. It was therefore fitting that this second odd couple should have combined to be the first leaders of the National Theatre; just as Olivier made the move to establish the actor-manager tradition at the very heart of British public cultural policy, that tradition was being supplanted by the success of Peter Hall's work at Stratford.

# The Art of Observation

Significantly, no heroic actor has emerged in the past thirty years to pick up Olivier's mantle (with the possible exception of Vanessa Redgrave), and no troika has developed to rival the extended impact of Olivier, Gielgud, and Richardson. Instead, in a shift paralleling the revision of values in the plays, the company system has created a remarkably versatile core group of British actors who have moved between the two major companies and into the West End, television, and film with ease and grace. Any such list, at its minimum, would include Ian Holm, Ian Richardson, Richard Pasco, Judi Dench, Alan Howard, David Warner, Diana Rigg, Albert Finney, Helen Mirren, John Wood, Paul Rogers, Paul Scofield, Ben Kingsley, Glenda Jackson, Michael Pennington, John Woodvine, Roger Rees, Patrick Stewart, Susan Fleetwood, Anton Lesser, Sinead Cusack, Jeremy Irons, Michael Gambon, Michael Bryant, Juliet Stevenson, Jonathan Pryce, Brian Cox, Fiona Shaw, Derek Jacobi, Ian McKellen, Anthony Hopkins, David Suchet, and Antony Sher. If we have lost the meteors, surely we have gained new constellations along with a broader view of the heavens.

•

TRADITIONALLY there have been three types of performance criticism: historical, biographical, and impressionistic. The first has been largely the province of theater historians, the second of professional biographers, and the third of press or magazine critics supplemented by the academics who provided annual summary reviews of productions for such journals as *Shakespeare Survey* and *Shakespeare Quarterly*. With the advent of serious attention to Shakespeare films and Shakespeare productions, particularly those by the Royal Shakespeare Company, a new form of performance criticism has quietly developed in the past twenty-five years. The explosion of contemporary performance criticism has its roots in the 1960s when the New Criticism began to yield its hold on Shakespeare studies. Critics like Northrop Frye, C. L. Barber, and Norman Rabkin began to absorb insights from anthropology, Freudian psychology, and quantum physics into their work with Shakespeare, opening up avenues of critical exploration of the Shakespearean dynamic much broader than those afforded by the methodology of the New Criticism. The expanses of Shakespeare's vision and canon have always been more open to a pluralistic approach than the work of poets like Donne and Herbert, whose lyrics found such congenial resonance with the New

[ 7 ]

Critical approach, and structuralists—whether grounded in Frazer, Saussure, Freud, Marx, Biblical studies, or Levi-Strauss—found Shakespeare an inviting territory. As these critics opened up potential new approaches to Shakespeare, they helped pave the way for serious discussion of contemporary film and stage performances of the plays as an essential ingredient in the postmodern dialogue about the workings of Shakespeare's art.

The publication in 1977 of Jack Jorgen's *Shakespeare on Film* and a year later of Richard David's *Shakespeare in the Theatre* marks the first book-length critical studies which took full measure of film and stage performances and treated them to extended analysis and discussion.[2] Within a decade of their appearance performance criticism and performance approaches to teaching Shakespeare in the classroom had become one of the dominant strains in Shakespeare studies. Under O. B. Hardison's leadership, the Folger Shakespeare Library became active in the performance movement by sponsoring a permanent repertory company in the library's theater, establishing a film and video archive,and supporting John Andrews's efforts to incorporate more descriptive and critical attention to Shakespearean performances around the world in the pages of *Shakespeare Quarterly*.

By 1989 performance criticism was so well established that one of Renaissance studies' most respected and inventive critics, Harry Berger, Jr., could focus an entire book on wrestling with issues related to text and performance, to the possible ways readers and spectators respond to Shakespeare on page and stage. The book's great achievement, I believe, lies more with its subtle and challenging reading of several key moments in *Richard II* than with its attempts to dismiss the claims of performance criticism.[3] Berger's quarrel is less with performance critics like Philip McGuire, Gary Taylor, and Barbara Hodgdon than with Richard Levin, whose *New Readings vs. Old Plays* hardly qualifies as a work of performance criticism. Levin's work attempts to use a performance norm to reduce and deflate some of modern Shakespeare criticism's most fanciful flights. I do not wish to claim an exclusive right for performance criticism nor to create a hierarchy between various branches of critical approaches to Shakespeare. Lively criticism is not determined by its category but by the intelligence, wit, and imagination of its author. Shakespeare critics as diverse as Stephen Greenblatt, Stanley Cavell, Coppélia Kahn, and, yes, Harry Berger, Jr., all are powerful, inventive voices in the contemporary polyphony which distinguishes and vitalizes

Shakespeare studies. The essays in this study attempt to build bridges between traditional criticism and the performance event whether on film or on stage.

My own tastes, in criticism as well as performance, are eclectic. Orson Welles's boast at age nineteen that "every single way of playing and staging Shakespeare—as long as the way is effective—is right" still hasn't lost its innocent bloom for me.[4] The problem is, of course, how to define and determine what is effective and why. I am as drawn, for instance, to Berger's sport with language ("The New Histrionicism," "a rousing Hotspurious finish," "death by crowning") as I am to the wonderfully outrageous comic details which distinguish the creation of Falstaff and Pistol, for instance, in Michael Bogdanov's productions of *1* and *2* *Henry IV* with the English Shakespeare Company. Berger, in my judgment, reacts too strongly to Levin's attempts to set performance *against* criticism. My effort is to link performance *and* criticism and to see the possibilities for performance *as* criticism.[5]

Berger's attempt to derail or "rerail" performance criticism came just at the moment when this study and several other performance-based works by critics as varied as Anthony Davies, John Collick, Peter S. Donaldson, Lorne Buchman, and Barbara Hodgdon were reaching fruition.[6] Four of these volumes are the first book-length studies of Shakespearean films since Jorgens's pioneering work. Davies's work is a study of the differences in film space and stage space particularly as those contrasts are reflected in Olivier's and Welles's Shakespeare films. Collick's Cultural Materialist analysis stands in sharp contrast to Davies's work. Collick, ambitiously, attempts to assess the cultural means of production surrounding the creation of major Shakespearean films from the silents to the Reinhardt-Dieterle *A Midsummer Night's Dream* to Olivier's *Henry V* to Welles's *Othello* to Kurosawa's *Ran* as an alternative to treating such films as the realized visions of the *auteur* director or as recognizable versions of mainstream critical thinking about Shakespeare's plays. Often the range of Collick's analysis strains in its efforts to make individual films carry the weight (and burden) of vast social and political ideas. I find his attempt to read Orson Welles's *Othello* in such terms particularly puzzling, but Collick's treatment of Kozintsev's and Kurosawa's Shakespeare films are much more successful explorations of how particular cultures appropriate and represent Shakespeare. However, I am perplexed by his judgment that Kurosawa's devastatingly destructive *Ran* "suffers for its optimism."[7]

[ 9 ]

Donaldson's *Shakespearean Films/Shakespearean Directors* works from the inside out as he explores, from a psychoanalytic perspective, elements in the lives of Olivier, Welles, Kurosawa, and Zeffirelli which resonate with their reconstruction of Shakespearean themes and images on film. If Collick paints his socio-political analysis with a broad brush, Donaldson works more like the old mole burrowing into flat surfaces and uncovering startling depths of perspective. Donaldson, through clearly working from a postmodern perspective, does not shy from calling his essays "readings," and I subscribe to his belief that "films are texts: replayable, repeatable, and subject to multiple interpretations."[8]

The final contribution to this new feast of studies in film criticism is Lorne Buchman's *Still in Movement*. Buchman isolates several key film devices such as *mise-en-scène* or the spatial field of the close-up as a means of understanding how filmmakers, particularly Welles and Kozintsev, have employed them to shape the unique ways Shakespeare is interpreted by film. Though his academic background is in theater, Buchman concentrates his analysis almost exclusively on film, confessing that "considerations of stage practice . . . arise, but they do so only to clarify how the drama becomes a product of the cinematic medium and how film activates the imagination of the spectator in a unique manner."[9]

It is more difficult, though not impossible, to make the same claim for stage performances that Donaldson does for films where we do not have the same liberty that the videocassette recorder affords for suspending time and lingering over a specific scene or image. Philip McGuire's *Speechless Dialect* taught us the interpretive necessity of reading the performance of Shakespeare's open silences (Hippolyta's reaction to Theseus at the opening of *A Midsummer Night's Dream*, Isabella's response to the Duke's marriage proposal at the conclusion of *Measure for Measure*, Lear's final moments, etc.) as a key to the way in which performances complete, extend, and confound traditional notions of what constitutes Shakespeare's text. McGuire's multiple examples drawn from a range of separate productions of these crucial scenes have the effect of stopping, or isolating, such performance moments for critical scrutiny.[10] McGuire's groundbreaking work is extended and enlarged in Barbara Hodgdon's exhaustive analysis of closure in Shakespeare's history plays. The generous reach of Hodgdon's critical intelligence and her intimate knowledge of British Shakespeare productions over the past two decades allow her to fashion the most ambitious synthesis of performance and criticism yet to appear. Hodgdon confronts the distinctions which attempt to divide reading and observing, text and performance, by remarking:

> On the one hand, there is a self-individuated private project, resulting in a text (the critical reading) that replaces the play with another text; on the other hand, a collectively understood and collectively mediated performance, a public project that *replaces* the play within a theatrical and cultural space. Although the final *products* (the critical reading, the performance) do indeed differ, the *processes* that generate each text, each "performance," so to speak, share more similarities than differences. Indeed, alteration, interruption, and intervention are features endemic to imagining and creating both sorts of text.[11]

Hodgdon rightly notes that when performances delete or rearrange lines from the text it's called "cutting," but when the same process occurs in any critical reading "it is called constructing an argument."[12]

The wealth of voices and perspectives contained in these studies, including Berger's skepticism, attest to the contemporary vigor of performance criticism. My own contribution to the enterprise is at once more personal and less theoretical, as it charts a developing dialogue between and among film and stage productions themselves as well as with their interaction with the world of literary criticism and theory, long viewed as antagonistic to the performance process.

Writing about performance in an extended and detailed manner is difficult but challenging. As Richard Poirier observed in 1972 in the preface to his collection of remarkably prescient essays, *The Performing Self*:

> Anyone who can describe any kind of performance with accuracy and fascination—in rock or in a sonata, in boxing or in ballet—has already developed an attentiveness and a vocabulary which can be adapted to a reading of, say, the plays of Shakespeare, a better reading indeed, than they have received from all but a few Shakespeareans.[13]

In Poirier's sense, all literature is performance, and poems and novels and essays dance for an audience of one with nothing mediating between our eyes and the page except our imaginations. The worlds of drama and film, however, present a series of complicated layers between audience and word, words which we read both by eye and ear. With Shakespeare, we are confronted by poetry made tangible by the actor's voice and body located in a specific landscape and defined by the sweep of pattern and movement and design which gives Shakespeare's world "a local habitation and a name." The performance critic has an entire host of deconstructive and reconstructive partners—from actor to designer to director with an assortment of professional technicians thrown into the mix—who already have had their play with the text and bring to him or her their version of that experience. These intermediaries become even more complex in the world of film, a complexity which heightens the director's power and ability to shape and edit the viewer's experience.

None of this is surely surprising, and much of it is covered with more wit and grace in Jonathan Miller's recent disquisition, *Subsequent Performances*.[14] What is surprising is that no critic has thought to see and stress the natural resonance between performance criticism and the central issues raised by postmodern literary criticism. For example, as criticism undertakes to deconstruct ideology and discover marginal voices and perspectives, so performance criticism directs our attention to silences and subtexts. The inversions of response consequent on the release of such marginal energies are radically illustrated by our interest in Russian and Japanese Shakespearean films. It is perhaps no surprise that many American and British critics see Kozintsev's *Hamlet* and *King Lear* and Kurosawa's *Throne of Blood* and *Ran* as the greatest Shakespeare films ever made, because they are experiences where the words (subtitles) march across the margins of a series of images ironically diverting our eyes and attention from the images, which are film's true text.

If this is a paradox suggesting that poetry, the *raison d'être* of performance, is rendered by performance at best expendable and at worst distracting, yet it is in some sense a paradox at the heart of performance, where the words spring to life only when released and captured in a symbolic landscape which resonates between word, actor, setting, and design. This paradox has been a frustrating one for Shakespeareans reared when modernism held sway but who have survived to struggle with such issues in our Age of Theory. I well remember a typical expression of that frustration voiced at the first Ohio Shakespeare Conference held in 1977. I had the enviable task of making some introductory remarks prior to a screening of Kozintsev's *King Lear*. I had just advised the audience of assembled Shakespeareans to keep their eyes on the entire frame to fully absorb Kozintsev's art rather than deflecting them to catch the subtitles flashed along the bottom. I said "Forget the words. They are Pasternak's reworked back into Shakespeare's. Keep your eyes on the images." This seemed to me perfectly reasonable advice, but it was too much for one of the conferees (a distinguished textual scholar) who rose to stammer in a voice choked with rage and incomprehension, "I must protest. This just won't do. I can't believe I've come all this way to a Shakespeare Conference to be told not to pay any attention to the words!"

My intent is to talk about words *and* images; if the latter are often given more emphasis it is only in an attempt to restore a better balance in our understanding of the ways in which Shakespeare stimulates the visual as well as the aural imagination.

·

I READ the famous opening line of Stephen Greenblatt's *Shakespearean Negotiations*, "I begin with the desire to speak with the dead," as his own melancholy means of distancing himself from those followers of Kott who have been relentless in wanting to make exclusive conversation with the "living Shakespeare."[5] Yet while Greenblatt's New Historicism explores Shakespearean territory far removed from contemporary performance criticism, both approaches surely participate in similar critical assumptions about the nature of the text and its exclusive province as a subject of Shakespearean inquiry. I would also challenge any reader of *Renaissance Self-Fashioning* or a chapter such as "Fiction or Friction" from *Shakespearean Negotiations* to deny that, even if they are not reading performance criticism, they are certainly reading criticism which takes great pleasure, and deservedly so, in its performance.

In fact, as we secretly acknowledge, all great criticism is a form of performance which at the same moment both rivals and reveals the text or texts it seeks to elucidate. Rather than seeing recent trends in literary theory in general and Shakespearean criticism in particular as a radical departure from past practice I prefer to highlight its continuity. C. L. Barber's work, in particular, has had a profound impact on many of the key contributors to postmodern Shakespeare criticism. Barber himself was a thoroughgoing modernist whose favorite twentieth-century writers were Eliot, Yeats, and Joyce and whose critical mentors were F. O. Matthiessen and I. A. Richards. What Barber added to the modernist approach was his interest in anthropology and Freudian psychology. Barber has clearly been the most influential American Shakespeare critic of his generation, as witnessed by the number of volumes which have been dedicated to his memory, the number of prefaces where his example and encouragement are given place of prominence, and the variety of critical camps who acknowledge the continuing vitality of his ideas by sparring with them at central moments in their arguments. His legacy has been further extended by the publication of Richard Wheeler's own magnificent restoration and completion of the two manuscripts Barber worked on throughout the years between 1960 and his untimely death in 1980, which allow Barber's voice and developing ideas to speak to a much larger audience than those of us fortunate enough to have been exposed to them in seminar, lecture hall, conversation, and correspondence.

Barber has not been acknowledged previously in print as an inspiration for many of us working in performance criticism, but he did extend his extraordinarily generous critical intelligence to our efforts as well. Such efforts he applauded not only for expanding the realm of Shakespeare criticism but because our work was grounded in a setting essentially social and communal: the theater. Barber used his influence in the Shakespeare Association of America to make panels and paper sections and seminars focusing on film and stage performances a regular part of its annual meeting. Barber's criticism and the grace with which he shared his critical intelligence with the larger community of Shakespeareans stands as a testimony to the continuities in the Shakespearean dialogue in our time.

Building on those continuities, the essays in this book seek to develop a dialogue between stage and film productions of Shakespeare and the critical discourse surrounding his plays. Studies devoted to films of Shakespeare's plays rarely make mention of how specific stage productions have handled similar scenes as the very recent work of Davies, Buchman, and Donaldson continues to reveal. It is even rarer to encounter an extended analysis of a stage production which sets it in detailed contrast with a film except, perhaps, to make comparison with a famous central performance such as Olivier's Henry V or Richard III. And as critical interest in performance has developed precisely because it had been ignored by traditional academic approaches to Shakespeare, little was done by the originators of the movement to bridge the two experiences, to be alert to, to literally *see*, relationships between critical ideas and production strategies.

This book, then, tries to tell a story, one with several interwoven strands. The overarching narrative line is that modern film and stage productions of Shakespeare's plays warrant and reward full attention in the continuing dialogue about Shakespeare's contribution to his own culture and to ours. The past thirty years have seen two revolutions at work in Shakespeare studies, one in performance and the other in criticism. As Shakespeare scholars have come to learn more about the art and craft of making films, they have come to an increased understanding of the contributions of filmmakers as diverse as Orson Welles and Laurence Olivier in the translation of Shakespeare into a new medium. Their films have had a cumulative impact upon Shakespearean performance far beyond any single stage interpretation because they exist to be continually reexperienced and reevaluated by new generations of performers and directors. As I indicate in my chapter on Polanski's *Macbeth*, when Antony Sher and Kenneth Branagh were preparing to play Richard III and Henry V at Stratford in the summer of 1984, the performances vividly lodged in their memories were not those of Alan Howard or Ian Holm, who had last played the roles for the RSC, but of Laurence Olivier, whose performances of three and four decades earlier had been permanently captured on film.

By looking specifically at such films as Polanski's *Macbeth* and Welles's *Chimes at Midnight* and *Othello* and the Reinhardt-Dieterle *A Midsummer Night's Dream*, I attempt to establish a dialogue among these films, critical ideas about Shakespeare ranging from E. M. W. Tillyard to the present, and interesting parallels between such films and recent British stage productions of the plays. Thus the chapter on Polanski's *Macbeth*, for example, looks back to explore the film's debt to Jan Kott's ideas about the play and then pushes forward to discuss the impact of that film on Adrian Noble's 1986 production of *Macbeth* for the Royal Shakespeare Company.

Peter Hall, the figure who has been the dominant force in the British theatrical world of the last thirty years, occupies a pivotal place in this study. Two chapters focus on Hall's work and attempt to assess his impact on Shakespeare productions in our age through readings of his film of *A Midsummer Night's Dream* (1969) and his productions of *Hamlet* (1976) and *Antony and Cleopatra* (1987), which bracket his work with Shakespeare during his years of leadership of the National Theatre. Through his creation of the Royal Shakespeare Company and his successful, if controversial, guidance of the National Theatre, Hall is universally recognized as having brought new ideas, new standards, and new energies to the ways Shakespeare is produced. Hall has been so successful that the revolution he led has now become the Establishment and so subject to easy dismissal by those who seek to lead the next turn in the cultural cycle.

Some cultural observers believe that the progress of Hall's work at the National and Trevor Nunn's at Stratford created two gigantic institutions, neither capable of being shaped by a single dominant personality and that both theaters are in danger of being swamped by their own success. Some have never warmed to the National Theatre's architecture, dismissing it as the Bunker on the South Bank, while others continue to deride the enormous expense of artistic energy and financial resources needed to keep three theaters going surrounded by platform performances, foyer concerts, several bars, two restaurants, and three bookstores. And Stratford has become equally omnivorous and complex, operating three theaters in Stratford, two in London (and for a while a third at the Mermaid), a season in Newcastle, and regularly creating touring productions to reach into small towns and communities which have no regular access to Shakespeare. While the cultural politics which inevitably swirl around two institutions so at the center of the national life can complicate the responses of British Shakespeare observers to their productions, to those of us who live far from the daily debate, such controversies seem irrelevant in the face of such exceptional recent productions as Deborah Warner's *Titus Andronicus*, Peter Hall's *Antony and Cleopatra*, Trevor Nunn's *Othello*, Ron Daniels's *Hamlet*, and Richard Eyre's *Richard III*.

As an analysis of Peter Hall's direction of Shakespeare occupies the center of this study, so it is perhaps fitting that Kenneth Branagh, born in the year that Hall founded the RSC, should be the focus of my final chapter. Branagh's film of *Henry V* stands as an excellent summary example of the themes and ideas which preoccupy this study. His film has its roots in Adrian Noble's 1984 production of *Henry V* (itself influenced by contemporary critical debate about the play), while also being deeply conscious of Laurence Olivier's famous film made during World War II. Branagh has not only created a film in the actor-director tradition of Olivier and Welles but established his own theatrical company as well. His example joins that of the director Michael Bogdanov and the actor Michael Pennington, who broke away from associations with both the RSC and the National Theatre to create the English Shakespeare Company in 1986.

The Bogdanov-Pennington collaboration in mounting the ambitious and inventive staging of *The Wars of the Roses* demonstrates the continuing vitality, vigor, and health of the Shakespearean enterprise. Bogdanov, and Pennington, clearly starting out to create an anti-establishment approach to producing Shakespeare far from the permanent center of the country's cultural life, ended up creating their own cultural monster which grew from three plays to seven, survived several major recastings, and emerged as a self-renewing work-in-progress, gaining energy and momentum from each new addition to the cast. The company and its production initially was imagined as a touring ensemble created to bring Shakespeare to English cities bypassed by the major companies, pitching and breaking camp each week or two like the circus, but grew to tour three continents, to challenge and delight audiences across Europe, North America, Australia, and Japan, and to make periodic returns to the Old Vic, ironically, the first home of the National Theatre.

If Hall is the classicist and Bogdanov the iconoclast in their directorial approaches to Shakespeare, the work of Ron Daniels and Adrian Noble can be seen as occupying the eclectic middle ground. The chapter on Daniels's *Romeo and Juliet* at Stratford in 1980, reveals another kind of observing. In this instance I was fortunate to be able to observe the process, the work-in-progress, as well as the final production as it emerged from almost eight weeks of rehearsals. Rather than presenting an extended critical analysis of the production, I have tried to let the rehearsal process speak for itself—as though shot in a series of close-ups with a hand-held camera—through selections from a diary I kept of the experience.

The chapter on Adrian Noble's work tries to give the flavor of the director I believe to be the inheritor of the tradition established, revised, and extended by Brook, Hall, Barton, and Nunn at the Royal Shakespeare Company.[16] Noble's work interests me because of its imaginative eclecticism, its clear ability to nurture startling performances from unexpected sources (Gambon's Lear, Sher's Fool, Stevenson's Rosalind, and Henson's Touchstone spring immediately to mind), and its affinity for creating company moments as electrifying as the individual ones we came to expect a generation earlier from Laurence Olivier. Noble also strikes me as a stage director intimately drawn to film culture and who has found ways to transform film devices into his stage productions: he is thus a director who extends and unites the Shakespearean legacies of Peter Hall and Orson Welles.

These essays participate in a dialogue they also seek to reveal between the realms of film, literary criticism, and stage productions of Shakespeare. The art of observation, as Othello and Heisenberg discovered, can be deceiving and even perilous. We often see what our imagination wills us to see. What we think we see is often a conjuring trick inspired by an artist's knowing nudge or whisper. Our seeing often subtly changes the performance phenomenon unfolding before us. The physicist and astronomer James Gunn, speaking of the problems associated with cosmological observations, notes: "Observers tend to overinterpret their observations. Theorists tend to overinterpret the observations even more."[7] Gunn offers an important corrective not only to his fellow cosmologists but to those of us working in performance criticism as well. Fortunately, in the world of performance the art of observation is a communal one: we see and respond together, and these essays attempt to articulate ways of recovering those pleasures we have shared in several modern film and stage productions of Shakespeare.

## CHAPTER TWO

# Chain Reaction:
# Polanski's *Macbeth* and
# Its Legacy

•

THOSE of us who began two decades ago to pay serious scholarly and critical attention to films based on Shakespeare's plays thought we were entering a ripe and rich period in the often contentious marriage of Shakespeare and film. The 1960s, after all, had brought us—to name just a few prime examples—Orson Welles's *Chimes at Midnight* (1966), Grigori Kozintsev's *Hamlet* (1964) and *King Lear* (1970), Peter Hall's *A Midsummer Night's Dream* (1969), Peter Brook's *King Lear* (1970), and perhaps most important, from a commercial perspective, Franco Zeffirelli's *Romeo and Juliet* (1968). Jack Jorgens concluded a much more inclusive list of that decade's achievements by commenting, "It is an impressive list, and it will continue to grow."[1]

Now, as the 1990s begin, we are buoyed by the success of Kenneth Branagh's *Henry V* and the appearance of Zeffirelli's *Hamlet*, but the last two decades indisputably failed to live up to Jorgens's prediction. The period from 1971 to 1989 brought us only four major films of Shakespeare's plays: Charlton Heston's *Antony and Cleopatra* (1972), which was never commercially released; Derek Jarman's *Tempest* (1980), which was a low-budget, highly personal, and idiosyncratic treatment which never received wide distribution; Akira Kurosawa's *Ran* (1985), which is the one assured post-1960s masterpiece and will rank with his *Throne of Blood* as one of the greatest reimaginings of a Shakespeare play within another language and culture; and Roman Polanski's *Macbeth* (1971).

What happened? The commercial and critical failure of Polanski's *Macbeth* had the combined effect of frightening off both the big-money producers—whose interest in Shakespeare had been momentarily quickened by the commercial and critical success of Zeffirelli's *Romeo and Juliet*—and major directors who might have been tempted to take a crack at Shakespeare had Polanski's film captured and expanded the audience created by Zeffirelli. The reception of Polanski's film only solidified the Scottish tragedy's theatrical reputation as a work doomed to devastating failure in production. The other factor which led to the collapse of independent production interest in Shakespeare was the BBC project to create television versions of the entire canon. Since Olivier's *Henry V,* interest in making large—or small—scale films of Shakespeare's plays generally sprang from a desire to translate or reimagine a successful stage production or single great performance into film.

Olivier's films of *Hamlet* and *Richard III* belong to this category, as do Tony Richardson's *Hamlet* with Nicol Williamson, Peter Brook's *King Lear* with Paul Scofield, and Kenneth Branagh's recent *Henry V.* The 1960s and early 1970s were also peppered with television adaptations of interesting stage productions. The Hall-Barton *The Wars of the Roses*, the Papp-Antoon *Much Ado About Nothing*, and Trevor Nunn's *Antony and Cleopatra* are three such notable examples. Rather than such successful stage productions becoming the models for future televized Shakespeare, the BBC series had the chilling effect of absorbing and dominating the market, so that the interest of rival, independent, networks—Thames TV for instance—became severely limited, giving us only Trevor Nunn's magnificent *Macbeth* and *Othello* from among many splendid Royal Shakesepeare Company productions over the past fifteen years and none of Peter Hall's work with Shakespeare over the same period at the National Theatre. We have been treated to a rival version of *King Lear* made by Granada Television with Olivier in his final Shakespearean role, but very few other such productions of merit have emerged during a period distinguished by dynamic stagings of Shakespeare's plays. The BBC chill became an even deeper freeze when the vast majority of their productions proved to be stilted and lifeless, even when the series was in the hands of the otherwise inventive and mercurial Jonathan Miller.

Interestingly, as we have lived through this fallow period in the history of Shakespeare and film, we have been blessed with an explosion of brilliant stage productions of Shakespeare in France, in Japan, in Russia, in America, and most prominently, in Britain. Contrary to the warnings about the negative effects of what we have come to call Director's Theatre on the performance of Shakespeare and the loss of the actor-manager tradition as exemplified by a Laurence Olivier, the last two decades have spawned perhaps the greatest single generation of Shakespearean actors in British theater history. It is true that the repertory system has precluded the emergence of two or three dominant stars who have defined Shakespearean acting in the contemporary world as Olivier, Gielgud, Richardson, and Ashcroft did for almost thirty years from the mid-1930s to the mid-1960s. But the ensemble system has produced a collection of actors unrivaled in the ease with which they move between Shakespeare, Ibsen, Chekhov, Shaw, Pinter, Shaffer, Hare, and Ayckbourn.

John Peter has written, in response to Peter Hall's *Antony and Cleopatra* (1987), that "golden ages of the theatre are usually in the past—but we may be living in one today."[2] Obviously, I agree with Peter's assessment and believe that such a golden age spans the past quarter century and can be dated from the moment Peter Hall was given direction of the Memorial Theatre at Stratford, a moment which was followed in a few years with a similar invitation to Laurence Olivier to accept direction of the new National Theatre. Thus we have the irony that the greatest heroic actor of our century was moving to reestablish the actor-manager tradition, now as an instrument of national cultural policy, at precisely the historical moment that such a tradition was to be made obsolete by Hall's subsequent success at Stratford and his move to succeed Olivier at the National in 1973.

If the success of the RSC and the National Theatre in the past two decades coupled with the magnitude of the BBC Shakespeare project has served, paradoxically, to shift interest in Shakespeare productions away from film and video to the stage, it is a further paradox of cultural cross-fertilization that many of those stage productions are distinguished by their cinematic qualities. It was film, after all, which gave us the concept of the *auteur* and raised the director to a stature to supplant screenwriter and star. If the repertory system has produced more great actors, but fewer stars, it has also produced a group of directors whose stage work is scrutinized as closely as the films of a Hitchcock, Ford, Fellini, or Bergman. Names such as Peter Hall, Peter Brook, John Barton, Buzz Goodbody, Jonathan Miller, Terry Hands, Michael Bogdanov, Bill Alexander, Ron Daniels, Barry Kyle, Adrian Noble, and Deborah Warner are as familiar to professional and lay Shakespeareans as are those of the actors featured in their productions. The modern mode of speaking Shakespeare's verse, pioneered at Stratford by Hall and Barton and Cicely Berry, stressed the colloquial and conversational qualities of his art rather than the rhetorical, which has more affinity with the flat, underplayed delivery of film dialogue than with an older stage tradition of declaiming, even singing, Shakespeare's verse.

The spare, sparse, monochromatic set and costume designs which dominated RSC productions in the early Hall years were derived, I believe, as much from the influence of the great black-and-white films of Bergman, Welles, and Renoir as from the more obvious influence of Brecht and contributed to create a modern, anticeremonial, antirhetorical approach to these plays. The emphasis was on the words and their meaning—rather than their sound or rhythmic beauty—and they issued forth from a background which was not allowed to distract from their primacy.

As films in the 1950s and 1960s came to dominate more and more our culture and in the hands of great directors to be regarded as essential works of art rather than passing entertainments, so they became an intimate and integral part of the cultural landscape inhabited by the younger directors who followed in the Hall-Brook wake. It is also the case that as films based on Shakespeare's plays became the subject of scholarly study and debate they too entered the general cultural dialogue more prominently, and with the advent of videotapes, they became a part of the permanent Shakespearean landscape. Such films have a power that reaches far beyond any stage production, which can live on only through memory and isolated summary. Thus it should come as no surprise that when Antony Sher and Kenneth Branagh were preparing to play Richard III and Henry V at Stratford in 1984 the face peering over their shoulders was not that of Alan Howard, who had played the roles most recently at Stratford, or of Ian Holm, who had done both in famous productions in the Hall era, but of Laurence Olivier whose film performances of these roles are still vitally with us.[3]

I want to turn now to an analysis of Roman Polanski's *Macbeth*, the last big-budget English-language film of Shakespeare to be made and released between 1971 and 1989 whose commercial failure significantly contributed to the collapse of a financial market for other Shakespearean projects. Interestingly, the film is far superior to its reputation and is as cinematically elegant and sophisticated, however violent and brutal, as any Shakespeare film in the canon. Jack Jorgens is quite correct to see "that Polanski has made quite a good film, thoughtful in its interpretation-translation of the play, filled with significant imagery, subtle connections, and imaginative creations."[4] He is also right to see that Polanski's countryman, Jan Kott, played an important role in the film's conception.

In the late 1960s many stage and film interpreters of Shakespeare had come under attack for accepting too fully the assumptions and readings of Jan Kott's *Shakespeare Our Contemporary*. If one wished to select a single noted critic whose assumptions about Shakespeare's world Kott's study most readily challenged and revised it would be E. M. W. Tillyard. It was Tillyard's *Elizabethan World Picture* which taught us to read Shakespeare's images of chaos as part of a larger cosmic vision whose ultimate end was the reestablishment of a proper hierarchial order implied in the concept of the great chain of being. It was also Tillyard who brought to us an awareness of the importance of the Tudor Myth in our understanding of some of the dominant patterns developed in Shakespeare's history plays. Tillyard's stress on the return to order in the final moments of the tragedies and the working out of Tudor providence in the histories stood directly in opposition to Kott's reading of the tragedies as experiences dominated by the grotesque and absurd and the histories as instances of unending power struggles captured by the phrase, The Grand Mechanism.

Examples of Kott's somber view can be found in Welles's *Chimes at Midnight* (1966), Richardson's *Hamlet* (1969), Brook's *King Lear* (1970), and Polanski's *Macbeth* (1971). Welles's masterful battle scene in *Chimes at Midnight* is not an epic clash of two vibrant heroes but a brutal, chilling comment on the horror of war in which only Falstaff, scurrying in and out of the battle like a giant armadillo to find pockets of safety, emerged with his discretion and valor intact. Tony Richardson's *Hamlet* stressed the cynicism and luxury of all the members of the Elsinore court, including Ophelia, and Nicol Williamson's performance, for all its brilliance of individual readings, makes it impossible for us to imagine his Hamlet as the glass of fashion and the mold of form in a Renaissance world Tillyard would recognize. Obviously, Peter Brook's *King Lear* is the movie most thoroughly saturated with Kott's ideas about that play; its unrelenting bleakness and pain sear and burn.

Polanski's *Macbeth* is also a film which makes interesting use of Kott's approach to Shakespeare. Polanski's adaptation is an example of the ways in which contemporary films as well as stage productions have made a fruitful dialogue with modern Shakespeare criticism rather than pretending that the realms of criticism and production are doomed to move in parallel, nonintersecting tracks. The film was made and released at a painful moment in its director's life and at a precarious one in his career, and many of the responses to it were highly colored by some of its surface violence, which invited parallels with the Manson family's murder of Sharon Tate and her house guests. Such responses also found justification in familiar elements of Polanski's film style, which draws heavily on melodramatic sensationalism. These responses were perhaps inevitable, and they do point to legitimate flaws in the film; they have, however, obscured much of the film's real achievements, achievements earned through a careful mixture of literary intelligence and skillful direction.[5]

One of the aspects of the film's interpretation of *Macbeth* which has been noticed by many reviewers is that it does not end with Macduff's "The time is free" and Malcolm's pledge to perform "what needful else/That calls upon us, by the grace of Grace"—the pieties of the restoration of legitimate order, degree, and harmony. Rather, Polanski cuts from Macbeth's severed head being swirled through a crowd of cheering soldiers, to Donalbain riding and then limping (the hunchback and limp having been established early not as a parody of Richard III but to quickly imprint Donalbain in our memories, for he is permanently absent from the play after Duncan's murder) to *his* appointment with the weird sisters. Polanski's ending, then, is decidedly in keeping with Kott's reading of *Macbeth* as dramatizing at its heart not the sanctity of order but the insatiability of power. I wish to propose that this moment is not just a clever idea inserted, perhaps, at the prodding of the film's literary adviser Kenneth Tynan but a moment carefully prepared for through the use of a series of visual metaphors and effective dramatic devices; elements of Polanski's art which reveal the film's affinity with contemporary criticism.

The film opens with a breathtaking shot of an empty beach at dawn, the sun (another image used successfully throughout the film) a pale glimmer on the horizon.[6] The witches are at their work, burying in the placid, glimmering sand a noose and a hand clutching a dagger—when Polanski borrows he borrows from the Renaissance as well as from Kott; the rope, the dagger, and the digging are, of course, traditional emblems of despair.[7] The dagger, we immediately understand, is that "false creation"; an emblem of Macbeth's vivid imagination and terrifying reality; the noose is "planted," but it will be Polanski's labor to make it grow. After the credits, rolled with the sounds of battle in the background, we return to the same beach now littered with bodies; Duncan's soldiers move amongst the dead and when one of the fallen whimpers and moves, his back is savagely flayed by a soldier wielding a mace and chain. After the reports of the "bloody man," the rebellious Thane of Cawdor is brought to Duncan manacled and chained but still wearing the chain and medallion symbolic of his title. Duncan, seated on horseback, disdainfully removes the chain from Cawdor's neck with his sword and tosses it, as though it were a political football, to Ross: "go . . . and with his former title greet Macbeth."

The implications are ominous. The emblem of rank and title is not an invitation to abide by proper degree but a chain of power which breeds ambition rather than reverence. The rewards of being a bloody man, a maker of "strange images of death" are ambiguous; for the fallen Thane of Cawdor, fighting on the wrong side, they bring immediate execution; for the new Thane they bring "borrow'd robes" and the promptings of horrid imaginings eventually made real.

At the moment Ross—the perpetual messenger, the bringer of always ambiguous news, the middleman playing his cards for a chain of his own—presents Macbeth with his new title and its emblem, Macbeth returns to his tent to lace on his boots; his new title is not to be personally satisfying but is to lead him on to another until he finds himself "bound in/To saucy doubts and fears." Polanski's camera tightens in on Macbeth's face and, as Lorne Buchman observes,

> We listen to an internal monologue that increasingly voices the thoughts of a man giving rein to his ambition. "Horrible imaginings" enter the hero's mind at exactly the moment he puts on the medallion of Cawdor. On stage, we key into his thoughts through asides and soliloquies; in film, the voice-over and closeup work specifically to make those thoughts fill the entire space. On the screen the action *is* thinking.[8]

Buchman rightly notes that Polanski repeatedly uses voice-over and closeup "to create, in spatial terms (both visual and aural), the smothering prison of the mind; Macbeth tyrannizes the world as he is tyrannized by the mind."[9]

It is appropriate that when Macbeth returns to Inverness with the news of Duncan's immediate arrival, Lady Macbeth removes his chain as she invites him to "feel now/The future in the instant."[10] The chain she removes as she entices him to the "sovereign sway and masterdom" of the crown should invite us, as I am sure it does Jon Finch's Macbeth, to recall Cawdor's death. Chained from neck to wrist and from wrist to ankle Cawdor is led up to a platform where his chain is secured to the castle wall. He gives Duncan one last, defiant glare and then leaps to his incredible downfall; his body left to swing suspended above the Forres courtyard. Polanski links power, rank, ambition, and appetite into a telling chain of destructive consequences.

The interconnections between power and appetite are reinforced by Polanski's handling of three crucial scenes: Macbeth's doubts and Lady Macbeth's resolve in 1.7, the murder of Duncan itself, and Banquo's banquet. Polanski uses, most intelligently, film's ability for sound-track voice-over in Macbeth's great vacillating soliloquy "If it were done when 'tis done, then 'twere well/It were done quickly." In fact, Polanski's setting of this scene and his movement of Finch in and out of voice-over is the most impressive and textually imaginative use of this device in Shakespearean films.

Macbeth is the most claustrophobic, self-absorbed, fantastical of Shakespeare's heroes, who can be transported to his inner regions at the least suggestion. Polanski imagines his Macbeth becoming rapt in his own alternating inner debate about the murder while seated next to Duncan at the banquet honoring his arrival at Inverness. As his thoughts reach "surcease, success," they are interrupted by a general toast being lifted by Duncan in his host's honor. Macbeth responds with a nod and immediately recaptures his train of thought and as his mind races on to "we'd jump the life to come," a wind suddenly blows through the room rattling the shutters and extinguishing the candles. When light is restored we realize that Macbeth has left the hall and is now standing on the balcony which rings the inner courtyard, and as he argues with himself that "in these cases/We still have judgment here" horses break loose from the stable and clatter out through the castle's gates. The camera cuts back to the feast, where Fleance is beginning to sing for Duncan, and then we are brought back to the balcony, where it has begun to rain, punctuated by a crack or two of lightning. As Macbeth insists that Duncan's "here in double trust" he breaks his stream-of-consciousness to speak out loud for the first time on "Then, as his host,/Who should against the murderer shut the door,/Not bear the knife myself." Polanski's device here captures the inner/outer, fair/foul alternating impulses which define Macbeth and the power of his imagination. Finch breaks into speech again on "I have no spur" just as that spur arrives to scold him back to the party, where after-dinner dancing has begun. Lady Macbeth moves her husband back inside and their famous dare/doubt exchange is uttered beneath their breaths without looking at each other as they both pretend to be absorbed in the dancers' performance.

# Chain Reaction

Polanski has clearly imagined his Macbeths as a young, handsome, bourgeois couple and the playing and setting of this exchange brilliantly captures his intentions as they talk about deep desires and base deeds while appearing to smile their way through the apparent enjoyment of a social ritual. When Macbeth breaks off their discussion with "I dare do all that may become a man;/Who dares do more is none," he moves away from her as she begins her remonstrance "What beast was't, then,/That made you break this enterprize to me?" and toward a nearby stoup of wine. As he lifts the stoup to fill his cup, Malcolm thrusts his goblet into view and his haughty look forces Macbeth—clearly pained—to do his bidding. After his cup is full, Malcolm with a teasing smile proclaims "Hail Thane of *Cawdor*." This moment, totally of Polanski's creation, is indicative of the subtle tensions between powerful egos his details serve to capture. Macbeth returns to his wife with the question, "If we should fail?" And Francesca Annis's Lady Macbeth replies most matter-of-factly, "we fail." After she has presented her plan she accepts Duncan's offer to dance, and it is Macbeth's admiration for her charmingly hypocritical performance which elicits his "Bring forth men-children only;/For thy undaunted mettle should compose/Nothing but males."

I think this sequence reveals the cinematic skill with which Polanski creates his vision and version of the Macbeths and prepares us for his decision to take us with Macbeth to the murder. Duncan's door creaks open and the next shot is of Macbeth, on the inside, rigidly framed by the closed door (the door closes on Macbeth as it does on the viewer; we, too, are now trapped and made culpable by our silent witness of the crime). Macbeth proceeds, reluctantly, to Duncan's bed and straddles the sleeping king while hesitantly drawing back the covers from Duncan's neck and chest with the tip of his dagger, and we are reminded of Duncan's use of his sword to strip Cawdor of his chain of misused authority. Anguished, Finch withdraws the dagger in contemplation and makes his fatal plunge only after Duncan has stirred awake into protest. At the moment of the murder Duncan's golden crown is knocked to the floor, and the camera follows its reeling, rocking course. We understand that Macbeth has traded his allegiance for the ring of a hollow crown.[11]

Polanski prepares for the banquet scene and furthers his interplay of visual metaphors through the invention of two revealing moments. He cuts from the crowning of Macbeth at Scone to the courtyard at Forres, where the camera focuses our attention on a caged bear as Macbeth welcomes "our chief guest" Banquo who is visible only at the rear of the frame. Macbeth, the baiting and the baited bear, the host at Inverness whose appetite has made him the false host at Forres, the man who understands that he can sustain himself only by feeding on others, is his own caged animal, his own chief guest in an appropriated palace. After the interview with the two murderers Macbeth retires to bed to rest his agitated mind; his rest is punctured by a nightmare. He dreams of Fleance standing with a mocking smile at the foot of his bed, placing Macbeth's crown upon his head, and then carefully removing an arrow from his quiver and gently using its tip to pull Macbeth's robe back from his throat and chest. The still dreaming Macbeth struggles to cry out but finds his mouth stopped by Banquo's hands; at this moment he awakes to find that it is rather Lady Macbeth's hands which are stifling his screams. This marvelous and effective sequence captures Macbeth's paranoid fears, his feelings of being mocked and rebuked by father Banquo and his progeny, his imaginative grasp of his first murder as he awaits the news of the second, and Lady Macbeth's role as the naive mocker and silencer of his alert but impotent conscience.

The banquet itself is arranged as a three-sided rectangle (as in Kurosawa's *Throne of Blood*) with Macbeth standing in the center area greeting his guests arriving from the just concluded bear-baiting.[12] When he is at last invited to sit, the camera moves to a chair we see is empty, then returns to Macbeth for his reply, "Where?" and when our eyes, now following Macbeth's, return to the table the chair is occupied. As its occupant turns to reveal himself as Banquo, Macbeth releases from his hand the golden goblet with which he had just given his cheer "Now good digestion wait on appetite/And health on both!" and the camera follows its crazy spinning on the floor and we hear its empty ring. This moment looks back to the camera's previous focus on Duncan's crown in the murder scene as well as forward to the witches' brew in 4.1, where Macbeth is made to drink their cauldron's concoction from an identical golden cup. Polanski's point is well made: the wine of life is indeed drawn, and this vaulting bragger over its lees is reduced to a paranoid monster. All this is made even more explicit as Banquo's ghost rises and pursues the backtracking Macbeth to his collapse at the foot of the column where the bear had been chained and hounded.

If Polanski's imagery is running somewhat in advance of Shakespeare's here (it isn't until 5.7 that Macbeth declares, "They have tied me to a stake; I cannot fly,/But, bear-like, I must fight the course."), it does so in the service of the playwright and the director.

Both have sought to realize Macbeth's ravenous appetite, insatiable yet empty. For it is an appetite which will not wait on "good digestion" and will not, has not, led to "health." Polanski's Macbeth makes literal Claudio's lines in *Measure for Measure:* "Our natures do pursue,/ Like rats that ravin down their proper bane,/A thirsty evil; and when we drink we die" (1.2.132–34).

After Macbeth's second visit to the witches, Polanski offers a crucial transposition of the text to reinforce the political and psychological images of ambition and appetite he visualizes at *Macbeth*'s core. I have already made brief mention of Polanski's conception of Ross as a potential Macbeth, waiting for his moment to seize the day. Ross begins as Duncan's harbinger of reward to Macbeth, and we are repeatedly reminded of his lingering presence waiting for proper acknowledgment and recompense in the new dispensation. It is appropriate, then, that Polanski should designate Ross as the third murderer and make his actions there ambiguous: he is seen, on horseback, at a distance, and as Fleance escapes, Banquo's final act is to shoot Ross's horse out from under him. Fleance, however, is escaping on foot, and Ross makes no attempt to pursue him. In the text, after Ross exits from the banquet scene we next see him in his exchange with Lady MacDuff prior to the entrance of the messenger who is followed quickly by Macbeth's marauders. Then he appears with Malcolm and MacDuff in England delivering, at first, his puzzling assurance that MacDuff's wife and children "were well at peace when I did leave'em" and then the terrifying news which we know (but wonder the circumstances of Ross's knowledge) that MacDuff's wife and babes have been savagely slaughtered. Polanski's Ross is made less puzzling. His interview with Lady MacDuff is not depicted as the visit of a well-meaning kinsman afraid to speak strongly against his monarch (as we might interpret his remarks in the text) but, rather, he appears as Macbeth's henchman who has used his family relationship with Lady MacDuff to gain access to Fife's gates; when he departs he leaves the doors open for the waiting assassins. Ross has been tyranny's messenger.

Polanski then moves, not to 4.3 with Malcolm and MacDuff in England, but to act 5 and the scenes which detail Lady Macbeth's madness and Macbeth's melancholia, "My way of life,/Is fall'n into the sere and yellow leaf."[3] Ross is *present* at Dunsinane to witness the decline of Macbeth's support. As Macbeth is seated in council receiving news of the flight of his supporters to England, Ross is with Seyton in the Dunsinane courtyard observing the desertion of

Lennox. Lennox's final act is to remove the medallion and chain from his neck (has he been the play's third Thane of Cawdor?) and to toss it to Seyton. Ross quickly grabs it and, indefatigable Thane-in-waiting that he is, delivers it to Macbeth now surrounded only by Ross, Seyton, and the murderers of MacDuff's wife and children. Finch toys with the chain for a moment, scrutinizes his final followers, and then casually slips it over Seyton's head. His final act of the authority he so bloodily pursued is to reward his valet with the same emblem of valor and loyalty he had received for his feats in defending Duncan's kingdom. It is the ultimate gesture of overreaching power's absurdity—whim motivated by spite—and creates, in some ways for Polanski's Macbeth, an even more telling movement toward "Tomorrow and tomorrow and tomorrow . . ." than does Lady Macbeth's suicide. Ross, taking it all in but missing the point, hurries off to get a new master. As a final ironic touch, Polanski has Seyton attempt to defend Dunsinane's gates from Ross's escape south only to be killed by a deadly crossbow. Seyton's fate, as well as Ross's, is paradigmatic of Polanski's interpretation of *Macbeth*. The great chain of being is overwhelmed by the great chain of power, and we all begin to weary of the sun.

The emptiness of the world Macbeth has drained of meaning is further reflected in the hero's final moments when Finch literally turns Macbeth into a machine of death. The deadened look in his eyes and the trancelike expression on his face become a performance mirror of Kott's concluding remarks on the character:

> For Macbeth attitudes are of no importance; he does not believe in human dignity any more. Macbeth has reached the limits of human experience. *All he has left is contempt.* . . . All he can do before he dies is to drag with him into nothingness as many living beings as possible. Macbeth is still unable to blow the world up. *But he can go on murdering to the end*"[14] (my italics).

The ending of Polanski's film—Donalbain's visit to the witches—then, has been carefully established by the world of power politics and restless ambition that the details and patterns I have sketched out seek to characterize. Polanski artfully interweaves his images of the chain of power, the cup of appetite, and the crown of ambition into a realization of a *Macbeth* "as brutal as it is beautiful."[15]

As I mentioned at the outset Polanski's *Macbeth*, rather than ushering in an expanded era of Shakespeare films, remained as the last big-budget English-language adaptation of a Shakespeare play to be released on film until Branagh's *Henry V* appeared late in 1989. The exciting and innovative work with Shakespeare in performance in the past fifteen years has been realized not on film or video but on the stage. One of the most interesting young directors to emerge in the post-Nunn era at the Royal Shakespeare Company is Adrian Noble, who in 1990 was named the artistic director of the company. In a later chapter I will discuss his productions of *King Lear* and *As You Like It*, but here I want to focus on his *Macbeth* (1986), because Noble is a director noted for the cinematic qualities which distinguish his vivid stage images, and we can see echoes of both Polanski's *Macbeth* and Kurosawa's *Throne of Blood* in the most successful mainstage production of *Macbeth* since the Olivier-Byam Shaw version in 1955.

As I will argue in detail later, it is a hallmark of Noble's imagination that he has been attracted to those Shakespeare plays which have seemingly received definitive modern productions. In the case of *Macbeth* he was up against two contrary traditions: the notorious intractability of the Scottish tragedy to yield itself to successful productions, placed against the great success of Trevor Nunn's studio version with Ian McKellen and Judi Dench in The Other Place in 1976.

Royal Shakespeare Company observers have long grown accustomed to productions set in a basic black box; in this instance, Noble and his long-standing design partner, Bob Crowley, made that black box explicit by building its three black timbered walls conspicuously ten feet in from the natural dimensions of the stage and which did not rise as high as the proscenium to underscore the specific space chartered to contain the play.

When we entered the theater we saw not only the black box but also a series of pikes, each holding a black, red, or white banner, buried in the stage floor. The pikes suggested the furious butchery of the battle which opens the play and the banners proclaimed the colors of the play's dominant images: night, blood, and milk. Noble returned to this visual tableau in the closing moments of the play as similar pikes, now bearing green banners, came slamming through the side and back walls of the set further trapping the mad king. This moment seemed an interesting visual echo, in stage terms, of the hundreds of arrows which come flying at Washizu in the final frames of Kurosawa's *Throne of Blood*.

In fact, as I have mentioned earlier, Noble's work can be distinguished among this generation of RSC directors by its affinities with film. Such affinities are revealed not just in allusions to the films which are a central part of contemporary Shakespeare culture, like *Throne of Blood*, but to images and techniques associated with film as well. Just as one could see the influence of Hollywood and Broadway musicals in Trevor Nunn's work long before his *Cats*—his *Comedy of Errors* and *Once in a Lifetime* spring immediately to mind—so one's mind flashes naturally to film analogies when watching Noble's work. I have already mentioned Kurosawa, and several other elements in Noble's *Macbeth* seem to me to be inspired by Polanski's film of the play. In fact, Noble's fine opening scene which found the witches wandering through a smoke-filled battleground defined by the upturned pikes and the bodies of the dead immediately summoned images of Polanski's witches moving through a similar landscape which, in a brilliant series of lapsed-time-frame cuts, gave way to the battle. In Polanski's case the witches' work precedes the battle, while Noble's staging had them conjuring their mischief out of the human hurly-burly which was already in progress. Both directors had the ages of the witches span youth to age to mirror the temporal vision they present to Macbeth: Glamis, Cawdor, King (hereafter)—past, present, future. The concentration of the action in a single, claustrophobic room was an indication that Noble was after the domestic drama and tragedy of Shakespeare's couple much as Polanski's use of the young and handsome Finch and Annis, perpetually caught in close-ups whispering their lines, was meant to emphasize.

Polanski's imaginative use of Fleance, in Macbeth's interpolated dream sequence, was picked up by Noble and extended throughout his production. Children were everywhere, mocking the Macbeths' barren marriage. The witches picked up a sleeping boy nestled in the arms of a fallen soldier in the opening scene; when Macbeth turned to sit in his throne after being crowned he found Fleance straddling it, and he reached out to embrace him saying at once both, "be mine" and "you, too, must go"; a group of children were released by the witches in 4.1 who played blindman's bluff with Macbeth as an emblem of their issue which stretches out to the crack of doom.

Noble has commented that "people go mad in rooms," which became a key conception for the tight, tense, trapped atmosphere his production created.[16] Noble's challenge was to keep us riveted by that single landscape and to keep it uncluttered by huge armies or cumbersome banquet tables. He clearly intended to find a means of transferring much of what Nunn's famed studio production captured but doing so in a vaster space, a house of 1500 rather than 150. The critics were universal in acclaiming this the first main house *Macbeth* to succeed since Olivier's in 1955. The opening sentences of Michael Billington's review spoke for many:

> You have to go back to 1955 to find a totally satisfying pro-
> duction of *Macbeth* on the main stage at Stratford; and even that
> one owed more to the genius of Olivier than the quality of the
> director. But Adrian Noble's new version breaks the spell.[17]

The production, like Nunn's, was performed without an intermission, making us all, "cabin'd, cribb'd, confin'd." The effect was to direct our unrelenting attention to the Macbeths almost as if the play were being presented in close-ups.

Jonathan Pryce and Sinead Cusack were interesting choices for the Macbeths, as his manic behavior was matched by her wide-eyed, sexy innocence, both caught in a doll's house made dark by the way each brought out the worst in the other. This was clearly a marriage which could only make murder, could only be consummated in the mutuality of Duncan's destruction, which led, of course, to divorce not union.

Pryce, like Macbeth, runs on alternating current. His performance startled because it created an unexpected black humor from his first encounter with the witches through to his dismissal of the "cream-faced loon" in the final act. Most exciting was his attempt to mock his reaction to Banquo's ghost as though his king were some mad, merry prankster. And a similar moment came when he let out a mock-horrific scream at the end of the "come seeling night" speech which gave both his wife and us a jolt.

Sinead Cusack matched his crazy psychic energy with her own sexy determination. There was a violent passion at work in their relationship, including Lady Macbeth having to absorb a vicious slap to the face on "Prithee, peace," a slap which she instantly knew gave her the upper hand, as Pryce's Macbeth was capable of great violence but even greater remorse. Billington, again, is accurate when he describes these Macbeths "as a Strindbergian couple locked together in love-hate. . . . you get a sense of molten intimacy in their domestic relationship. You feel that for the Macbeths naked power has become a substitute for parenthood."[18] Irving Wardle captured the essence of Sinead Cusack's conception in language which could apply equally to Francesca Annis's performance in Polanski's film: "Sinead Cusack plays her as a corporation wife, blind to everything except the banality of her husband's advancement, and reduced to mute horror when she sees the monster she has let loose."[19]

Noble's stage images are so powerful that they often function as film images do, lingering in one's mind long after the words which may have called them into being. It is interesting that although Noble's use of the long pikes, now festooned with green banners, that come crashing through the three sides of the set in search of the madman trapped within reminded me of Kurosawa's arrows in *Throne of Blood*, they summoned yet another remarkable film image for Billington: "And, at the last, the walls crowd in on Macbeth and are pierced by symbolic green flags like the hands grabbing at Catherine Deneuve in Polanski's *Repulsion*. If you didn't speak English, you could understand the play from the visual symbols."[20]

Billington has focused on one of the two Polanski films (the other was *Rosemary's Baby*) which surely led to his interest in *Macbeth* among Shakespeare's tragedies and on those elements in Noble's staging which linked madness, murder, and claustrophobia: "People go mad in rooms." Further, Billington senses a key element in Noble's art as a stage director which links him with the world of film: his use of striking visual symbols and images as vivid illustrations of Shakespeare's text.[21] When Noble remounted his *Macbeth* with a new cast in the 1988–89 RSC season, he underlined his indebtedness to Polanski by casting Nicholas Selby as Duncan, the actor who had played the same role in Polanski's film seventeen years before.

Polanski's film may have contributed to a long interruption in the history of filmed Shakespeare, but it, like other Shakespeare films, lives on to enrich the ongoing exchange about modern modes of Shakespearean performance, and it may well have been a subterranean source for the most exciting and successful large-scale stage production of *Macbeth* in our time.

## CHAPTER THREE

# The Long Good-bye:
# Welles and Falstaff

•

I F POLANSKI'S *Macbeth* represents the end of the richest era for the release of sound-filmed Shakespeare, Orson Welles's *Chimes at Midnight* represents that period at its zenith. Anthony Davies accords Welles's film highest honors: "*Chimes at Midnight* and Olivier's *Hamlet* are the two films which most successfully fuse the elements of theater and cinema in the field of Shakespearean film."[1] Michael Anderegg, writing in *Film Quarterly*, also hails Welles's achievement: "*Chimes at Midnight* has come to be recognized, over the last decade or so, both as one of the most intelligent and imaginative of films adopted from Shakespeare and as one of Orson Welles's finest achievements, a film at least equal in energy and brilliance to *Citizen Kane* and *The Magnificent Ambersons*."[2] In a painstakingly thorough study, Robert Hapgood demonstrates how significantly Welles's film participates in a phenomenon which distinguishes the best English-language films of Shakespeare: most began life as stage productions which matured into successful film conceptions. Hapgood concludes his analysis by citing André Bazin as a means of measuring Welles's achievement:

> As it [*Chimes at Midnight*] emerged from its stage versions to its final realization on screen, Welles's adaptation achieved, in essentials, that difficult double feat that Bazin envisages: it respects its Shakespearean theatrical original while also respecting its modern film idiom—and in such a way that, when it is at its best, Welles's vision and Shakespeare's coincide.[3]

My particular interest in Welles's achievement lies in the ways in which his film participates in the rich and ongoing critical debate concerning Falstaff's role and meaning in an understanding of Shakespeare's second tetralogy.

[ 35 ]

In our time we have been rewarded with a variety of diverse and provocative interpretations of Shakespeare's most famous comic creation. To mention only some of the more familiar and recent: Falstaff as Braggart Soldier and Vice (J. Dover Wilson); Falstaff as Saturnalian Lord of Misrule (C. L. Barber); Falstaff as Emblem of Supreme Charity (W. H. Auden); Falstaff as Parodist and Holy Fool (Roy Battenhouse); Falstaff as Centaur (Douglas J. Stewart), and Falstaff as (M)other (Valerie Traub).[4] The vigor of the continuing critical dialogue about Falstaff is signal witness to the power the second tetralogy exercises for modern audiences and readers. It is therefore surprising that our age has not produced a series of definitive or imaginative stage interpretations of Falstaff to match the wit and intelligence of the critical exchange about Falstaff's central importance to the plays which give him life.[5]

The staging of *1* and *2 Henry IV* and *Henry V* by the Royal Shakespeare Company in 1975 found its interpretive center in Alan Howard's development of Hal rather than in Brewster Mason's portrayal of Falstaff. The great production in the trio was *Henry V*, which was justifiably applauded by international audiences and critics. Significantly, it was also the first of the three plays to be performed at Stratford, though Alan Howard has indicated that "when we began rehearsals we worked on *Henry V* for one half the day, and *Henry IV, Part One* for the other half. And gradually one began to see that the whole question of acting, of assuming roles, which is so central to the early Hal, is carried through into *Henry V*."[6] Howard makes no mention of what Hal may have learned about "assuming roles" from his master teacher, protean Falstaff. Stratford Festival Canada's productions of *1* and *2 Henry IV* in the 1979 season followed the pattern set by the RSC by magnifying Hal's relationship with his father while minimizing the importance of his imaginative invigoration when in Falstaff's company.

A few concrete examples from the two productions will help to illustrate what I'm exploring. In Terry Hands's direction for the RSC, the blocking emphasis in *1 Henry IV* was far more thoughtful and interesting in the scenes between Hal and his father than they were in the Hal-Falstaff exchanges, so much so that 3.2 emerged as more subtle and complex than its wonderful parody in 2.4. Hal entered brandishing a tankard, a prop he continued to use with effect at moments intended to remind his father that he was determined to be his own man. In contrast, Emrys James's king made several faltering and embarrassed moves to embrace his son early in the scene but repeatedly pulled back when confronted with Hal's insistence on keeping a wary distance. The only furniture in the scene was the king's chair positioned at center stage, and the two men did a delicate dance around it ending up in it together in a loving embrace on Hal's promise to "die a hundred thousand deaths/Ere break the smallest parcel of this vow" (3.2.158–59). Both leapt up to regain composure and control on Blunt's entrance (which received the intended laughter), but their pact was further sealed (and their identities were merged) when Henry IV took Hal's tankard and downed its contents as he delivered, "A hundred thousand rebels die in this" (3.2.160). For those fortunate enough to see all three productions (once given on a single Saturday in March of 1976), a stroke of casting became further evidence of the productions' intentions to create a vital, living relationship between father and son, king and prince. Hands cast Emrys James as the Chorus in *Henry V.* Seeing that production in close sequence with *1* and *2 Henry IV* gave the quite remarkable impression that the old king had been rewarded miraculously with his own deep wish: "Not an eye/But is a-weary of thy common sight,/Save mine, which hath desir'd to see thee more" (3.2.88–89)—not only to see his son's great success but to herald and champion it as well.

In Peter Moss's Canadian Stratford production of *1 Henry IV* the father-son relationship was again heightened and resolved in a fashion which led one to believe that their reunion was both a fitting climax and extension of Hal's tavern frolic. In this instance the comparison between Falstaff and Henry IV was made manifest by the casting and costuming of Lewis Gordon as Falstaff and Douglas Rain as king.[7] Gordon is physically slight and even with the appropriate padding was not measurably larger than Rain's Henry. The resemblance between the two was further strengthened by having both characters sport nearly identical gray-white beards. When the two were both present on stage in act 5 and enlarged by their armor they might have been mistaken for brothers. Moss underlined his efforts to create a bond twixt father and son by some damaging surgery to the concluding lines of the play. In the aftermath of Shrewsbury, after Falstaff has waddled in with his prize, Henry turns to Hal for a report on the day's success: "How goes the field?" Hal replies with his graphic description of Douglas's reaction to seeing his men scurry for safety on the "foot of fear":

> The noble Scot, Lord Douglas, when he saw
> The fortune of the day quite turn'd from him,

The noble Percy slain, and all his men
Upon the foot of fear, fled with the rest,
And falling from a hill, he was so bruis'd
That the pursuers took him.
(5.5.17-22)

Hal and Henry share a boisterous laugh at Douglas's sad fall and exit arm and arm as the lights fall. The production sacrificed a great deal to end on that shared laughter, for it obliterated Hal's generous pardon, his expression of a noble charity to a worthy warrior-opponent, and his demonstrated political graciousness soon to be contrasted with his brother John's cold-blooded actions at Gaultree Forest in *2 Henry IV*. These are but a few examples of the ways in which both productions failed to find imaginative strategies for exploring Falstaff's importance to these plays, while employing a number of devices to dramatize fresh approaches to Hal's relationship to his father.

An important exception to this pattern of diminishing Falstaff to underscore other values in these plays can be found in Orson Welles's film, *Chimes at Midnight*, retitled as *Falstaff* for its American release in 1966. It has been only in the past decade that Welles's film has received the critical attention it deserves, an attention crowned by Bridget Gellert Lyons's recent edition of the complete filmscript.[8] Prior to the work of Davies, Anderegg, Hapgood, and Lyons, only Jack Jorgens and Dan Seltzer had presented treatments of the film which respected it as an interpretation of Shakespeare.[9]

Critical inattention to the film can be traced to its lack of availability rather than to its merits. Prints of *Chimes at Midnight* are expensive and difficult to locate, circumstances severely inhibiting the scholar's access to its achievements, though the growing film library at the Folger has helped to redress this problem. The *New York Times*'s film critic, Vincent Canby, underlined this situation in a column devoted to Welles when he was honored with the American Film Institute's Life Achievement Award: "Some of Welles's achievements are already easily recognized (*Citizen Kane* and *The Magnificent Ambersons*) but some spend most of their time in vaults, films like *Falstaff-Chimes at Midnight*, which may be the greatest Shakespeare film ever made, bar none."[10]

Like Canby, I believe that Welles's *Chimes at Midnight* is an excellent contemporary contribution to our understanding of Falstaff. Welles is, of course, working with his own integration and dramatization of ma-

terial lifted from the second tetralogy. His major emphasis is on
*1* and *2 Henry IV* with brief borrowings from *Richard II* and *Henry V.*
Welles uses short selections from Holinshed as a narrative device
to link this material together. I do not propose to delineate or defend the exact manner in which Welles has organized and rearranged
specific scenes, brief exchanges, or individual lines from Shakespeare's four plays in the making of his film, for such material is
readily available in the published filmscript and Jack Jorgens's in-
dispensable summary of that material.[11] I wish merely to explore
how Welles captures Hal's emergence from the two fathers who
threaten to submerge his own unique identity either through guilty
rule or gilded license, with a particular emphasis on Welles's treatment of Falstaff. Daniel Seltzer's synopsis of Welles's achievement
is instructive:

> Welles's movie is essentially a kaleidoscopic revisualization of
> Shakespeare's two plays. Scenes are set in new sequence, many
> of them cut entirely, others formed of the original text intact
> but with lines from elsewhere in the plays inserted for con-
> ceptual emphasis—either ironic or corroborative, some of the
> characters eliminated, but those remaining never destructively
> over-simplified. Amazingly, into two and a half hours of film
> time, Welles has set forth the psychological reality of these
> plays, taking as his dynamic center the same core of deep human
> emotion that energizes Shakespeare's texts—the struggle within
> Prince Hal simultaneously to love, resist, and to survive two
> parents, one his father and the other a surrogate, and to choose
> from among several life styles one that is uniquely and trium-
> phantly his.[12]

I agree with Seltzer: *Chimes at Midnight* is a compelling contemporary attempt to capture Shakespeare's resonances, not a
self-aggrandizing effort to reshape Shakespeare's plays into a bastard-
ization celebrating Welles's cinematic genius. Seltzer is mistaken,
however, when he declares that Welles "has placed his emphasis
where it is in Shakespeare, and so often is not in modern productions—upon the prince himself. The king, Falstaff, and Hotspur
move about him, come tangent to him, but never do we forget what
these scenes are about."[13] Welles's two titles, if nothing else, point
to the centrality of Falstaff, not Hal. The original title (*Chimes at
Midnight*) explicitly places the passing of Falstaff at the heart of his
interpretation.

Welles's interest in Falstaff and the Henry plays dates from 1938, when at the age of twenty-three, he and John Houseman mounted an ambitious but unsuccessful stage production of this material, entitled *Five Kings*, for the Theater Guild. In his fascinating book on Welles's stage career, Richard France offers this account: "Central to Welles's understanding of the chronicle plays was his use of the character of Falstaff to completely dominate the stage. He was for Welles the production's major expressive element. While enlarging the stature and importance of Falstaff, Welles reduced the character of Prince Hal."[4] Twenty-eight years later Welles had not changed his mind about the need to focus on Falstaff. In an interview conducted just prior to the film's release, Welles indicated that "you discover in the making of the film that the death of the King, and the death of Hotspur, which is the death of chivalry, and Falstaff's poverty and Falstaff's illness run all throughout the play. Comedy can't really dominate a film made to tell this story, which is all in dark colors."[5] When asked if he agreed that his film could be seen as a lament for Falstaff, he replied, "Yes, that may be true. I would like to think that."[6] Seltzer's description of Welles's portrayal of Falstaff: "jovial he can be, but predominantly he is sad," is a perceptive comment on Welles's performance.[7] What Seltzer fails to realize is that such a reading extends beyond Welles's interpretation of the character to cast a cold eye on the entire film. An analysis of several crucial scenes in the film will demonstrate that Welles's overriding visual and structural emphasis is to signal farewell, to say a long good-bye to Falstaff, rather than to celebrate Hal's homecoming to princely right reason and responsible rule.

The opening shot of the film frames Welles's way of organizing his own shaping fantasy of Shakespeare's material. The camera looks out from a ridge over a snow-covered landscape; there we pick out two figures slowly working their way through the snow toward an ancient and imposing oak tree, equidistant between our vantage point and the travelers. The composition of the shot is arresting, and its quality of stark black and white, coupled with its immediate evocation of landscape as symbolic and psychological territory (years past Macbeth's sere and yellow leaf) owes as much to Bergman as it does to Shakespeare. We follow the figures as they move toward and around the oak, and then we cut to a medium close-up as they enter a heavy-beamed and timbered room and settle themselves before an immense roaring fire. The two figures are a striking contrast: one huge and placid, the other frail and nervous. The camera shoots between them to the warmth of the fire as Alan Webb's Shallow rasps, "Jesus, the days that we have seen."

The frame, through which Welles presents his film, is not Shakespeare's "so shaken as we are, so wan with care," with its focus on Henry's burden and political dilemma; it is the personal filter of the play's other Olympian pretender, Falstaff. The intention of this partial, or open-ended, frame is to create the impression of a flashback. Its effect is to allow us to see that this is Falstaff's story. We are to witness the glory of his days and to partake in the sorrow of their passing. The winter landscape, the two stoic figures seeking the warmth of the blazing fire, the scene of slow, uphill struggle culminating in stasis—all speak profoundly to Welles's observation that by focusing on Falstaff his Shakespearean material leads him into dark colors; it is Falstaff's winter which dominates the texture of the film, not Hal's summer of self-realization.

Though I think the atmosphere of loss and lament can be identified throughout the film, I would like to describe five key scenes which most fully embody the farewell atmosphere of Welles's interpretation. Welles stresses the importance of leave-taking in his conception of the relationship between Hal and Falstaff: "I directed everything, and played everything with a view of preparing for the last scene. The relationship between Falstaff and the prince is not a simple comic relationship . . . but always a preparation for the end. And as you see, the farewell is performed about four times during the movie, foreshadowed four times."[18] I do not deny that Welles's view of Falstaff is a sentimental one, but it does not indulge in the hyperbolic excesses of Falstaff's romantic apologists from Morgann to Auden to Battenhouse. Because Welles is intelligent enough to let us see Falstaff's cowardice as well as his discretion, he manages to avoid misleading us into regarding his fat knight as no more than a harmless comedian spinning his anti-establishment jests for any well-paying dispensation. Welles is on record as having said that he regards Falstaff as more witty than funny and his film squares with that assessment.[19] Welles's Falstaff is a threat as well as a treat, and our sorrow at his rejection is tempered but not supplanted by the film's consistent awareness of that fact.

After the opening sequence, the credits are rolled against a background of marching troops and jaunty martial music, giving a vigorous pace to these shots in significant contrast to the tempo and landscape of the Falstaff-Shallow beginning. The film then moves to Westminster and the clash between Henry IV (beautifully played by John Gielgud) and Northumberland, Worcester, and Hotspur. Gielgud's elevated presence (captured by the actor's tone and haughty demeanor and by the camera's low-angle perspective) in the Spanish cathedral at Cardonna, with the light streaming in from the clerestories in carefully divided segments and his breath flowing visibly forward in the same cold divisions, is a remarkable visual achievement. At once we grasp all the textual images associated with Henry IV and his rule: care, division, distance, concern, austerity, calculation, emotional repression. When the film cuts from Westminster to the Boar's Head, our focus is immediately upon Falstaff snoring in his bed (the two fathers, thus, at once placed and defined). The horseplay between Hal and Falstaff which follows is enlivened by the camera's careening progress as it tracks Falstaff in pursuit of Hal. Falstaff thunders down a narrow, twisting staircase into the tavern's great room, arched by giant beams and filled with long tables. Every time the camera is in this setting it is alive with the energy of festive motion. Tracking, cutting, rapid shifts of angle: the camera's activity becomes a metaphor for the frenetic pleasure this locale releases in its celebrants. But the significant movement, repeated three times in the film, is Hal's progress *through* the tavern atmosphere, trailed by a cajoling Falstaff, out into its courtyard. In this first pass through the Boar's Head, the tavern is empty, but Hal's desire to escape is paramount.[20]

Once we are outside Welles provides us with a dual landscape. In the foreground we have the entrance to the tavern proper, at mid-distance are the gates opening out from the inn-yard, and in the extreme background we see the imposing ramparts of a castle. Welles chooses to shoot the opening of Hal's "I know you all" soliloquy from a medium long shot in which we see (1) the castle ramparts, (2) Hal poised at the inn-yard's gates, and (3) Falstaff slightly out of focus framed in the Boar's Head entrance, looking quizzically toward the heir apparent.

Welles's strategy here is both disconcerting and revealing. Hal is speaking directly into the camera—to us—but our perspective is complicated because we also see Falstaff over his shoulder. Here the landscape provides meaning. Hal is literally poised between the tavern and the castle, as his soliloquy makes metaphorically manifest. He is speaking to us, not to Falstaff, and thus we are associated with the castle in the foreground, incorporated into the drama as that audience who demands an explanation for his riotous behavior. Hal thus separates us from Falstaff, making us members of the prince's party by confiding to us his regard for the past and his plans for the future. The moment is further enriched, and our sense of being suspended with Hal enlarged, by the way in which Welles has Keith Baxter break up the concluding couplet of the soliloquy. The penultimate line "I'll so offend to make offense a skill" is delivered with Hal pivoting to face Falstaff, and "offend" is underlined by Baxter's wink, which draws a smile from the old misleader of youth. Then Baxter turns back to the camera and to us to confess, in a whisper, "Redeeming time when men least think I will." In Welles's strategic use of topography and spatial relationships, Hal here stands caught between the tavern and the castle, between Falstaff's inviting smile and the bleak landscape leading toward the fortifications of responsibility. As Hal leaves he moves through the inn yard gates shouting his farewell to Falstaff, whose mind is absorbed, not with the implications of this leave-taking, but with the morning's promised "offensive" at Gad's Hill. The camera cuts between Hal riding off and Falstaff planted at the threshold of his domain accepting the first of his long good-byes.

The farewell motif is repeated in a minor, but wildly comic, key in the Gad's Hill robbery scene—one of the film's most beautiful visual moments. The scene is shot in Madrid's Casa de Campo park; the ground is covered with leaves, and narrow trees stand tall and bare in late autumn's austere beauty. The invention and pace of Welles's tracking shots become an integral part of the comic zest and jest exploding from the multiple collisions of this pack of fellow travelers. Falstaff and crew have adorned themselves in the voluminous folds of hooded white terry cloth robes, and they approach their prey in the guise of prayerful supplicants. Hal and Poins wear romantic capes and broad-brimmed black hats as they swoop down to rob the robbers of their booty. (This scene in film and text works in ironic counterpoint with the later battle at Shrewsbury, where it is Falstaff who proves the counterfeit and robs Hal of his purse-y.) At Gad's Hill, Hal says good-bye by simply showing Falstaff his backside as he scurries away, remarking to Poins:

> Falstaff sweats to death,
> And lards the lean earth as he walks along.
> Were't not for laughing I should pity him.
> (2.2.103–5)

This mixture of tough-mindedness and sentiment prefigures the tone and stance Hal will adopt in his famous (and mistaken) eulogy of his fat friend delivered at Shrewsbury:

What, old acquaintance, could not all this flesh
Keep in a little life? Poor Jack, farewell!
I could have better spar'd a better man:
O, I should have a heavy miss of thee
If I were much in love with vanity:
Death hath not struck so fat a deer today,
Though many dearer, in this bloody fray.
(5.4.101–7)

When the film returns to the Boar's Head, it is to capture 2.4, the celebrated tavern scene where Hal and Falstaff exuberantly mock rebels and rivals, kings and kingdoms, vanities and vices, and most significantly, fathers and sons. In one great intuitive sweep, Shakespeare accomplished the dream of every comic writer—to give us the parody before the reality. Welles's Falstaff, firmly planted atop a tavern table with a tin pot for a crown, literally becomes, through the camera's low angle perspective, a titanic figure well deserving of Hal's hyperbolic slander—"the roasted manning-tree ox with the pudding in his belly." This is the moment, in both play and film, when Falstaff is at his zenith as Auden's emblem of life and laughter-giving charity. But that moment fades as soon as Hal sees which way Falstaff's wind is blowing. Hal insists that they change places and parts, thus displacing his surrogate father at the very instant that he assumes the mock persona of his real father. Now the camera provides us with repeated overhead angles as Hal-Henry admonishes Falstaff-Hal for the villainous company he keeps. Welles holds the climactic moment: "Banish plump Jack and banish all the world." "I do. I will." for several beats before the monstrous watch comes banging at the door. This frozen moment works in spite of our awareness that Hal's threat must be interrupted before it can be absorbed by Falstaff, because the camera catches on Welles's face the same quizzical expression that we witnessed peering at us in the background of the "I know you all" soliloquy.

Welles's critical intelligence captures an important dimension of Shakespeare's meaning, a dimension that frequently escapes other interpreters of Falstaff. For all of Falstaff's Orwellian alertness to the sham hollowness of political rhetoric, for all his ability to see through and comically explode the pieties of power, the one person he does not see through is his own pupil, Hal—the most powerfully shrewd character in the play. Welles makes us see Falstaff's inability to comprehend Hal's projected threat of banishment. In that suspended moment, when the watch does come knocking on the door, however, the screen is filled with activity and the camera bursts into motion as the Boar's Head patrons race for cover from the law's intrusion. In the text, Hal instructs Falstaff to hide behind the arras, but Welles has him disappear through a trapdoor (a neat stage analogy) into the tavern's bowels. This scene becomes a perfect foreshadowing of the eventual rejection scene where King Hal sends Falstaff toward that grave which "gapes for him thrice wider than for other men."

Adroitly, Welles now cuts directly to 3.3 as though it were the following morning with all its marvelous otter play with Mistress Quickly and the debate over Hal's supposed indebtedness of 1000 pounds to Falstaff. There is great poignance in Falstaff's rejoinder that Hal owes him his love, which is surely worth a million. Hal is drawn into a gigantic bear hug on this line, illustrating the exuberant and warm tactile relationship Falstaff and Hal share in the film, an aspect of Hal's behavior that is skillfully contrasted with the aloof and distanced space Henry IV insists on keeping even in his fondest exchanges with his son. When, during that companionable embrace, we get the exchange concerning Falstaff's jest that he fears Hal only as he fears "the roaring of the lion's whelp," Hal asks, "And why not as the lion?" The camera closes in on Falstaff as he responds, "The king himself is to be feared as the lion: dost thou think I'll fear *thee* as I fear thy *father*?" With Falstaff's question left swaying in the unanswered air, the camera slowly pulls back to a medium close shot. Falstaff then collapses into a chair, where his ample lap is quickly filled by Doll Tearsheet (another skillful interpolation from *2 Henry IV*) come to mourn his imminent departure to recruit his charge of foot. Tearsheet is played by Jeanne Moreau, and as this remarkable French actress puts her inviting pout into framing Shakespeare's words we are treated to a marvelous, and I'm sure unintentional, reward of international casting. As she caresses Welles and coos to him Shakespeare's loving "Ah, Jack you whoreson tidy Bartholomew boar-pig," Moreau's "whoreson" emerges distinctly as "Orson."

When Hal moves to take his second leave from Falstaff and the tavern world, he passes through the central room, now alive with customers whose festive presence repeatedly impedes his attempt at exit and release. Once he has emerged from the labyrinth of revelry, he is framed by the same landscape we witnessed earlier in his first departure. This time Hal turns and shouts back at Falstaff, "Farewell thou latter spring, all-hallown summer!" As Hal makes this second exit from Falstaff and his tavern rule, he is not riding to soothe a ruffled father but to confront a fiery rival—Hotspur. If the first farewell was an indication that Hal was called upon to move in other worlds than the tavern, the second reminds us that if those other worlds pose a threat to Falstaff ("Should I fear thee as I fear thy father?"), they also present a threat and a challenge, in the person of Hotspur, to Hal. As Hal departs now we know that he isn't simply taking leave of Falstaff but is moving irrevocably toward engagement in his father's world of political responsibility. Nevertheless the film's focus is on Hal's sad good-bye to the Boar's Head and Falstaff rather than on a jaunty welcome (represented in the text by Vernon's hyperbolic description of Hal in arms but cut in Welles's film) to honor's battlefield.

The Shrewsbury battle scene is one of the film's justly celebrated visual achievements, and Pauline Kael is right to see it as belonging with sequences from Eisenstein, D. W. Griffith, Kurosawa, and John Ford.[21] From a Shakespearean's viewpoint, it corresponds directly with Jan Kott's chilling, middle-European reading of the history plays as dramas reenacting not the sanctity of hierarchy but the brutality of armed aggression: The Grand Mechanism. There is little doubt that Welles meant to endow his Shrewsbury with a very different tone and atmosphere from the romantic and stirring version of Agincourt that Olivier achieved in his justifiably admired film of *Henry V.* Shakespeare presents multiple perspectives on Shrewsbury's significance: Worcester's cold Machiavellianism, Henry IV's shrewd military strategy, Hotspur's heady intemperance, Douglas's exasperated professionalism, Falstaff's knowing cynicism, and Hal's practical assurance that this is his day to seize. Abandoning Shakespeare's multiplicity, Welles concentrated on a modern extension of Falstaff's understanding that war's appetite is fed by "mortal men," that war can make all of us "food for powder." Welles attempts to capture what war is like for the men in the trenches rather than for those mounted on dashing chargers gliding athletically toward their opponents. Olivier's film version of Agincourt was a patriotic evocation of Hal's unsullied triumph (all lines revealing his darker side having been cut, including "Kill all the prisoners"), shot in a manner to highlight his vitality and pluck. Welles's treatment of Shrewsbury, by contrast, is a slow, painful, exhausting depiction of mud-laden soldiers enacting some primal destructive rite.[22]

When asked how he managed the intense, blow-by-blow effect of the battle scene, Welles responded:

On the first day I tried to do very short pieces, but I found the extras didn't work as well unless they had a longer thing to do. They didn't seem to be really fighting until they had time to warm up. That's why the takes were long, since there was no way of beginning the camera later and cutting. But I knew I was only going to use very short cuts. For example, we shot with a very big crane very low to the ground, moving as fast as it could be moved against the action. What I was planning to do—and did—was to intercut the shots in which the action was contrary, so that every cut seemed to be a blow, a counter blow, a blow received, a blow returned. Actually it takes a lot of time for the crane to move over and back, but everything was planned for this effect and I never intended to use more than a small section of the arc in each case.[23]

Welles's battle is stunning in its horror, and the camera clearly sympathizes with Falstaff's comic cowardice as he scurries in and out of harm's way looking like a giant armadillo in his ill-fitting armor. The clash between Hal and Hotspur is not prolonged. Both men are exhausted, their swords as heavy to their arms as a boxer's fists become in the fifteenth round of a title fight, and Hal outlasts his spirited rival because he has husbanded his energies more resourcefully than Hotspur. The battle world Welles gives us represents Falstaff's perspective on war and honor, just as Olivier's Agincourt sprang from his understanding of Henry V's daring determination.

After Falstaff has counterfeited death back into life, Welles jumps us into 2 *Henry IV* and creates a post-Shrewsbury scene which contains the third of our leave-takings, this time in a new landscape and with an interesting reversal of perspective.

For the first time in the film we see Hal, his father, and Falstaff together. When Falstaff drags the body of Hotspur into the camp where father and son, king and prince, are congratulating themselves on their victory, Welles has Gielgud give Falstaff a disdainful glare as the king moves away from the crowd which is gathering to admire Falstaff's prize.[24] The sky is filled with large, somber clouds moving elegantly across the horizon. A camp wagon, holding a butt of wine, is positioned in the center of the frame. The composition of this shot is reminiscent of countless John Ford and Howard Hawks Western scenes. In fact, the roll of the clouds across the sky here mirrors the famous graveyard scene in Hawks's *Red River*, where, as the story goes, Hawks had instructed John Wayne to speed up his lines so that the camera could capture the cloud which was passing overhead. In an interview I conducted many years ago with Hawks, I asked him if he thought Welles's scene was derivative (Welles has repeatedly stressed his indebtedness to both Hawks and Ford), and his charming reply was "Yep. I always thought Orson was just using Shakespeare to disguise the fact he was making a Western in that picture."[5]

For this setting, Welles draws on the men's sense of postbattle camaraderie as they gather for refreshment and tale-telling (as in the campfire scenes which conclude most harrowing days on the cattle drive in Westerns), a setting ideally suited to Falstaff's talents. Now that the actual danger has passed, the setting seems to say, Falstaff is ready to usurp the center of attention by dramatizing his version of the day's events. He moves eagerly toward the wagon and a waiting cup of sack and then turns to deliver his famous disquisition on the inventive powers of "sherris-sack." This speech is, of course, a soliloquy in Shakespeare's text, but Welles presents it with Hal poised in the background, in a stunning reversal of their positions in the two Boar's Head farewell scenes we have already examined. This is an incredibly full moment in the film. One father, Henry IV, has exited on the arrival of his surrogate. As Falstaff reaches the brilliant climax of his essay—"If I had a thousand sons, the first human principle I would teach them would be to foreswear thin potations and addict themselves to sack" (4.3.121–23)—Hal drops his tankard on the barren ground and moves off to follow his father's path. Falstaff is left to search for an audience and a reaction in an empty landscape. This third good-bye is an unspoken one, but once again it leaves the camera focused on Falstaff's uncomprehending face, perplexed by Hal's failure to be overwhelmed by his performance.

The fourth good-bye is, of course, the one which both plays move toward, the coronation scene, where Hal accepts the role of his public father and rejects the threat of his private one. Welles's visual construction of the scene is, again, based on a reversal of the pattern established in Hal's earlier farewells at the Boar's Head. If earlier it was Hal who had to push his way through the tavern crowd (those foul and ugly mists which seem to strangle him), now it is Falstaff who has to fight his way through an imposing congregation of soldiers, armed with long pikes, to confront his son-king. To reach the lion's whelp, Falstaff must pick his way through the labyrinth of pomp and power. As he falls to his knees to receive the tap which will put the laws of England at his command (as well as those resources necessary to repay the 1000 pounds he has conjured out of Shallow), Welles's camera pulls back to shoot Hal's austere "I know thee not old man" through the interstices of the pikes of power. When the procession has passed on and over our large supplicant, Falstaff makes a resigned recovery for his expectant companions and then, in the company of his page, moves away from us down a long, tunnel-like passageway, slowly diminishing in size. This is the last shot we have of this vast physical presence moving away from the audience he had courted and entertained, swallowed by the shadows.

The final scene of the film returns to the Boar's Head inn-yard where Mistress Quickly, Bardolph, Pistol, and Falstaff's page are positioned at the same tavern entrance where we witnessed Falstaff responding to Hal's initial farewell. Now the scene is funereal. The camera closes in on Margaret Rutherford as she blubbers her way through one of the most memorable eulogies in the history of literature. "And then I felt to his knees, and so upward and upward, and all was cold as any stone." Bardolph, Pistol, and the other pallbearers move away to an immense cart upon which rests the largest coffin in the history of film. Slowly and with great effort they begin to push it out through the gates. Once again, the castle ramparts define and limit the upper edge of the frame. This is the film's final long good-bye: the camera lingers over the laborious procession wheeling away the body "that when it did contain a spirit, a kingdom for it was too small a bound." As we participate in this sad farewell to Falstaff, Holinshed's words (in the voice of Ralph Richardson) emerge to proclaim a bitterly ironic contrast to what our eyes are telling us: "Thus began the reign of King Henry V, famous to the world in all ways." As the new dispensation proclaims itself, the coffin rumbles on its inexorable path to the grave. The new king is headed for France and Citizen Falstaff is dead.

Welles builds his film around his conception of Falstaff. Fully aware that great works of narrative art construct a necessary and significant relationship between their central characters and the landscape they inhabit, Welles has said:

> The people must live in their world. It is a fundamental problem for the film-maker, even when you are making apparently the most ordinary modern story. But particularly when you have a great figure of myth like Quixote, like Falstaff, a silhouette against the sky of all time . . . you can't simply dress up and *be* them, you have to make a world for them.[26]

[ 49 ]

From our first view of Falstaff working his way through a wintry landscape, to the horrors of the combat at Shrewsbury, to the titanic coffin making its way to the grave, Welles's images all contribute to the creation of a world enriched by Falstaff's presence and diminished by his loss.

Kenneth Tynan has written in admiration of Welles that "Orson coming into a room is like the sunrise."[27] In *Chimes at Midnight*, we do see a son rise, but our last and lingering image—a silhouette against the sky of all time—is of a great genius being carted off to the grave.

## CHAPTER FOUR

# One Murderous Image:
# Welles's *Othello*

•

I F WELLES'S *Chimes at Midnight* participates in a lively dialogue with contemporary productions of *1* and *2 Henry IV,* his *Othello* brilliantly anticipates the labyrinthian turns of postmodern literary theory. In fact, a postmodern approach to the New Critic's text might be aptly summarized by André Bazin's famous reaction to Welles's *Othello,* describing its impact as "extremely fragmented, shattered like a mirror relentlessly struck with a hammer."[1]

The major schools of current literary theory have their sources in the writings of Marx, Freud, Lacan, Saussure, Levi-Strauss, Bakhtin, Barthes, and Derrida. These gusts of theoretical fresh air have wafted through English departments in the past twenty years, shaking, if not uprooting, the firm hold of what used to be called the New Criticism as the reigning method of textual analysis and classroom pedagogy. The New Criticism was brilliantly American: practical, focused, nontheoretical, easily cloned, with its ideology neatly disguised as close reading. The text was supreme, existing in splendid isolation from subtext or context, from history or biography, from culture or politics, from audience or author.

All major contemporary revisionist theories have challenged the New Criticism's text as the exclusive focus of critical discourse. Film and performance criticism of Shakespeare deserves to be regarded as a contributing partner to the postmodern enterprise; such critics have struggled to define and articulate the tacit play and tension between text and performance. Film and performance criticism played with currently fashionable ideas, such as intertextuality, long before these ideas began appearing in general literary exchange.

In fact it is surely one of the goals of current theory—when practiced at its most lofty level—to rival, if not supplant, the text. In reading the books and articles of our leading postmodernists, one is tempted not simply to ask with Stanley Fish "Is there a text in this class?" but to ask "Is there a text in this text?" This is not a new or novel question for those of us in film and performance criticism, particularly when dealing with Orson Welles's adaptations of Shakespeare, where the traditional critical complaint has been "Is there a text in this film?"

Welles was the first great postmodern reader of Shakespeare, straddling like a colossus the territory between Twain's King and Duke and Derrida. In a sense, current literary criticism has simply caught up with issues and ideas that film and performance critics have been struggling with for years.

In two recent articles, Ihab Hassan has sought to capture the key tenets of postmodern discourse.[2] Hassan identifies and details eleven such tenets or "traits" and divides them roughly into two camps: deconstructive and reconstructive. Three terms in each group are particularly useful for thinking about Shakespearean films, particularly Welles's. Briefly summarized they are as follows: on the deconstructive side, according to Hassan, are:

INDETERMINACY: All poststructural literary theories reject determinate meaning of the text.

FRAGMENTATION: Such theories trust only the fragment, rejecting all notions of organization or synthesis.

DECANONIZATION: For Hassan this term signifies the rejection of all master codes, conventions, and authorities and signals the critic's urge to "deconstruct, displace, decenter, demystify the logocentric . . . order of things."[3]

On the reconstructive agenda we find the following central terms:

HYBRIDIZATION: This denotes the mixture and mutation of genres in parody, travesty, pastiche, or the development of hybrid styles and forms—the nonfiction novel, paracriticism, paraliterature, mixed media, happenings, the new journalism.

CARNIVALIZATION: This is Bakhtin's key contribution to such criticism, which celebrates literature's ludic and anarchic qualities. Through its emphasis on play and carnival, Bahktin's work has obvious affinities with Shakespeare, as already revealed in several recent studies.[4]

PERFORMANCE: The very nature of the postmodern ethos invites participation. Indeterminacy insists that the reader-auditor-critic (as the rereader) is essential to the creation of the very text itself.

Though I must confess that much of the terminology of postmodern criticism strikes me as heavy-handed and graceless, it nevertheless raises central questions about Shakespeare's text in precisely the same way a previous generation of critics raised questions about films or performances of Shakespeare's text. Hassan's deconstructive triad of indeterminacy, fragmentation, and decanonization are now seen as accurate descriptions of our cultural enterprise, while twenty years ago they represented the very terms used to dismiss Welles's films by academic Shakespeareans. The irony is delicious. And, of course, Hassan's three reconstructive terms—hybridization, carnivalization, and performance—all speak directly to the central critical issues Shakespeare film and performance critics have been articulating for the past two decades. Later in this essay I want to return to these terms to illuminate Welles's achievement in *Othello*.

For now, however, it is important to remember that Welles's Shakespeare films emerge from America's own unique frontier experience in decoding and reciphering Shakespeare. Welles's exposure to Shakespeare was a central part of forming the legend of a midwestern prodigy. His youthful recitations of Shakespeare to Chicago society marked him as exceptional. He was sent to the progressive Todd School, where at age twelve he played *both* Cassius and Mark Antony in a production of *Julius Caesar* which won top prize in a school drama competition and was performed at Chicago's Goodman Theater.

If Shakespeare was a key ingredient in Welles's early sense of his superiority and his precociousness, it was crucial that he came to Shakespeare as a drama student. Welles first "read" Shakespeare as script for performance (long before the New Criticism's ascendancy), not as a determinant text available only to the literary critic's trained appreciation.

Welles's *Othello* differs from his two other Shakespeare films in that it did not grow out of previous stage versions. We often forget that while Welles's work with the WPA and his own Mercury Theater firmly established him as a vital stage force, his most voluminous work during that period—as writer, director and actor—was in radio. It is perhaps paradoxical that Welles's work in radio may have played a more important role in his development as a filmmaker than did his more famous work as a theatrical director. Radio demanded that material—whether novels, short stories, or plays—be reshaped to fit the demands of its format. New narrative devices were accepted without question as Welles adapted classical material for a new medium and a popular audience. It was this experience, I would argue, which allowed him to assume that a text written in a particular genre automatically had to be transformed when adapted for another medium. It also led, I believe, to his repeated use of both aural and visual narrative framing devices in his films.

Welles's reshaping of his Shakespearean material for film was a natural extension of his work with classical texts in his radio series. In fact, this series ran concurrently with his work in New York for the WPA and the Mercury Theatre as well as his later move to Hollywood, where his initial energies were devoted to creating a screenplay of a classic text, *Heart of Darkness*. Radio gave Welles even greater liberties to play with a text than did theater because he could create rather than meet or disappoint audience expectation—the form was plastic because it was so unique and one-dimensional. Welles knew he was involved in what Hassan calls hybridization, and the charge that his manipulation of Shakespeare's text in *Macbeth* and especially in *Othello* and *Chimes at Midnight* was an act of outrageous self-aggrandizement is a stale misreading of his achievement.

Welles's *Othello* is his most cinematically complex and baroque adaptation of Shakespeare. It is his most maddening work for scholars because it remains unavailable for public screening and has only recently been released on video. To have this rich treasure locked away from audiences must be regarded as the textualist's revenge. The battle over the film's rights stands as an ironic analogy to the "base Judean who threw away a pearl richer than all his tribe." It is a further irony that while only scholars are allowed access to the film within the confines of the Folger Shakespeare Library or the U.S. Library of Congress, or the British Film Institute, we have Michael MacLiammoir's brilliant diary record of the film's progress, *Put Money in Thy Purse*, and Welles's own film about the making of his *Othello* done for West German television in 1978. So we have two intriguing texts about a text we cannot see—which may, in fact, be a postmodernist's dream: tantalizing marginalia beautifully bordering an empty page or, in this case, an empty frame.

We are, however, fortunate to have several contemporary critical studies of the film which take it seriously as film *and* as Shakespeare.[5] Jorgens and Buchman both see that one of the film's great achievements is the development of camera styles to contrast Othello's and Iago's subjective psychological states. Buchman has several strong readings of the camera's perspectives in individual scenes as he details the gradual triumph of Iago's style over Othello's. He provides a rich and full description of Welles's wild film inventiveness in depicting Othello's seizure and collapse after Iago's poison has begun its work.[6]

# One Murderous Image

A shot-by-individual-shot examination of the sequence leading up to Othello's "trance" reveals the intelligence of Welles's design. His vision encompasses a series of cage images to reinforce Iago's triumph in imprisoning Othello's imagination within Iago's own diseased conception of the world and a continuation of a startling use of chiaroscuro to frame both the racial issues at work in the play and their metaphoric reaches into the subterranean destructive forces Iago unleashes in Othello.

Another example of Welles's ability to capture Shakespearean meaning on film is detailed in Jack Jorgens's evaluative description of the beginning of the famed "seduction" scene—filmed in a single traveling shot with the camera mounted on a jeep, which serves as a marked contrast to the rapid pace of Welles's cutting throughout the rest of the film. Jorgens is attentive to the sounds and silences in and around the words which illuminate Welles's vision:

> Yet some effects are only apparently simple, as in the centerpiece of the film—a traveling shot of nearly one and a half minutes duration of Othello and Iago walking together, stride for stride, along the ramparts of the fortress. Iago questioning, pausing, refusing to reveal his suspicions, questioning again. It is a good shot because the acting is good, and the seeming endlessness of their motion suits the dramatic moment. It is a great shot because of its overlaying of several *aural and visual* rhythms, each in conflict with the others, which builds to a growing sense of unease in the viewer: the regular *beat* of the boots on the stone and the accompanying movements of their bodies, the rhythm of the *waves beating* against the shore, the uneven bursts of speech and silence, the irregular appearances of cannon in the notches of the wall, the regular patches of sunlight thrown on the walker's feet, and the pattern of the irregularly spaced rocks in the sea beyond the ramparts.[7]

To build on Jorgens's analysis, Welles has those footbeats carefully punctuate the two key words Iago skillfully plants in Othello's mind and which Othello echoes back to him: "honest" and "think." The camera's final movement is to zero in on a medium close-up of Othello, for the first time alone in the frame, as he swallows Iago's hints and takes the hook: "Why there's more in this . . ." The first cut has the camera now positioned behind Othello's head looking at Iago in the right side of the frame as he delivers his second variation on the reputation theme: "Good name, my lord . . ." Welles then cuts back to Othello in shadows on the left side of the frame with the right half capturing light playing on the ramparts wall: "By heaven I'll know thy thoughts" followed by a cut to Iago for "O beware my lord, of jealousy/It is the green-eyed monster," with the camera cutting back to a low-angle shot with Othello's face framed by the sky—the last shot we will have of him in this sequence against light and space. As Davies rightly sees,"Welles's manipulation of the two men in space and in relation to the natural outdoor sunlight is part of the general strategy whereby Iago moves into oblique light and Othello into the trap of darkness."[8]

Welles's Othello plunges into that trap by moving down into the fortress, pausing only in an archway for a reaction shot to Iago's "I know the country's dispositions well," and then continues restlessly on to his own chambers trying to escape the images Iago has planted at the very moment he relinquishes himself completely to Iago's vision: "Now art thou my lieutenant." "I am bound to thee forever."

This crucial exchange immediately is followed by Othello removing his robe which Iago takes as Othello examines his reflection in an unusually shaped mirror as Iago deadpans: "I see this has a little dashed thy spirits."[9] The next shot is the supreme one in the sequence. It captures Iago, Othello, and Othello's distorted reflection in what MacLiammoir refers to as the "Carpaccio Mirror," which also catches a gridlike shadow from the latticework in the chamber, as Iago delivers the "conception . . . clime . . . degree" line. This sends Othello to his knees as Desdemona enters and tries to soothe his clearly disturbed spirit and mind. He rises on "your napkin is too little" and pulls at his breastplate in a futile attempt to relieve his transformation, which sends him back to the mirror in vain search to recapture "my perfect parts which do attest me right" only to have Desdemona—who has followed him—caught in the mirror as well. Othello pivots and takes Suzanne Cloutier's alabaster face in his hands and examines it with deep puzzlement as Emelia in the rear of the frame picks up the handkerchief. Othello releases Desdemona and turns and throws the curtains back which surround the bed. Cut to new scene with Emelia coming down stairs toward her husband teasingly saying "I have a thing for you."

Peter S. Donaldson has a brilliant reading of this sequence which culminates in his understanding that "the eye is literally and figuratively a mirror. Welles seems to know this; his use of mirrors resembles the lover's game of finding one's image reflected in another's eyes. . . . For Welles, fantasies of omnipotence and transcendence are often associated with the power of the film medium. But he is also aware of the capacity of the medium to degrade and diminish, and he associates it, as here in *Othello*, with the failure of love."[10] Donaldson links this failure to a psychoanalytic understanding of the relationship between mirrors and mothers which leads him to conclude: "It is not conflict with rivals or with internalized Oedipal guilt that plagues Welles's character; it is the failure of the maternal object to mirror and to satisfy."[11]

I have attempted to provide the sequence of events in this scene in greater detail than Jorgens, Buchman, and Davies but to the same purpose: to indicate the care, organization, discipline and understanding they reveal about the ways in which Welles puts his cinematic intelligence to use in illuminating Shakespeare. From the relatively open and smooth traveling shot which began the sequence, to a series of medium close-ups which catch Othello's face in the shadows, to Othello's plunge down into the fortress to seek relief only to find imprisonment, to Welles's repeated use of the mirror to capture both Othello's loss of assured identity and the powerful masculine vanity that identity was based upon, all these sequences capture Othello's disintegration. A disintegration made complete by the arrival of Desdemona and her inability to displace the image of her Iago has created for Othello and Othello's uncomprehending inability to discover her flaw, her imperfection, her dishonesty in her face. Othello moves from the mirror, to Desdemona's face, and then flings aside the curtains of the marriage bed where now he sees only his own contamination.

This is a complex and subtle rendering of Shakespearean meaning which surely anticipates many of the key critical ingredients associated with postmodern theory I outlined earlier. Decanonization, fragmentation, and hybridization are all at play here as Welles refashions, rearranges, reshapes the text to translate it into the technical resources and finished images which are at the heart of the film. A pluralist reading might see a triad at work in the play, with Desdemona and Iago being envisioned as the principal "readers" of Othello's text. Desdemona is, of course, the liberal-humanist reader who responds to Othello's narrative in a traditional fashion: she sees "his image in his mind," she urges his narrative forward, she responds as a sympathetic auditor by simultaneously pitying and being thrilled by his tale. She idealizes his text and wishes to merge with it, marry it, to earn a place in his story.

Iago, on the other hand, is the deconstructionist. He wants to re-write Othello's text—which has made him marginal—and does so, with critical cleverness, by taking Othello to school in the principal teaching methods of the New Criticism. He begins by asking innocent and leading questions about the surface narrative ("Did Michael Cassio, when you wooed my lady,/Know of your love?") of Othello's courtship as a method of establishing what countless undergraduates would label, with a groan, the text's deeper, hidden, meaning. A meaning which, in the new critical lexicon, is meant to reveal the artist's brilliant control of irony and ambiguity in blending the form and content of his text, but which in Iago's perverse deconstructionist reading ("I am nothing if not critical") is meant to release Othello's destructive power: "I'll chop her into messes." Iago, in my reading, becomes a vicious parody of the postmodern critic, weaving the fragments of his destructive fantasy so skillfully that he moves from margin to center, refashioning Othello's view of self and the world.

What Iago, of course, releases in Othello is his own subconscious fear that, through his marriage, his own highly idealized sense of self, his own carefully created text, has become stained. This fear in an ego so powerful, once released, becomes monstrous. Stanley Cavell's understanding of Othello's murder of Desdemona is illuminating: "He cannot forgive Desdemona for existing, for being separate from him, outside, beyond command, commanding, her captain's captain."[12] Cavell sees that Othello's instability is rooted in his buried fear of sexuality conceived as the stain of imperfection which Othello translates into the idea of sacrifice. Desdemona's gift of her virginity, her willingness to become imperfect through the seaming of their union "is the sacrifice he [Othello] could not accept, for then he was not himself perfect. It must be displaced."[13] Cavell is writing long after Welles's film, but he is following Welles's understanding of Othello's buried fear that Welles captures through key filmic images; these come to define Welles's Othello.

From the film's opening overhead shot of Othello's face, created as if the camera shutter were gradually opening, to the final overhead shot of Othello and Desdemona on their marriage-murder bed, the key perspective of the camera is looking down, often peering into underground vaults and sewers. Jorgens is excellent in detailing the horizontal and vertical levels Welles employs, but we are most frequently placed, by the camera, above the action, where we are forced to peer down through latticework holes, or windows, or twisting staircases to try to see what is submerged. The two most famous examples are 2.3 and 5.1, the drunken brawl Iago manipulates to discredit Cassio and the fight between Roderigo and Cassio which ends with Iago's murder of Roderigo.

Welles condenses the three scenes of act 2 into one long arc which extends from Othello's arrival in Cyprus, where he climbs the steps up from the harbor to the ramparts of the fortress to greet his "fair warrior," on to the festive blare of trumpets as Cassio announces "Othello's pleasure" that the destruction of the Turkish fleet and the consummation of his marriage be celebrated with "sport," "revels," and the "full liberty of feasting," to the first shot (within the narrative proper) of the huge cage sitting empty on the wharf, to Iago urging Cassio to drink, to Othello gathering Desdemona into his embrace in their bedchamber, to Iago moving through scenes of revelry, to the sudden move into an underground world where the Roderigo-Cassio chase and fight is carried out. Welles moves us from the top of the battlements and the triumphant reunion of Othello and Desdemona, to the very bottom of the Cyprus world, where men slosh through a sewerlike environment, disturbing the general celebration and, more importantly, bringing an abrupt end to Othello's and Desdemona's lovemaking.

As I have indicated, our first introduction to the underground world is from above as the camera peers down through a latticework cover and gives a glimpse of the figures struggling below who are framed by the barlike shadows cast by the cistern's cover. The chamber itself was one of Welles's great discoveries in the Moroccan town of Mazagan near Mogador, where the majority of the Cyprus scenes were shot. Michael MacLiammoir's vivid description captures the appeal of Welles's find:

> Its beauty, of undeniable and bewildering quality, is equalled by its enormous size, foetid, clinging air, and general aspect of nameless doom. . . . it was built in the early half of the fifteenth century by Portuguese artists of satanic genius. . . . ominous dark ceiling of stone is supported by scores of heavy pillared arches that soar into the dusk like wings of bats; every sound causes faint echoes to reverberate from unexplored recesses; squat doorways lead the eyes. . . . to swiftly descending staircases; surrounding cloisters, half visible in the gloom, seem to be full of deep murmuring, yet a damp, dripping silence engulfs you as you step fearfully over the threshold.[14]

Here, and in the later, more famous Turkish bath scene, Welles has found a stunning visual equivalent for Shakespeare's images which chart Othello's progress from "an unhoused free condition"—constantly equated with the liberty and power of the sea—to "a cistern for foul toads/To knot and gender in."

The shadows and sounds of Cassio, Roderigo, Montanto, and Iago sloshing through this Byzantine sewer (dubbed as "Portugal's answer to Poe" by MacLiammoir) becomes a perfect counterpoint—a perverse reverse image—of the "profit yet to come" between Othello and Desdemona. The "foul rout" promoted by Iago's clever misrule is extended by Welles through a maze of pillars to become a Jungian nightmare of Othello's wedding dreams. The fighting and sloshing through a maze of pillars concludes with an overhead shot down into the sewer which captures Roderigo's little white dog forlornly wandering through the water in search of his master. We then cut to Othello and Desdemona up on the battlements having been roused from their bed by the chaos below. Welles immediately cuts again to the sewer, where Roderigo has returned to claim his dog. Welles, by framing the awakened Othello and Desdemona with the sewer shots of Roderigo and his dog, is making a wickedly playful association of gulls and their pets as well as reminding us that Iago has set in motion events which will release much greater destructive powers than drowning cats and blind puppies.[15]

Roderigo's dog threads his way through the film and makes the journey from Venice to Cyprus. My first reaction to its presence—influenced perhaps by Welles's ludicrous attachment to his own poodle in his latter years—was that it was a sentimental intrusion. I should have better trusted Welles's artistic instincts. In my fruitless search through Carpaccio for a source for the mirror in Othello's dressing chamber I did make an unexpected find—Carpaccio's use of a small white dog in several paintings, most prominently in "The Vision of St. Augustine" and "A Miracle of the Relic of the True Cross." In the latter the dog appears on the bow of a gondola maneuvered by a black gondolier.

The next scene, again fashioned by Iago, which makes imaginative use of an overhead perspective of violence breaking out in a cage-like atmosphere, is the infamous Turkish bath setting for 5.1. This was actually the first scene shot in the film because the costumes had not yet arrived in Morocco and Welles seized on the expedient of shooting in a locale that would require only towels. The mandolins underscore the frenetic excitement of the scene, which lasts just less than

two minutes and which contains thirty-eight cuts.[16] The atmosphere
of the bath shares the dankness of the sewer scene, the sense of water
dripping everywhere, the violence exploding in an enclosed space as
well as the use of Roderigo's dog, this time coddled by Iago as he
urges Roderigo to attack Cassio. The latticework of the cistern cover
is here echoed by the slats in the floor through which Iago repeatedly
stabs his sword in search of Roderigo scurrying for protection beneath. Shots of the sword plunging through the slats accompanied by
the quickened pace of the mandolins give way—once Iago's task is
accomplished—to the quiet dripping (oozing) of the water and a final
shot of Roderigo's dog. In the frenzied editing of this sequence, the
overhead shots through the slats extend Welles's repeated use—in a
wonderful variety of contexts—of barlike shadows to capture the way
in which the Othello world closes in on itself and how the expanse of
Othello's vision gives way to the impasse of Iago's.

This movement is underlined by Welles's cut from the Turkish
bath to Othello shutting the door, made of iron bars, of his bed
chamber as the camera cuts to Desdemona framed against a latticework window as she asks:

> Dost thou in conscience think, tell me, Emelia
> That there be women do abuse their husbands
> In such gross kind?
> (4.3.63–65)

Emelia departs after her reply, given as she helps Desdemona on
with her nightgown, and we are thrust into total darkness as we hear
"It is the cause" as the camera slowly pans to Othello's face as he
approaches his victim. That approach moves him by and through the
visual devices Welles has used to establish the landscape of the play:
shadows, the latticework window, a many-pillared room which bears
an eerie polished resemblance to the ceiling and pillars of the cistern
(but which in fact is the crypt in a small thirteenth-century church in
Viterbo south of Rome).

Then as he pushes his way through the curtains which surround
the bed, Othello—with a logic Stanley Cavell's reading of the play
would endorse—strangles Desdemona with the famous "spotted"
handkerchief, and we are given a wonderfully surreal overhead shot
of Desdemona's face moving, struggling for breath, through the
handkerchief. After the murder we again get a series of shots, including one of Iago's cage hanging from the battlements, that we have
come to associate with Othello's circumscription: Othello framed by

shadows, archways, bars, as the camera spins out of control in a manner similar to Othello's fit, this time capturing the chamber's vaulted ceilings as Othello finally recovers his balance and lifts Desdemona from the floor and places her on the bed. In so doing he looks up at Cassio looking down at him through a large round opening in the ceiling. We are now looking down into Othello's sewer-cistern-dungeon, and Welles shoots the entire "soft you, a word or two" speech from this overhead perspective. Othello's face has become entirely swallowed by the surrounding shadows as he finishes his speech and collapses on the bed as a cover is placed over the hole in the ceiling shutting off the camera's access to Othello's ruined world.

Many commentators have been quick to pick up MacLiammoir's remark that Welles's conception of Iago derived from what he believed to be Iago's impotence. It is no surprise that Shakespeareans, trained as motive hunters, should zero in on this contribution to the continuing debate about Iago's character. What has gone unnoticed, however, and what is so much more crucial for an understanding of Welles's *film* is MacLiammoir's report of how Welles concluded his discussion of the Othello-Iago relationship. "I like Orson's design for the growing dependence of Othello on Iago's presence, the merging of the two men in one murderous image like a pattern of loving shadows welded."[7] MacLiammoir's brilliant description of Welles's intent was written during a rehearsal period in Paris three months before actual shooting began, yet it suggestively captures the heart of Welles's achievement.

Welles's notion of the merging of Iago and Othello into "one murderous image" was far in advance of modern criticism's understanding of their relationship. C. L. Barber and Richard Wheeler echo Welles's understanding: "He [Iago] must live through Othello, become him by destroying him."[18] Barber and Wheeler also get at an important dimension of Shakespeare's play which Welles's art captures, the refusal to make Iago a scapegoat for Othello's own murderousness: "To hide what is on the bed and center only on the evil of Iago is to turn away from the full horror."[19]

Welles uses the black and white of his medium to create a vivid chiarascuro "pattern of loving shadows welded." After the shadows have melded so murderously that they "put out the light" Welles cuts back to the opening, precredits, funeral procession with Othello and Desdemona being carried to the harbor. The procession is framed in silhouette against the horizon—our first readjustment to a light/dark contrast since the beginning of the murder scene. We are given an interesting shot of the battlements and Iago's cage swinging from the top of the tower's wall all reflected in the harbor. The shot is clearly a studio contrivance but one meant, I believe, to call our attention, yet again, to the nature of Welles's medium. Film is a reflection, a series of shadows projected on a wall, and Welles has employed the very nature of film as the key metaphor for capturing Shakespeare's play. Framed by the shades of Othello and Desdemona and by a reminder that their story is a casting of shadows, the final image is an uncanny presentiment of deconstruction's marriage of presence and absence. By the end of the film the only light that remains is that reflected in the harbor's water, a reflection which captures Iago's suspended cage swinging over the mourners below. The shadows cast from the projection booth flicker and go out.[20]

## CHAPTER FIVE

# Babes in the Woods:
# Shakespearean Comedy
# on Film

•

O NE OF the great achievements of modern Shakespearean criticism is the way in which it has liberated the comedies from secondary consideration within the canon. The work of C. L. Barber, Northrop Frye, John Russell Brown, Jan Kott, and Leo Salingar has created an intellectual and theoretical landscape for the comedies as rich and suggestive as the finest work done on the tragedies in the past thirty years. The work of these critics has had a profound effect not only in academic circles but in the world of performance as well.

The program notes for productions of the comedies over the past twenty-five years at major repertory theaters are saturated with quotations from these contemporary critics, quotations which move far beyond decorative commentary into the worlds of structure, pattern, and movement. Of course program notes can be deceiving; often they are mere window dressing unrelated to the actual production's values and emphasis. But it is, I think, possible to establish and document crucial relationships between current critical ideas and production strategy in such notable productions as Peter Hall's two *Dreams* at the RSC, followed by Peter Brook's famous production of the same play with the same company; John Barton's *Twelfth Night* and *Much Ado About Nothing;* and productions of *As You Like It* at Stratford Festival Canada, the National Theatre, and the RSC directed by Robin Phillips, John Dexter, Terry Hands, and Adrian Noble. What marked all of these productions as being in a modern idiom was their design incorporation of the seasonal rhythms embedded in these plays, their highlighting of the sterile court-liberating green world contrast, their underlining of the disguise motif as metaphor for sexual confusion and transformation, and their common adoption of a tone or atmosphere in which wit held sway over farce. Jack Jorgens has demonstrated admirably that a similar interchange between critical formulation and production approach can be identified in the two English-language films based on Shakespeare's comedies made during the 1960s: Franco Zeffirelli's *Taming of the Shrew* and Peter Hall's *A Midsummer Night's Dream.*[1]

To demonstrate what liberating perspectives modern Shakespeare criticism has provided contemporary directors of the comedies it is instructive to turn to the beginnings of sound filmed Shakespeare, to Reinhardt and Dieterle's *A Midsummer Night's Dream* and Paul Czinner's *As You Like It.* These two films, released within a year of each other in the mid-1930s, exploit and explore quite different strains and strands in Shakespeare's comic world than those exposed by Frye, Barber, or Kott—or Hall, Dexter, or Barton. For Reinhardt, Dieterle, and Czinner, visual spectacle takes precedence over verbal subtlety, broad farce substitutes for cool wit, allegorical possibilities are sacrificed to literal-minded explanations, and finally there is a decided tendency to translate Shakespeare's release of potent and disturbing imaginative turmoil into the safer confines of domestic folly and fancy.

None of this is, surely, surprising. Any casual survey of the criticism written about Shakespeare's comedy from the Victorians well past the Edwardians reveals a strong bias regarding these plays as picturesque idylls, all delightful daydream without shadow or substance. Couple this critical stance with film's natural attraction to spectacle, and one understands the context of Reinhardt, Dieterle, and Czinner's approach to their Shakespearean material. Neither film was a success when first released, but there is little quarrel among contemporary film and Shakespeare enthusiasts that the Reinhardt-Dieterle *Dream* has aged remarkably well and is clearly the superior work. Part of its current charm contributed considerably to its initial failure. My students, rather than finding Dick Powell, Olivia de Haviland, Mickey Rooney, Jimmy Cagney, Victor Jorey, and Anita Louise disastrously out of place in Shakespeare's dream, delight in the eclectic mixture of famous faces and acting styles familiar to them from their early years of watching late-show movies on television. And today Mickey Rooney seems as ubiquitous as Puck: popping up in *Sugar Babies*, Dr. Pepper commercials, and the Arts and Leisure section of the Sunday *New York Times* with magical regularity.

Jack Jorgens has argued that the Reinhardt-Dieterle *Dream* is "the first production on stage or screen to give anything near full weight to the play's darker elements."[2] However, although the intimations of love's nightmare can be discovered in the midst (and mist) of an overriding emphasis on spectacle in which stunning visual effects and Mendelssohn's cloying score are given more than equal billing with Shakespeare's text, it must be noted that the film repeatedly retreats from the rich suggestions of the darker side of Shakespeare's tale to seek the comfort of a more literal-minded and reductive narrative.

One particularly damaging example of this tendency is a series of actions which follow Bottom's emergence from the brake, transformed by Puck from ham to ass. After his companions scatter in amazement, Jimmy Cagney's Bottom stands alone in his wonder at their reaction. Rooney's Puck, in keeping with his characterization of the part as the wild child, hurls a rock at Bottom which glances off his head. Cagney reaches to comfort his wound and literally feels his transformation; this sends him to his knees to examine his reflection in a woodland pond. Sight confirms feeling and brings forth sighs, sniffles, and tears turning Bottom's song into a lament, a whimper for solace rather than a boisterous insistence that Bottom is Bottom and cannot be shaken by what he believes to be his companions' practical joke: "I see their knavery. This is to make an ass of me; to fright me if they could. But I will not stir from this place, do what they can. I will walk up and down here, and will sing, that they shall hear I am not afraid" (3.1.121–25).

Instead of Titania's being awakened by a Bottom in full bray we have her responding to the sobs of a forlorn child propped pathetically against a tree. Bless thee, Bottom, thou art translated indeed! Certainly, Bottom's beauty is his obliviousness; his absolute lack of self-consciousness is his most stunning quality. The film's translation of Bottom here is ass backwards; we are moved to sentimental pity rather than engaged in comic wonder. Titania responds as maternal Beauty touched by the soulful Beast, rather than as exotic Imagination become infatuated with imperturbable Reality. Bottom is seen— by Titania and the film—as a literal babe in the woods, and this reading is underlined by the way in which Reinhardt-Dieterle link Bottom with Titania's "sweet changeling"—the son of the Indian vot'ress whose custody quarrel has caused the debate and dissension between Oberon and Titania and made a breach in nature.

# Babes in the Woods

The directors make much of the physical presence of the little changeling boy by dressing him up as a miniature Rajah complete with a bejeweled turban looking as though he wandered into Shakespeare's woods lost from the set of a Kipling film.[3] Through a series of actions in which Titania fondles and caresses her little prince while Oberon looks on with eyes flashing fire, Reinhardt and Dieterle make it clear that Oberon's jealousy derives from his displacement as the sole object of Titania's affection. Shakespeare's rich clash between Titania's female loyalties and Oberon's ire at having his male dominion challenged is transformed into the melodrama of a domestic sibling-parent rivalry.

The climax of this "interlude" comes when the Indian boy finds himself abandoned by Titania as she begins to devoutly dote on Bottom. The lad stands alone in a woodland clearing crying as Oberon rides in on his black stallion to sweep him up and away with a triumphant laugh. If, in *A Midsummer Night's Dream*, Shakespeare is, in C. L. Barber's fine phrase, "making up fresh things in Ovid's manner,"[4] then Reinhardt and Dieterle, in their film of the play, are making up some stale clichés in Hollywood's fashion. In the midst of a bold attempt to create on film a visual metaphor for Shakespeare's green world, Reinhardt and Dieterle are foiled by trying to impose literal narrative on the suggestive reaches of Shakespeare's imagination. The dark and erotic possibilities of the visual landscape they create falls victim to the light and recognizable tale they ask it to contain. The possibilities they seized upon, and which Jack Jorgens celebrates, for film's ability to envelop us in Shakespeare's rich twilight world evaporate as a result of their inability to imagine narrative metaphors as powerful as their visual images. As much as we enjoy and delight in the exuberance of their achievements we must still be prepared to assess their failures to transcend early sound film's tendency to grind its material into the grist of domestic melodrama.[5]

A similar pattern can be seen at work in the other mid-1930s attempt to capture Shakespearean comedy on film. Paul Czinner's film of *As You Like It* is much tamer than Reinhardt and Dieterle's *Dream* but suffers from a similar attempt to create a studio spectacular court world placed in contrast to an Arden too easily recognized as film's version of a pastoral idyll: deer, rabbits, flocks of shaggy sheep, pleasant cows, neatly cultivated gardens with ponds arched by picturesque wooden bridges, and a charming cottage ringed by a white picket fence. The film is perhaps most remembered for eliciting from its now famous Orlando, Laurence Olivier, his assessment—based on his experience making the film—that Shakespeare and film were not meant for or made for each other.

Czinner's film has not attracted, quite properly, the critical attention or curious interest that has been devoted to the Warner Brothers *Dream*, yet its flaws echo the concerns I have raised about its more respected counterpart. In this instance the generating source for the film's approach to Shakespeare is clear, so clear it is acknowledged by the opening credits, which carry the announcement: "Treatment Suggested by J. M. Barrie." The story of Barrie's involvement is interesting. In January of 1934, at the age of 77, he was taken by his godson to see *Escape Me Never*, a new play which featured the Austrian actress Elisabeth Bergner in the role of its young heroine. Miss Bergner and her husband, the film director Paul Czinner, had just come to London to avoid the Nazi atmosphere beginning to dominate in professional circles in Germany. Barrie and Bergner were introduced, Barrie became enchanted, and determined to write a play for her: *The Boy David*, which was to be his last. In the period between Barrie's inception of *David* and its completion, Bergner and Czinner made their film of *As You Like It*. The relationship between the aged playwright's infatuation with the gamin-like Bergner and his lifelong preoccupations with never-never lands, with lost boys appearing miraculously at open windows, and with exploring the territory of what every woman knows (i.e., that she's a clever boy) all contributed importantly to the conception of Czinner's *As You Like It*.[6] The final, marvelous irony to this tale is that *The Boy David*, after a stormy period of rehearsals (Augustus John was employed to do the sets, but was dismissed after a series of violent disputes with Barrie) opened the night after Edward VIII abdicated and was completely upstaged by the saga of England's most glamorous lost boy.

In the absence of any written record of Barrie's contribution to Czinner's approach to *As You Like It*, one is invited to read that relationship through an analysis of key moments in the film. The film displays the tendency, already seen at work in the Reinhardt-Dieterle *A Midsummer Night's Dream*, to minimize the intellectual vibrancy of Shakespeare's comedy and to maximize opportunities to treat it with sentimental clichés which flirt with cute rather than clever. *Peter Pan* is a rich and rewarding fable, and one might profitably explore its engagement with magic and belief and childhood powers of displacement as they relate to Shakespeare's treatment of similar themes in his comedies. However, to superimpose its narrative development on the far more complex and daring reaches of *As You Like It* confuses rather than clarifies important dimensions of the two plays. Some concrete examples may help to illustrate my concerns.

The opening shot of the film is an overhead which pans the camera down through the branches of a tree into a busy barnyard. Parenthetically, this use of the camera as providing the viewer with a superior, overhead, perspective gradually moving us down and into the action is repeated throughout the film (most notably to introduce us to Arden and to bring us into the final scene of prenuptial festivity) and is, perhaps, an interesting technical metaphor for Barrie's preoccupation with bringing excitement and adventure into his worlds through an open window as he does in both *Peter Pan* and *What Every Woman Knows*. The barnyard is filled with the activity of farm workers making their way through the clutter and cackle of chickens, ducks, and geese. The camera tracks through this familiar farm landscape of workers at their tasks to seek out a solitary figure seated at the end of a long table, head buried in hands. Slowly the head rises to reveal the young Olivier, stunningly handsome, and totally forlorn. Our sympathy is immediately engaged by his lost expression accentuated by a single spit curl dangling down his forehead. Our attention is absorbed by the camera's lingering image of this solitary, passive figure. We are confronted with a paralyzed lost boy, not Shakespeare's Orlando whose forthright debate about the powers of fortune and nature and his heady and perceptive self-analysis about the effects of his brother's repressive actions create a portrait of a generous, independent civility threatened by unnatural hardship. (I should add immediately that Laurence Olivier's performance is what makes this *As You Like It* worth watching, and the expression which plays in his eyes and along his lips when Ganymede asks him to call him/her Rosalind is film acting at its most intelligent and witty.)

Czinner similarly reduces our initial impression of Rosalind. When, in 1.3, Celia is trying to distract her cousin through the wonderful exchange about petticoats, burrs, and holiday foolery we are treated to a clever transposition of two words in the text which reveal Barrie's concerns rather than Shakespeare's. In the text, when Celia queries Rosalind about her private thoughts, "But is all this for your father?" Rosalind responds, "No, some of it is for my child's father." Rosalind, as always, is beyond convention and into life, beyond melancholy for her exiled father and into full anticipation of the consequences of her overthrow at the wrestling match, beyond sentiment and into wit. Czinner's film, however, banishes wit and replaces it with the safer confines of sentimentality by having Rosalind respond, "No, some of it is for my father's child." The focus is reversed, turned inward toward self-pity rather than translated outward into experience. Elisabeth Bergner's Rosalind lacks resilience and independence; rather she is dainty, vulnerable in the extreme, skittish, cute. When Duke Frederick emerges in this scene to pronounce his decree of banishment, Bergner sinks to the floor and dissolves in tears. It is Celia who undertakes to comfort her and initiate the plans for liberation.

Once in Arden and in her masculine usurp'd attire, Miss Bergner plays more coy than boy. Her accent, perhaps a charming addition in another role, plays havoc with Rosalind's attempts to challenge and test Orlando's romantic assumptions about wooing, wedding, and wives. She stretches her vowels out toward eternity, and w's are her doom. She wants Celia to answer her insistent questions about the poet carving her praises throughout the forest, in "one verd." She chastizes Orlando that "men have died from time to time, and verms have eaten dem, but not for love." And when she tries to instruct him on the nature of wives, her advice emerges as, "The viser the vayvarder." Finally, what happens to her combination of vowels and w's in the "howling of Irish wolves against the moon" cannot be captured by imitation or transcription.

My final example is what ties Barrie most conspicuously to Czinner's approach. In the film's concluding sequence, once again introduced with an establishing overhead shot, we are treated with a folk extravaganza as the "country copulatives," preceded by the ubiquitous sheep, stream in to celebrate the multiple weddings. At the end of the procession comes Rosalind hand in hand with a lovely boy of three or four sporting diapers and wings! This child, who we come to discover is Hymen, is clearly the product of Barrie's imagination regarding what results when earthly things, made even, atone together. Our lost boy, and the lost girl turned boy turned girl again, have gone to the woods and in their union have created the only precious quality in Barrie's world—childhood.[7]

Both these 1930s films get swept away with the release of Shakespeare's comic art into the tricks of strong imagination; neither catches our modern understanding that such tricks are always at the service of clarifying larger issues of social and individual maturation. Shakespeare's flight to the woods is not a regressive trip back into childishness but a journey into new and exciting and dangerous realms of adult experience. It is a wonderful irony that at the moment when these two 1930s attempts to translate Shakespearean comedy onto film failed to capture the dynamics of Shakespeare's comic art Hollywood was producing a series of comedy/romance films which Stanley Cavell has brilliantly demonstrated are the true modern progeny of Shakespeare's way of working in the comic form.

Cavell's *Pursuits of Happiness: The Hollywood Comedy of Remarriage* makes deft use of modern critical formulations about Shakespeare's comedies, particularly Frye's ideas about the structure of romance and the mythos of spring, to unpack and release the rich comic subtleties of such films as *Bringing Up Baby, It Happened One Night, The Lady Eve,* and *The Philadelphia Story.* As Reinhardt-Dieterle and Czinner were domesticating and reducing the wilder reaches of Shakespeare's comic imagination, directors like Howard Hawks, Frank Capra, and George Cukor were finding modern extensions for the essence of Shakespeare's comic understanding. I agree with Carolyn Heilbron that Cavell's book is one of contemporary film criticism's triumphs and "is also perhaps the best marriage manual ever published."[8] Cavell grounds his perceptive and witty readings of these great films in his understanding of their debt to Shakespeare's art. Here, for instance, is an extended example of Cavell's mind at work and play conjuring parallels and resonances between *A Midsummer Night's Dream* and *The Philadelphia Story:*

> *The Winter's Tale* also harps on the idea of dreaming, but it is *A Midsummer Night's Dream* that more closely anticipates the conjunction of dreaming and waking, and of apparent fickleness, disgust, jealousy, compacted of imagination, with a collision of social classes and the presence of a whole society at a concluding wedding ceremony, a presence unique among the members of our genre in *The Philadelphia Story.*
>
> And *Midsummer Night's Dream* is built from the idea that the public world of day cannot resolve its conflicts apart from resolutions in the private forces of night. For us mortals, fools of finitude, this therapy must occur by way of remembering something, awakening to something, and by forgetting something, awakening from something. In the language of *The Philadelphia Story* this is called getting your eyes opened, and the passage both to the private forces of night and to the public world of consequences may be accomplished by champagne, or some other

concoctions of liquors and juices. Dexter offers Tracy a Stinger, made he says "with the juice of a few flowers." In *Midsummer Night's Dream* the eyes are analogously closed and opened by what it calls the liquor or juice of certain flowers or herbs, used externally. It is upon such application that Titania becomes enamored of an ass. Tracy presumably became enamored of her ass by the more up-to-date agency of what we call "the rebound," what Dexter calls "a swing"; but she wishes to do with her creature what Titania wishes to do with hers, to "purge [his] mortal grossness so,/That [he shall] like an airy spirit go." Tracy is shown to try purging, or anyway covering, George's lower-class grossness so that he can go like an airy aristocrat on horseback (or rather to cover his failed attempt to cover his grossness) by rubbing dirt into his new riding habit.[9]

Cavell uses Shakespeare as a means of deepening our pleasure in these films, just as critics such as Barber and Frye opened our eyes to levels of individual and social meaning in Shakespeare's comedies which escaped previous commentators. Cavell also demonstrates that a sophisticated comedy of romance and remarriage is at the heart of Hollywood's popular legacy, thus belying the notion that the wit and subtlety and structure of Shakespearean comedy—unlike the passion and violence of the tragedies—is incompatible with film.

The most successful modern attempt to translate Shakespearean comedy onto film is Peter Hall's *A Midsummer Night's Dream*. Here we have another example of a director coming to film Shakespeare after having directed several successful stage productions of the play. In this instance, as Michael Mullin has shown, Hall's conception and approach to the play was honed by two productions of *A Midsummer Night's Dream* during his tenure as director of the Royal Shakespeare Company.[10] The film, in many ways, can be seen as a culmination of his work with the company, and it features many of the actors who came to prominence under the repertory system inaugurated by Hall at Stratford: Ian Richardson, Ian Holm, Judi Dench, David Warner, Diana Rigg, Paul Rogers, Derek Godfrey, and Helen Mirren.

Even though Hall's film captures the earthy, erotic, even nightmare qualities of Shakespeare's *Dream* as articulated by modern critics like Jan Kott and was structured to mirror the seasonal confusions caused by Oberon and Titania's dissensions, it proved, on release, to be far in advance of its audience's expectations. Twenty years later it stands as the most intelligent and successful—particularly to generations of university student audiences—achievement in Shakespearean comedy on film. It also stands as an interesting synthesis of Kottian ideas about the play linked with an attention to the language of the text inspired, Hall tells us, by F. R. Leavis's formalist criticism. Hall maintains that he shot so much of his film in close-ups because he found it "the only way to scrutinize the marked ambiguity of the text."[11]

Jack Jorgens provides a fine reading of the film, and he is particularly good at demonstrating how adventuresome Hall is in using film techniques which correspond to eclectic elements in Shakespeare's own art and style.

> Hall's magic, like Shakespeare's has a purpose. The assaults on our viewing habits and the violations of conventions serve as an analogue for what happens to those other dreamers, the lovers, Bottom, and Titania. . . . For dreamers and audience in this film, the patterns of logic break down. . . . In being true to the dream experience, Hall has gone some distance toward what Peter Brook and others have called for—a style which liberates Shakespeare's multi-layered, fluid, imagistic verse from slow, literal, naturalistic film textures and images.[12]

Hall borrows from Godard by using jump cuts, a hand-held camera, and imaginative and unusual placement of his actors in the frame; breaking up long speeches or interchanges between two characters by shifting the background without transition between locations; and using multiple-color filters for the camera lens, especially on Titania's "These are the forgeries of jealousy" speech. Thus Hall playfully breaks our realistic expectations for film narrative even as he further confounds our expectations for Shakespeare's *Dream* by plopping his actors down in a real woods, where the ground is dank and dirty, the night distempered, and the air permeated by contagious fogs.

Hall's wood is both jungle and maze, and we are, like the lovers, trapped within it and never privileged by the camera with a perspective superior to theirs. Hall understands that Shakespeare's woods in the *Dream* is not a benign pastoral landscape sentimentally set in contrast with the patriarchal rigidity of Athens. The woods, with its seasonal dislocations caused by a kind of marital squabble over the raising of a child, becomes a mirror for the confusion and pull of sexual and gender loyalties experienced by the lovers. They have fled into a dream which rapidly turns to nightmare as they experience all the agonies of puberty compressed into a single night. As the lovers become more disheveled and mud-caked, so they become more exposed, vulnerable, and comic. They, too, are going through a ritual of transformation which the woods makes possible not through a natural benevolence but through an absence of social rules and structures. This landscape is "other"—mirroring our inchoate dreams and desires. Shakespeare's forest is the space, in C. L. Barber's helpful formulation, which allows for the confusing release of desire typically suppressed or controlled by the social structure, so that through the expression of that emotion issues of human interaction can become clarified.

As Jorgens points out, Hall's use of the buildings and grounds surrounding Compton Verney, the English country home where he shot the film during six weeks of a chilly and damp September, reveals his secure understanding of the structure of Shakespeare's text. After the credits have rolled against the backdrop of sky and pond in a series of shots which mirror the seasonal changes in Titania's famous speech and which feature a series of sounds from nature, primarily birds and crickets, accompanied by the call of the French horns associated with Theseus, Hall gives us a shot of Philostrate marching down the formal path to the main house with the house's servants lining the path in two neat rows. Athens is superimposed on the screen as Hall provides us with his own visual joke to mirror Shakespeare's eclectic mingling of Ovid and Warwickshire. The scene with Theseus, Egeus, and the lovers is shot within the main house with the subsequent exchange between Lysander and Hermia begun within and moved without for the meeting with Helena. Plans for escape to the woods are formulated with the two of them seated in a boat on the pond. The movement, then, is from house to grounds to pond to woods, each landscape becoming more fluid and less ordered, beautifully capturing the dynamics of Shakespeare's text.[13]

Appropriately, the play's great middlemen and mediators between art and life, imagination, and reality—Bottom, Quince, and crew—are discovered making their plans under a lean-to attached to an outbuilding, a halfway house between Theseus's court and Oberon and Titania's woods. Hall often uses bird noises to accompany his transitions between scenes. We hear the sound of a duck taking flight from the pond as a move between 1.1 and 1.2. And then we hear chickens cackling as the mechanicals disperse at the end of 1.2, which gives way to the hoot of a solitary owl as Hall cuts to the first forest scene. Hall reveals a sure understanding of his craft, both as

[ 74 ]

filmmaker and interpreter of Shakespeare, in his deft merging of landscape and text which gets at Shakespeare's exploration of the relationship between desire and decorum, imagination and reality, art and life, without sacrificing the essential humor which triggers our pleasure and delight. The film's final series of shots, featuring Puck's epilogue, move him through the film's central landscapes as the camera follows his progression in a semicircular fashion. From Philostrate's deliberate stride up the straight path to Puck's final series of movements from woods to pond to house, Hall's film embraces Shakespeare's ever-widening comic circle as it expands to include at its very center and heart, the wooing of Bottom by Titania.

Hall's *A Midsummer Night's Dream* stands as the finest realization we have of a Shakespearean comedy on film. He gives us text *and* interpretation in which he skillfully employs his film intelligence to augment our pleasure in Shakespeare's art. Throughout my discussions of contemporary film and stage productions of Shakespeare I have attempted to articulate influences and resonances between these two worlds of performance. I find it interesting that no performance critic, in discussing perhaps the single most famous Shakespeare production in the past twenty years—Peter Brook's *A Midsummer Night's Dream*—has paused to consider its relationship to Hall's *Dream*. After all both directors worked side by side to develop the Royal Shakespeare Company in the 1960s, both were leaders in the Shakespeare revolution which replaced the actor-manager tradition with that of the university-educated director, both were heavily influenced by continental production ideas, and particularly by the work of Jan Kott, whose *Shakespeare Our Contemporary* found resonance with theater directors long before it found sympathetic readers among academic Shakespeareans. One of the great pleasures for Shakespeare observers of my generation has been to see the way in which productions at the Royal Shakespeare Company comment on one another, and no pair of productions provides such a remarkable dialogue as the two *Dreams* imagined by Peter Hall and Peter Brook. In both cases it is obvious that Hall and Brook were escaping the established production tradition for the play dominated by the fairies all wrapped about in gauzes and by Mendelssohn's score. Hall was explicit in describing his break with that tradition:

> I've tried in the *Dream* to get away completely from the expected Shakespearean setting, which is essentially nineteenth century and Pre-Rapahelite. . . . That's how the *Dream* has

always been presented, culminating in Reinhardt's stage productions, and his film of the 1930s.[14]

Hall, certainly inspired by Kott's essay "Titania and the Ass's Head," signaled his revolutionary intentions by shooting on location in a cold, muddy, English countryside and stressing the text's earthy, erotic qualities made manifest by Judi Dench's naked Titania, played as the gentlest and most all-embracing earth mother. So Hall broke with tradition by actually taking us to nature and rubbing our noses in it through the exasperating confusions of the lovers.[15] Brook, faced with the results of Hall's interpretive decisions, clearly decided on taking a completely opposite tack, and one which emphasized the very performance, or self-reflexive, nature of Shakespeare's play. If Hall, through the medium of film, found a means of accentuating aspects of the play nearly impossible to capture in a stage production, so too Brook would find an equally daring means of obliterating generations of staged conceptions of the play. As J. L. Styan has observed, Brook's emphasis was on the magical performance aspect of the play, and Styan's description of the production's famous white box set allows us to see immediately that Brook's conception makes as radical a break with *Dream* tradition as did Hall's:

> Sally Jacobs's set was variously seen as a three-sided white box with a white carpet, a squash court, a clinic, a scientific research station, an operating theatre, a gymnasium and a big top. Two doors were cut into the back wall, two slits in the sides, two ladders set in the downstage edges, and a gallery or catwalk round its top allowed the musicians and fairies to gaze down at the players fifteen feet below in the box. . . . Into this space the immortals could indeed descend on trapezes or manipulate flexible metal coils on the end of rods to suggest trees for John Russell Brown, "this was a machine for acting in," and at the same time the actors acting in it were the visible puppets of the machine.[16]

Brook's theatrical imagination has zoomed us light-years away from Hall's Warwickshire woods, but that journey which translates the *Dream* into such a contemporary space would not have been possible without Hall's equally audacious decision to take us deep into the forest of the night. Once these productions had broken with the tradition for staging the *Dream*, they become the new standards against which subsequent productions were forced to set themselves. All four of the most successful *Dreams* of the past two decades—Alvin Epstein's at Yale in 1975, Ron Daniels's at the RSC in 1981, Liviu Ciulei's at the Guthrie in 1985, and A. J. Antoon's for the New York Shakespeare Festival in 1988—found their interpretive energy in responding to either Hall's or Brook's approach to the play.

The only film of a Shakespeare comedy to be released in the 1980s was Derek Jarman's *Tempest*, which made as significant a break with Hall's approach to a Shakespearean comedy-romance as Hall had made with Reinhardt-Dieterle and Czinner. Jarman's *Tempest* is, along with Peter Greenaway's *Prospero's Books*, the most idiosyncratic and personal of all sound-filmed Shakespeare. It shares, in the energy and direction of its approach to Shakespeare's text, the critical assumptions of the postmodernists mirroring ideas from such disparate camps as the deconstructionists and the cultural materialists.

Jarman's film, particularly when considered in the context of the BBC series which dominated film and video productions of Shakespeare in the 1980s, came as an outrageously invigorating breath of fresh air. Jarman shot the interiors of his 90-minute color film at the Palladian Stoneleigh Abbey in Warwickshire and the exteriors on the Northumbrian coast near Banburgh Castle on a budget of $325,000—a feat almost as magical as Prospero's.

With one notable exception (Arlen's "Stormy Weather") all the words are Shakespeare's. We get something more than half the text, and though it is often rearranged and reassigned, the play's essential plot divisions and developments remain. Nevertheless, the film is decidedly Jarman's re-creation of the text in his own, highly individualized, cinematic style. Jarman dreams over and through Shakespeare's play in a manner which mixes elements from the work of Cocteau, Welles, Kenneth Anger, and Ken Russell. Dream, nightmare, and imprisonment are the key elements in his visual and verbal approach to his Shakespearean material.

The tempest itself emanates from Prospero's nightmare, with the mariner's cries of "we split," "cold," and "all lost," echoing through Prospero's disturbed soul as he struggles to awake. In this opening sequence the film cuts repeatedly between Prospero's tossings in bed as he fights to free himself from a gauzelike covering which threatens to suffocate him, and shots of Alonzo's ship struggling for survival in the tempest-tossed sea. Sounds of heavy breathing broken by quick gasps are heard on the sound track amidst the storm and the mariner's shouts; these sounds recur periodically during the film, particularly when Prospero is in solitary contemplation of his project or is about to summon Ariel; they serve as a reminder that the film conceives of the play as a product of Prospero's nightmare or dream vision. This notion is rounded off neatly at the conclusion of the film, which ends not with Prospero's epilogue but with "Our revels now are ended," Jarman's means of underlining that this tempest has progressed from the nightmare of Prospero's revenge through his dream of Miranda and Ferdinand's meeting and marriage to the gentle and generous realization that we all "are such stuff/As dreams are made on, and our little life/Is rounded with a sleep."

By setting the chief scenes of his film within the empty, decaying Stoneleigh Abbey rather than on an open isle, Jarman extends his framing nightmare-dream-sleep device into the heart of Shakespeare's tale and discovers there an imprisoning claustrophobia, a feat I found exciting and imaginative. The play, after all, has much to do with many forms of literal and figurative bondage, and Jarman's film makes one see that Prospero's dream of revenge is as much being bounded in a nutshell as is the nightmare of his rude exile. Even his magic cannot make Jarman's Prospero a king of infinite space, for he progressively covers every inch of wall and floor space with chalked diagrams, astrological chartings, and geometrical designs and formulas ever increasingly finding himself in a closed universe of his own devising. Heathcote Williams, who plays Prospero, is a professional magician as well as an actor but his performance eschews the sleight of hand for the rougher magic of the mathematician.[17] When one interviewer expressed disappointment that Prospero didn't break his staff, Jarman responded (surely with a twinkle), "Ah, but you see he does break his piece of chalk."

As much as I admired the visual shape and design Jarman gives his film, I found several key performances (or rather conceptions of characters realized through performances) to be curiously at odds with the film's scenic beauty and intelligence. Jack Birkett's Caliban had a splendid look—huge and moon-faced with a menacing smile—but the menace disintegrated too often into a high-pitched giggle or lisping whine and drained the character of its power, a power further eroded by Birkett's campish prance, which made his Caliban more eunuch than monster capable of rape. One moment when this posture worked, however, was in the scene where Prospero threatens Ferdinand: "I'll manacle thy neck and feet together:/Sea water shalt thou drink . . . " here played with Caliban in the background feverishly turning a huge hurdy-gurdy pouring forth carnival music accompanied by Birkett's raucous giggle!

On the other hand, Karl Johnson's Ariel was a marvel: controlled, alert, intelligent, and haunting with no resort to punk or camp idioms, which his character might have more easily invited than Caliban's or Miranda's. David Meyer's Ferdinand emerging naked from a cold, blue-filtered sea to find his first warmth and comfort in the straw beside Caliban's stable fire was likewise more striking for its straightforwardness and simplicity.

Two scenes in the film, entirely of Jarman's invention, created the most publicity and controversy when the film was released. The first consisted of a silent flashback to the days of Sycorax's reign over the island with Ariel in manacles and Caliban sucking contentedly at her ample breast; the second contained a lavish production number (courtesy of Busby Berkeley via Ken Russell) with a chorus line of dancing sailors arranged to set off the blues singer Elizabeth Welch's wonderful rendition of Harold Arlen's "Stormy Weather." I found Caliban at his mother's pap intrusive and unnecessary but thought Miss Welch's "Stormy Weather" inspired. Its refrain of "Keeps rainin' all the time" became a wonderful modern equivalent for Feste's corrective to *Twelfth Night's* midsummer madness: "the rain it raineth every day." This moment worked because it created a witty resonance with all those other moments in the comedies where, in the midst of the festive celebration of love and romance, Shakespeare carefully places reminders that holiday is not every day, that men are April when they woo but December when they wed, that maids are May when they are maids but the sky changes when they are wives.

It is interesting to note, however, that the character who Jarman has the greatest difficulty in reimagining is Miranda. Her innocence puzzles Jarman and so his film resorts to a set of attitudes reminiscent of those adopted by Reinhardt-Dieterle and Czinner. She, like Mickey Rooney's Puck, emerges as something of a wild child, obsessively riding a large rocking horse, squealing with delight when Caliban discovers her bathing, sucking her thumb, twisting her fingers in her unkempt locks, dressing up in a child's version of a starlet's tiara-crowned outfit, imagining herself parading down the King's Road in the latest display of punk pastels. Jarman, who sees so much so well in his film, cannot translate Miranda into a modern idiom. In brazenly trying to avoid the sentimental, he allows his art here to become petulant rather than playful. His treatment of Miranda becomes, for all its attempts to be hip, curiously akin to the patterns I traced in the 1930s efforts to first capture Shakespeare on film in words as well as images.

Peter Hall's *A Midsummer Night's Dream* remains film's most daring and successful marriage of image and text and can be seen, in retrospect, as the culmination of his work with Shakespeare during his Stratford period. After an intentional exile from directing Shakespeare for six years, Hall reemerged as the leader of the largest and most ambitious repertory theater in the world, Britain's National Theatre.

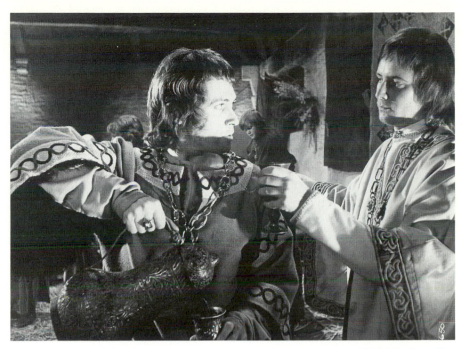

1. Malcolm (Stephen Chase) insists on being served by Macbeth (Jon Finch). Polanski's *Macbeth*.

2. Macbeth (Jonathan Pryce) stirs both his passion and guilt with Lady Macbeth (Sinead Cusack). Adrian Noble's RSC production.

3. Doll Tearsheet (Jeanne Moreau) gently scolds her "whoreson tidy Bartholomew boar-pig," Falstaff (Orson Welles). Welles's *Chimes at Midnight*.

4. Othello (Orson Welles) and the Carpaccio mirror. Welles's *Othello*.

5. Bottom (James Cagney) and Titania (Anita Louise). Reinhardt/Dieterle's *A Midsummer Night's Dream*.

6. Bottom (Paul Rogers) and Titania (Judi Dench). Hall's *A Midsummer Night's Dream*.

7. Kenneth Anger as the little changeling boy. Reinhardt/Dieterle *A Midsummer Night's Dream*.

8. Prospero (Heathcote Williams) with his mathematical projections. Jarman's *Tempest*.

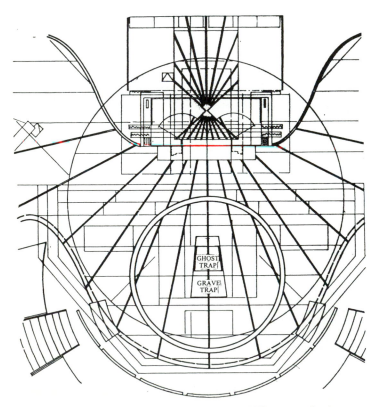

9. John Bury's stage design for Peter Hall's National Theatre production of *Hamlet*.

10. Romeo (Anton Lesser). Ron Daniels's RSC production of *Romeo and Juliet*.

11. Juliet (Judy Buxton). Ron Daniels's RSC production of *Romeo and Juliet*.

12. The Fool (Antony Sher) and King Lear (Michael Gambon) in their music hall routine. Adrian Noble's RSC production of *King Lear*.

13. Lear (Michael Gambon) "fantastically dressed in wildflowers." Adrian Noble's RSC production of *King Lear*.

14. Rosalind (Juliet Stevenson) on her way to Arden. Adrian Noble's RSC production of *As You Like It*.

15. Celia (Fiona Shaw), Oliver (Bruce Alexander), and Rosalind (Juliet Stevenson) play "Call me Spielberg." Adrian Noble's RSC production of *As You Like It*.

16. Falstaff (John Woodvine) and Hal (Michael Pennington) trade hyperbolic slanders. Michael Bogdanov's ESC production of *The Wars of the Roses*.

17. Falstaff (John Woodvine) on the joys of serris-sack. Michael Bogdanov's ESC production of *The Wars of the Roses*.

18. Richard III (Andrew Jarvis) ignoring Buckingham (Michael Pennington). Michael Bogdanov's ESC production of *The Wars of the Roses*.

19. Henry V (Laurence Olivier) in his cart rallying his troops *before* the battle of Agincourt. Olivier's *Henry V*.

20. Henry V (Kenneth Branagh) in his cart *after* the battle of Agincourt. Branagh's *Henry V*.

## CHAPTER SIX

# Militant Classicist:
# Peter Hall and
# Shakespeare

•

W HEN PETER HALL assumed the directorship of Stratford's Memorial Theatre and founded the Royal
Shakespeare Company in 1960 he established a bold
new direction in the modern staging of Shakespeare. Hall came to
Stratford committed to building a permanent ensemble of actors
who, through intense training and discipline, could discover a contemporary approach to Shakespeare's rhetoric. As he explained in
his 1964 essay "Shakespeare and the Modern Director" the core problem centered on Shakespeare's language and modern assumptions
about meaning:

> Shakespeare's language and his form are, of course, foreign to
> us. Modern actors naturally distrust words. They know them as
> grey soiled things and, as any politician will tell you, rhetoric is
> now suspect. Actors also (in a time when the artist's freedom of
> self-expression is canonised) resent the disciplines of blank verse
> or alliterative prose. Techniques have, therefore, to be learnt and
> developed until Shakespeare's form is a discipline which sup-
> ports rather than denies self-expression.[1]

Hall struggled to find a way to respect the integrity of the plays *and*
to make them meaningful to a modern audience, to provide both text
and context:

> I'm trying to express Shakespeare as I honestly understand
> him. And without going to the conscious excesses of performing
> in modern dress, or turning verse into prose, or re-ordering
> the plays in terms of psycho-analysis, I must admit that I am a

modern. So are the scholars whose re-interpretations I study, so are the audiences who watch my productions.[2]

As Hall and his successor, Trevor Nunn, have repeatedly admitted, their tutor to the contradictions and ironies of the modern world was F. R. Leavis. Hall approvingly records in his *Diaries* the following paragraph from a *Time* article about his leadership of the National Theater:

> By the time he finished Cambridge, Hall had already directed several plays and, perhaps more significant, studied English under F. R. Leavis. Even though Leavis hated theatre, he made a lasting impact on Hall with his scrupulous examination of a text, particularly for its ironies and ambiguities and the sense that a work of art must be placed in a social context. Hall more or less applied that lesson in his celebrated *Wars of the Roses* productions, where the protagonists were not seen as gallant warrior kings but as bloody power buccaneers. Hall clearly believes that to immerse an audience unforgettably in a play, the cast and director must locate and pinpoint the vital element that T. S. Eliot once called "the present moment of the past."[3]

During his years at Stratford, Hall's search for the present moment of the past did not preclude imaginative tampering with Shakespeare's text, as witness the immediate and lasting impact of the Hall-Barton *Wars of the Roses*, though he was rarely guilty of the excesses Kenneth Tynan impishly mocked him for early in his directorial career:

> Having closely compared Peter Brook's production of *Titus Andronicus* with Peter Hall's production of *Cymbeline*, I am persuaded that these two young directors should at once go into partnership. I have even worked out business cards for them:
> Hall & Brook, Ltd. The Home of Lost Theatrical Causes. Collapsing plays shored up, unspeakable lines glossed over, unactable scenes made bearable. Wrecks salvaged, ruins refurbished: unpopular plays at popular prices. Masterpieces dealt with only if neglected. Shakespearean juvenilia and senilia our specialty: if it can walk, we'll make it run. Bad last acts no obstacle: if it peters out, call Peter in. Don't be fobbed off with Glenvilles, Woods, or Zadeks: look for the trademark—Hall & Brook.[4]

However, by the time Hall was named to succeed Olivier as the director of the National Theatre in 1973, he had substantially revised his methods of examining the present moment of the past in a Shakespearean text. Hall's post-Stratford directing of Shakespeare has been distinguished by two guiding principles: presenting the full text (1) with no cutting, rearranging of scenes, or reassignment of lines and (2) without pointedly setting the play's action against a specific cultural or historical context outside of the Renaissance. Hall, in a recent interview with Michael Billington, refers to this approach as "militant classicism."[5] In his fourteen years with the National, Hall has directed six large-scale Shakespeare productions (*The Tempest*, *Hamlet*, *Macbeth*, *Othello*, *Coriolanus*, and *Antony and Cleopatra*) and three studio productions (*Cymbeline*, *The Winter's Tale*, and *The Tempest*, which were originally staged in the Cottesloe but did transfer for a limited run to the Olivier in August 1988).

In general, critical response to Hall's work with Shakespeare at the National prior to his *Antony and Cleopatra* has not been as positive as that during his years at Stratford. Hall's directing triumphs have been outside Shakespeare: *No Man's Land*, *Volpone*, and *Amadeus*. These successes share, however, with his Shakespeare productions his determination to extend his Stratford experience by linking the star actor tradition with ensemble principles.

I want to examine the two productions which best define Hall's mature work with Shakespeare and which, fittingly, span his tenure as director of the National Theatre: *Hamlet*, which opened the new South Bank building in March of 1976, and *Antony and Cleopatra*, his final large-scale Shakespeare production, which opened in 1987. This is an appropriate moment to reassess Hall's approach to Shakespeare during what has come to be known as his classical period following his years of experimentation at Stratford. The 1976 *Hamlet* can now be seen as marking a crucial sea-change in Hall's work with Shakespeare. Because the productions which followed it—*Macbeth*, *Othello*, and *Coriolanus*—were not great successes, interest in Hall as a major contemporary interpreter of Shakespeare waned. However, the richly deserved positive response, by critics as well as audiences, to his *Antony and Cleopatra* allows us to look back at the 1976 *Hamlet* to better assess its virtues and its relationship to Hall's eventual triumph with *Antony and Cleopatra*. Historically, this production of *Hamlet* is significant because while originally planned to open on the Olivier Theater's thrust stage, delays in construction forced Hall to open it at the Old Vic (the National's home since inception in 1962) and then to move it (in March of 1976) into the Lyttleton, the new National's proscenium theater. Eventually this *Hamlet* found its way to the Olivier's wide open spaces, thus making it the production which literally straddled the transition from the Olivier era to the Hall era in British Shakespeare; from the Old Vic to the New National.

Hall was returning to this seminal text ten years after directing it at Stratford, where, next to *The Wars of the Roses*, it was his most heralded and popular production, particularly with the young. Stanley Wells has provided a full account of Hall's work in his *Royal Shakespeare*. Wells is quite correct in stressing the ensemble impact of the production, where critical attention was drawn as often to Tony Church's Polonius or Brewster Mason's Claudius or to Glenda Jackson's Ophelia as to the title character:

> Undoubtedly the most significant, as also the most controversial, piece of casting was that of David Warner as Hamlet himself. He was only twenty-four years old, and at this time was very much a 'modern,' as opposed to a classical, actor. He was exceptionally tall, but unheroic in build; his face, though expressive, was not conventionally handsome. He did not cultivate grace of movement or beauty of voice, and his verse speaking was a law unto itself. He had been very successful as Henry VI in Peter Hall's production of *The Wars of the Roses*, and somewhat less successful as Richard II. The roles are significant; both of them rather passive, languid, pathetic characters. To cast him as Hamlet was itself a major interpretative decision. It was obvious that this would be no princely, romantic embodiment of the role. Mr. Warner was, frankly, a gangling, spotty young man with traces of a Midlands accent. No make-up artist would transform him into anything remotely resembling the young Gielgud, and it was clear that Mr. Hall could not wish him to effect such a transformation.[6]

In 1965 Hall had selected a Hamlet to fit both his interpretation of the play and the larger conception of ensemble playing he had already gone far in achieving at Stratford. By contrast, in 1975 he was reaching out to link the tradition of star actor with that of the powerful director wedded to ensemble principles. Hall selected Albert Finney to lead the company into its new home.[7] Finney was the most explosive of the younger actors looked to as the heirs of the Olivier, Gielgud, and Richardson tradition. I found the production a compelling mix of idea and passion though many perceptive reviewers failed to see how Hall's ideas about the play and Finney's often startling performance meshed. The following account tries to establish the way in which Hall's design and direction illuminated how power, corruption, and fragmentation frustrate and crush individual sensibilities struggling to develop and cohere. The production, in retrospect, signaled an important development in Hall's approach to Shakespeare which he has followed during the past fifteen years.

The following entry from Hall's *Diaries* was dictated on the morning after the production opened and underlines his own high expectations:

> This is the closest I have reached to the heart of a Shakespeare play in my own estimation; it is the production which over the last fifteen years has the least gap between my hopes and the facts on the stage. It is also pure and clear. And the production is the closest I've ever got to a unified style of verse speaking which is right. I feel now I know how the verse should be treated. In Stratford days what I did was intellectual. Now I have found a way of doing it which is based on feeling and passion. It has been a very satisfying experience.
>
> The audience were very attentive and the actors did well. All in all it was our best performance. The last scene has never gone better and I felt an actual tragic purgation in the house. The reception was really thunderous. I've heard it as much for Callas, but that's about all. Everybody very elated. I believe we're going to have a contentious press, but on tonight's evidence we have achieved something big. Man leaving performance (snorting): "*Hamlet* is not as contemporary as that. . . ."[8]

As Hall anticipated, there were a few snorters among the critics as well. Some reviewers were enthusiastic about Finney's performance, calling it rough and electrifying; others felt he raced through the part with little indication of its range or complexity. Surprisingly, there was even less comment about Peter Hall's staging of the play, other than to note that he was presenting an uncut *Hamlet* and trusting his audience to sit still for a single intermission which did not come until "How all occasions do inform against me." Mel Gussow's remarks in theSunday *New York Times* were typical: "Somewhere in Peter Hall's weighty production, there must be a purpose other than to present a leading actor in an uncut *Hamlet* in the nation's first theater. Perhaps the director and actor envision a commoner prince. If so, the vision has not been realized."[9]

Benedict Nightingale had a more positive response to Finney's performance, calling it "passionate and powerful, full of scalding humor and savage contempt." However, he joined Gussow in failing to see any design to Hall's direction: "It is Finney's evening, partly because of his own magnetism, partly because Peter Hall is determined to allow him his head. In recent years we've grown used to seeing Shakespeare's plays tailored with little sermons on subjects dear to his directors. But Mr. Hall's production excludes nothing, emphasizes nothing, refashions nothing. The actors are presented with a bare stage and a totally uncut text, and then more or less left to get on with their jobs."[10] I believe Gussow and Nightingale missed much that Hall did with a stage which was undressed but hardly bare, and I want to describe what we saw as we entered the theater and how it became the nutshell which bounded us all in Hamlet's bad dreams.

Hall's *Hamlet* incorporated three structural devices: a wall which ran across the stage approximately two-thirds of the way from proscenium to the rear wall and which was broken at its center by a set of double doors topped by a triangular pediment, a white circle (some thirty feet in diameter) painted on the stage floor which ran from the double doors to the edge of down stage, and a series of eleven white lines which ran at radial angles from stage front through the double doors where they met and then fanned out again in mirror approximation to their position in front of the wall. Five of the lines intersected the circle. The audience became aware that the lines continued beyond the wall during the few scenes when the doors were open. The most effective use of our awareness of the lines' further path was during Hamlet's "To be or not to be" soliloquy when Hall positioned Ophelia at the point where the eleven lines intersected while Hamlet, far down stage, confided his metaphysical dilemma to the audience. At such moments we were invited to see Hall's device as life lines which could not flow and interconnect properly; the wall and double doors were symbolic of the larger political and mythic reaches of the play, reminding us of the formidable public issues and relationships at work in the text which deny the forms of contact, communication, and interchange which would be taken for granted in a world less out of joint.

Hall's use of these three devices universally failed to draw comment from the play's reviewers, yet my experience of the production found them central to his way of working with the text. Francis Fergusson, in his essay on *Hamlet* in *The Idea of a Theater*, comes to the play from a reading of *Oedipus Rex*. That context leads him to remind us that the play is not the prince. Fergusson repeatedly stresses the political and social ramifications and resonances of Hamlet's world as a means of correcting the Coleridgean or Freudian tendency to concentrate all our energies on Hamlet's inner drama.[11] Two worlds, the political and the personal, are intimately intertwined in the play, constantly impeding and infringing upon each other, and Fergusson rightly reminds us of the larger dimensions of Hamlet's struggle. The way in which Hall's simple but effective use of the wall and its center doors was incorporated into our visual sense of the production worked to remind us of Fergusson's insight. The double doors and their triangular pediment were loaded with the suggestion of the House of Atreus. Nothing else in Hall's production was meant explicitly to invite parallels with Greek drama, but his determination to present the text without emendation supports the notion that this was meant to be not a tidy, but an epic *Hamlet*.[12]

It is instructive to note that Hall's interest in emblem and design had grown since his Stratford years. In his interview with Judith Cook just prior to directing *The Tempest* in 1973, Hall indicated that he had taken a six-year exile from directing Shakespeare and was coming back to him with a fresh perspective:

> I've become very interested in emblematic theatre. And that has led me to the meaning of the baroque theatre, the baroque opera, the masque and the theatre of Inigo Jones. I think we are perhaps a little puritanical as a nation about the visual theatre. We are apt to think that as soon as Inigo Jones came into the Jacobean theatre, the writer was driven out. I don't believe that. The emblematic, visual side of the theatre—if you have a great artist doing it—is immensely potent.[13]

As a means of illustration let me cite three examples of the way Hall utilized the emblem he created on the stage floor. In both the nunnery and closet scene Hall had Hamlet use the obvious circle motif to its fullest. The periphery of the circle was, appropriately, Hamlet's territory. In both scenes he stalked and circled, probed and accused the female figure planted in the center. Neither scene was played with its potential for physical violence, as each is so often performed. Finney's Hamlet was too wary, too committed to his peripheral role as scourge and minister. He moved about the edge of Hall's circle throwing his taunts at the women who had been placed by others in a position they did not seek. Both Gertrude and Ophelia are central to Hamlet's deepest inner life, provoking his outrage and disgust. In this production, Hamlet's ambiguous relationship to both was made manifest by the way in which all three characters are seen to occupy an alien territory. The center is rightfully Hamlet's. Claudius (Denis Quilley) and his Minister of the Interior, Polonius (Roland Culver), assign that space to wife and daughter as a means of determining why Hamlet's center will not hold. But Hamlet avoided the center, preferring to make his anguished rounds. Both women were fixed by Hall, Gertrude (Angela Lansbury) literally wedded to a chair, in a center where their gestures repeatedly suggested they were nervous and uncomfortable—surrogate usurpers. Hamlet repeatedly moved in toward them, and then at the moment he discovered the hollowness of their center ("Where's your father?" "At home". . . . "What have *I* done that thou dar'st wag thy tongue/ In noise so *rude* against me?") he backed off from physical engagement to his distanced prowl.

In the nunnery scene Finney initially treated Ophelia (Susan Fleetwood) with great tenderness and his "Where's your father?" was tossed off as a mad, almost comic, evocation of the silly old man rather than in response to any telltale movement in the wings. Hamlet took his cue for the scene's reality simply from Susan Fleetwood's guilty reaction. He immediately dropped her hands and retreated to the edge of Hall's circle, where he made a complete perambulation as he delivered his stunning attack ("If thou dost marry, I'll give thee this plague for thy dowry") on the bewildered woman trapped in the circle's center. As this example serves to illustrate, I found Hall's use of such space repeatedly illuminating.

Another instance will serve as a further example of Hall's intentions about this center space. In 4.5 Laertes charged in with sword drawn and assumed the center of the circle. Claudius did not move in toward him but worked his way on the left edge of the painted circle. He lured Laertes from the center to the periphery on "Be you content to lend your patience to us," skillfully having avoided a clash with Laertes's momentary appropriation of the center. When we returned to the two poisoners in 4.7, their positions were reversed. Claudius was at the center and Laertes *moved in* to join him on "I'll anoint my sword"—further proof that not only does the center corrupt but the absolute center corrupts absolutely.

Hall's repeated use of the center and the circle was meant to remind us that those in *Hamlet* who comfortably assume the center are feigners. As another instructive example, when Rosencrantz and Guildenstern entered through the open doors in 2.2 Hamlet was on stage left of the circle as he began to unravel their clumsily weaved up folly. When he launched into the brilliant explanation of his loss of mirth, which quite escaped his obtuse and inept undergraduate inquisitors, he cut through the circle on "What a piece of work is man." This was another moment when Hall's staging subtly reinforced the intellectual motion of the text. As Rosencrantz and Guildenstern made the move to embrace Hamlet as, in Conrad's Marlow's phrase "one of us," Finney's Hamlet stranded them on an empty island. By cutting through the circle he spatially cut them off at the same moment he offered his radical dismissal of the paragon of animals.[14]

Hamlet moved back into the center, momentarily, at the conclusion of his interview with Rosencrantz and Guildenstern to proclaim that he was "but mad north-northwest: when the wind is southerly I know a hawk from a handsaw," and then bolted toward the closed double doors to throw them open to welcome the players. Here came fresh air indeed. Hamlet led the player-king to the center for their evocation of a previous fall and loss. This was one moment in the production when Hamlet seemed to revel in the center. He could now momentarily enjoy that alien territory because he shared it with one who openly acknowledged that he was a feigner. The ability to weep for Hecuba was underscored several scenes later when Hamlet forced tears from his uncle-mother, our player-queen, when she occupied the same space.

I want to mention two casual props Finney used to create his Hamlet: a scholar's cloak and a sea-blue scarf. The cloak was used not only to identify the solemn black of mourning but also as an emblem of the Wittenberg Hamlet can't discard once back in the provinces. Finney appropriated this common prop as a gestural symbol of his Hamlet which could be used to swirl out to threaten and estrange as well as curl in to hide and protect. He was most adroit at using his cloak to underline the expanse and impasse of Hamlet's nutshell. The scarf was employed to add a dash of romanticism. In the early scenes, it was tied rakishly around Finney's neck—the only spot of color in his somber demeanor or costume. The scarf was acknowledged, appropriately in the most self-conscious of Hamlet's soliloquies ("O what a rogue and peasant slave am I") as Finney used it to deflate the exaggerated self examination which concludes with "Who does me this?" When we next saw the scarf it was wrapped around Finney's forehead when he staged his performance of the mousetrap: no longer an undergraduate's affectation but now a sign that Hamlet realized that he, too, was a player who must use his every resource to show scorn her own image, including radical defiance. The scarf also served as a bandage for Hamlet's cerebral struggle with Claudius, a struggle which takes its toll and creates its own interior wounds: "My wit's diseased." At the conclusion of the play-within-the-play Finney untied his scarf and whirled it above his head as he leapt onto the raised platform where the *Murder of Gonzaga* had been played out. I was reminded of Olivier's filmed leap into Claudius's vacated chair swirling a lighted torch; Finney's gesture here spoke to the play's move to strip away false faces and hidden realities, while Olivier's intention was to extend the play's imagery of false fire and forced illumination: "Lights, lights, lights!"

The play-within-the-play was staged with a deeply raked platform erected at the outer upstage edge of the circle. Three chairs were positioned in the center of the circle in mirror approximation of their arrangement in 1.2 where the careful observer immediately noticed that the size of the chairs resembled those of the three bears: Claudius's was slightly larger than Gertrude's and Hamlet's was similarly smaller than his mother's, revealing Claudius's own strong sense of political geometry. The other members of the court were seated on benches on the edge of the circle. Hamlet, again uneasy with being positioned in Claudius's center, moved his chair to stage left to join Ophelia. I mention this only as another example of the identification of the center as Claudius's usurped province.

In the closet scene, Gertrude was seated on a chair at the center of the circle in an interesting departure from traditional staging. As Hall commented about his decision to cut the bed:

> A closet is a withdrawing room, a place for disrobing, not the bedroom. It's a stage tradition . . . to have a bed . . . but a bed is not really what the scene is about. It's difficult to play around it, and you rapidly get to Freudian images, but only Freudian images.[15]

As Hamlet verbally thrust and parried to uncover her culpability, the ghost rose from the elevator trap located immediately behind Gertrude's chair. The effect was astonishing because the audience shared Hamlet's perspective and his startled reaction as the ghost's silver helmet suddenly appeared as though sprung from Gertrude's head. Richard David's description of this moment vividly presents how Hall captures the Shakespearean resonances at work here:

> Growing more distraught, he [Hamlet] ranges impatiently about her chair; when, behind them both and masked by them,

the Ghost rises from the trap. Now the Ghost had descended by
the trap at the end of his interview with Hamlet, but that effect,
in full view, had seemed contrived. His reemergence in the
closet scene was quite unexpected and a real piece of theatrical
legerdemain. Hamlet, by now kneeling at his mother's knee,
looks at the Ghost over her shoulder; she, all tenderness for her
son suddenly seized in this paroxysm of madness, has no consciousness of his father's presence. The three reactions, Hamlet's
intense, Gertrude's all maternal solicitude, the Ghost in painful
hope against hope that sufficient memory of their bond may lin-
ger in his wife to make her aware of him, built up a strange
chord, complex yet with each component note distinct and beautifully balanced; and the inspiration of this moment continued to
inform the remainder of the scene in which the interchanges between mother and son, irretrievably separated yet bound by
shared regrets, gently modulated into a sad autumnal calm.[16]

Here Hall's stage emblem vividly captured Shakespeare's exploration of the destructive consequences of this fatal family triangle and
provided us with a startling Freudian image, after all.

The only moments when the center was held in steady focus were
when it was occupied by the ghost and the gravediggers—the dead
and the quick. Hall allowed the furious pace of his production to slow
only at those moments when we were receiving the grave truth from
king and clown.

In the final act the gravedigger digs Ophelia's grave in the circle's
heart and Hamlet, in his wry banter with death's great clown, reveals his reconciliation with death's inevitability. A moment later,
he strips off his gray seafarer's cloak to declare: "This is I,/Hamlet,
the Dane" as he jumps into the grave to acknowledge his love for
Ophelia. These open declarations of public power (King) and private commitment (lover) at the very center of a significant social
ritual announce the end of his repressed struggle which had pushed
him to the edge of personal and social alienation. Finney trium-
phantly appropriated the center from this moment on, and in the
following scene he moved Horatio in from the periphery to the
center, where he confidently confided to his friend his action in
sealing the fates of Rosencrantz and Guildenstern. In the duplicitous
fencing match, Hall provided a final original touch. Hamlet and
Laertes were each provided a resin box into which they stepped
before each play of the bout. The match was robustly staged to

advantage Finney's vigor, but the consequences were to place white footprints, in helter-skelter fashion, all over the carefully conceived circle and its intersecting radial lines. "Only connect" is what Hamlet cannot achieve except in death. Eventually the circle and the lines, Hall's design, were obliterated by the furious footsteps which led to the play's final devastation.

Hall's geometric understanding of Hamlet's fractured mind and world was beautifully mirrored in Finney's performance. His prince may have been soiled but was never sullen. All of Hamlet's bitterness and disgust with Denmark's rank and gross unweeded garden were given full voice in a radical reversal from David Warner's 1965 interpretation. Finney's Hamlet was volcanic, wild and whirling in and beyond words. Hall's own initial reaction to Finney as "a powerful, passionate, sexy Hamlet, glowering with resentment," was an apt description of the performance as it matured through rehearsals.[17] What kept the performance focused was Hall's design, keeping this Hamlet persistently on the prowl of the periphery of the circle of Claudius's court until the interim, finally, became his.

Hall's subsequent work with Shakespeare in the years between this *Hamlet* and *Antony and Cleopatra* has been unevenly received, but each of his productions followed the *Hamlet* pattern of linking a star actor with members of the permanent National Theatre Company: Finney (again) in *Macbeth* (1978), Scofield in *Othello* (1980), and McKellen in *Coriolanus* (1984). This practice has continued, most notably in his *Merchant of Venice* with Dustin Hoffman (1989) as Hall has moved from the National to the West End and created his own, private production company. Each production presented an uncut text with no rearrangement of scenes or reassignment of lines; each sought to employ a scene and costume design which did not intrude or startle or make any obvious statement of directorial intent. In each of these three instances, for a variety of reasons, the mix of the talent or personality of the star actor and Hall's style failed to fuse to create a production which galvanized the growing community of professional Shakespeare watchers. Finney's bad-boy charm wasn't fruitful for Macbeth, and he was badly mismatched with Dorothy Tutin's Germanic Lady Macbeth; Scofield's Othello was eagerly awaited and politely received, but again there was an awkward mismatch of actor and part as Scofield's natural reserve was clearly embarrassed by the eruption of Othello's raw passion and the production was interesting primarily for allowing us to witness a great actor struggling *against* the character he was meant to imagine and inhabit; the *Coriolanus* failed to mesh Ian McKellen's histrionic performance with the tight ensemble playing Hall clearly desires to achieve.

Hall refused to compromise his principles, and his faith was vindicated by his production of *Antony and Cleopatra* with Anthony Hopkins and Judi Dench. John Peter begins his review in the *Sunday Times* with the following large claim:

> Golden ages of the theatre are usually in the past—but we may be living in one today. Peter Hall's production of *Antony and Cleopatra* (Olivier) is the British theatre at its spellbinding and magnificent best. This is a big, heroic play in every sense, and Hall's control over it is complete. The huge spans of the action tense up, arch and unfold like great symphonic movements and the poetry of this sensuous, athletic text tolls with burnished conviction. Hall reminds us, and we do need reminding, that the bedrock of classical theatre is the text; that the life of the play is first and most essentially in the words of the play, and that visual splendour and the excitement of action need to be justified by a sense that the words are both felt and understood.[18]

Peter is right to focus immediately on the text for, as we have seen, Hall's preoccupation from his very first days at Stratford concentrated on the text and finding for his actors a modern, effective approach to speaking Shakespeare's verse. Nowhere is this more important than in *Antony and Cleopatra* and the late romances. Here, Shakespeare is working at the height of his power and fashions a poetry both intense and elliptical characterized by his ability to forge a new verse style. He typically makes meaning by surrounding a single polysyllabic word of latinate origin with a series of Anglo-Saxon monosyllables, thus marrying and merging the two key strands of his language at the very moment he creates complex meaning through the simplest expression. The finest example of this process comes in Cleopatra's final moment: "Come, thou mortal wretch,/With thy sharp teeth this knot intrinsicate/Of life at once untie." (5.2.303–5). Cleopatra's life has been intricate, tied up personally and politically with those Roman generals sent to subdue her, and now, true to her paradoxical nature, this creature of flux chooses her ultimate release ("Husband I come") by naming herself "wife" and dying "after the high Roman fashion." Shakespeare's late, subtle, incandescent images can only be captured by actors working at the top of their craft, and in this instance, Hall was able to achieve the right blend of star performers, new faces, and such veterans of National Theatre productions as Michael Bryant, Desmond Adams, Peter Gordon, and Basil Henson, whose association with the company reach back almost as far as Hall's.

It is significant to note that in this production Peter Hall was not working with his scenic designer of long standing, John Bury, but with Alison Chitty who had designed many NT productions in recent years but none with Hall. Even so the design bore interesting parallels with Hall's NT *Hamlet*. The inspiration for Chitty's design, which extended beautifully into Hall's conception, was Veronese's painting "Mars and Venus Bound by Cupid." As Michael Levey comments, "All Veronese's people are a common stock, instinctively aristocratic, handsome, healthy. All give an air of being in costume for a gorgeous pageant in which nature has fitted them to take part. In his portraits Veronese manages to suggest splendour without ostentation."[9]

Splendor without ostentation, instinctively aristocratic, handsome, healthy, common stock all are apt descriptions of Hall's realization of *Antony and Cleopatra*. Interestingly, he used a detail from the Veronese "Mars and Venus" which included Mars, Venus, and Cupid for the program cover and the poster for his production. However, he had the painting, which is a mixture of white, cobalt, and mauve, reproduced in the dominant autumnal earth tones of his production: orange and ochre. It is also interesting that the elements left out of his reproduction of Veronese's painting also came into play in Alison Chitty's set. Veronese positions his figures against the background of a Roman ruin which is distinguished by a broken lintel supported by a satyr caryatid. Chitty's design—beyond being bathed in deep reds, burgundies, and browns projected through the lighting with a dappled effect—took inspiration from Veronese's background.

Her basic set consisted of three large sections of a circular wall which followed the natural curve of the Olivier's thrust stage; each section was mounted on tracks which allowed it to be set at various distances from the apron to expand or contract the basic playing space. The central section contained a large set of wooden double doors distinguished by brass door knobs. The door was framed on stage right by a large section where the wall's plaster had peeled away to reveal large rough quarry stones beneath, while stage left of the double doors was a Doric column rising to hold up the fragment of a lintel which extended about one-third of the distance across the door frame. This piece of broken lintel corresponded with Veronese's ruin with the exception that a plain support column had replaced his caryatid.

The rich, dark, blood-red earth tones cast by the set were reflected in the costumes of Antony, Enobarus, Cleopatra, and the other Egyptians, who were all dressed in shades of burgundy, auburn, and amber with the men in white blouses open at the throat. Cleopatra and her women wore their hair in cascading ringlets of curls rather than in the straight, long pageboy headdress typically associated with Cleopatra. This was clearly a Renaissance lass unparalleled. Though Cleopatra's wrists were loaded with gold and silver bracelets, the traditional serpent jewelry—either in upper arm bracelet or as crown— was quite intentionally absent. As Alison Chitty commented, "If I can design this production without having snakes on anybody's head or without anyone's knees showing, then I will have achieved something. . . . What I aim for is a root world that holds the story. It's not very literal, more sculptural I suppose. In this case I've ended with something rich, dark, blood red."[20] By contrast, the Romans were all in gray and blue with their coats neatly buttoned to the neck.

The opening scene immediately established the Rome/Egypt contrast as Philo and Demetrius entered in their buttoned-up Roman outfits to lament Antony's loss of measure; "tawny" was given special emphasis, and the double doors burst open on "gypsy's lust." We were greeted first by the raucous sounds of Eastern wind and string instruments and then bursts of laughter followed by the rustle of silk as Cleopatra swirled through the doors leading her Antony— mounted on Mardian's shoulders—by a rope. The forestage quickly o'erflowed with a cacophony of sound and movement. Antony delivered both his "There's beggary in the love that can be reckoned" and "Then must thou needs find out new heaven, new earth" from his perch on Mardian's shoulders which allowed him to take in the Olivier's substantial space with an expansive gesture. Hall has said, "What I like best about the Olivier is its feeling of a universe," and when Hopkins tumbled down and caught Cleopatra (she was in constant motion during the first half of the play, and he was always having to reach out to capture and still her) and playfully wrestled her to the floor, we were immediately folded into their universe.[21]

The music stopped and Antony released his embrace on the word "Rome," which immediately caused Judi Dench's Cleopatra to become the aggressor as she then threw her leg over Antony's thigh to prohibit him from escaping her clutches as she taunted him about his

Roman obligations and allegiances. She straddled him on "As I am Egypt's Queen", but he rolled her over on "Let Rome in Tiber melt" and placed his right hand under her thigh and pulled her to him on "This is my space." He did not manage to subdue her until "No messenger but thine," which Hopkins gave a brilliant reading by delivering "No messenger" as a firm command, slowing shaking his head, and then after a long pause, a quick wink before a very tender "but thine," which brought them to their feet for a wistful "Tonight we'll wander through the streets and note/The qualities of people." On "Come, my queen" they both swirled through the double doors with Cleopatra in the lead flanked, a half pace behind, by Charmian and Iras.

Hall's staging of this scene was a perfect rendering of the intellectual movement of the text from the Roman preface to the Egyptian scene, to the vitality of Antony and Cleopatra's relationship spiced by its instability and excess, to the nagging echoes of Rome and wife, to the fullness of Antony's wonderfully naive commitment to whatever world he happens to inhabit, to the fluid flow and spark of Cleopatra's wit and sensual charm. Our first view of Antony, mounted on a eunuch's shoulders, tethered and led by a woman while proclaiming love's dominion as an imaginative space beyond our finite experience, brilliantly established the ambiguous territory Shakespeare's text relentlessly explores: is such behavior divinity or dotage?[22]

Certainly in this staging Hall and Hopkins were right to know the specific space Antony proclaimed as his. I have too often seen Antonys vaguely look about the general location as impetus for "This is my space." Hopkins and Hall were right to locate that space quite precisely as Cleopatra. Hall and Judi Dench also found an inspired body language for Cleopatra. Rather than making her lazy and languid as if all her sexual energy issued forth from an inert earth mother (some ancient precursor of William Faulkner's Eula Varner Snopes), Dench placed motion and movement at the heart of her interpretation of the character. She was the fluid, fertile, overflowing Nile with an essence which cannot be stilled, silenced, or contained. The only time she came to rest in the first act was when she stilled herself at the climax of Charmian's taunts about Julius Caesar. Dench delivered "My salad days,/When I was green in judgment, cold in blood,/To say as I said then" in an absolutely measured tone straight out to the audience, and she paused to allow it to register before stirring into action again on "But come, away/Get me ink and paper."[23]

If Dench's movement of her body gave her Cleopatra energy and sweep, her voice brought depth, command of experience, and mature heat to her performance. She created a creature come from the Nile, who could sing both high and low. She could move the timbre of her voice from the throaty muskiness of a blues singer, to moments of chromatic dissonance by finding an intentional crack between registers, to moments of gentle, haunting reminiscence or vision. The latter was made most memorable in her evocation of her dream of Antony again taken center stage and straight out over Dolabella's skeptical head to the audience. Dench could make her voice move from whiskey to perfume in an instant and have us all pay our hearts for what our eyes eat only.[24]

I would not have imagined Judi Dench as a powerful Cleopatra: she does not possess Suzman's allure or Mirren's ripe sexuality, but her performance repeatedly found ways to make manifest Enobarbus's telling comment on the paradoxical nature of Cleopatra's attraction:

> I saw her once
> Hop forty paces through the public street;
> And having lost her breath, she spoke and panted,
> That she did make defect perfection,
> And, breathless, pow'r breathe forth.
> (2.2.234–38)

Through voice and motion Dench found her way of making defect perfection. She was always registering and reacting, moving in toward her Antony, then swirling away. She could and did "faint with alacrity" on the floor, into Antony's arms, in concert with Charmian and Iras, who were choreographed to follow her movements a half beat behind their queen, which further added to her multiplicitousness. She approached and retreated; she rose and collapsed; she swirled in and flew out; she transformed herself from a creature of the Thames into the serpent of old Nilus.

As I have mentioned, Cleopatra was at the center of Hall's structural and spatial conception of the play. In the first half we watched the energy and movement of her performance and Antony's unsuccessful efforts to contain her variousness, her infinite variety. In the second half, Cleopatra's sense of play was finally stifled by the recklessness of Antony's disintegration. In Anthony Hopkins's performance Antony became a reeling, careening force completely given over to, and victimized by, his passions and manic shifts of mood. Cleopatra then became the lens or filter through which we focused on

Antony's destruction. It was she who tried to reach out to capture and cradle and still her Roman, who had lost all sense of measure, all sense of inner balance. Her unpredictability had been a carefully crafted performance: her means of expressing personal power in the midst of political powerlessness. Her variousness infected Antony and from 3.7 on he became, physically and emotionally, an electrical particle bouncing about chaotically in a charged magnetic field.

Their only moment of mutuality, of union in this life, came in 4.8 when Antony returned smiling from "The world's great snare uncaught" to be reunited with his "great fairy." Hall allowed this moment to be held and cherished, burnished with the glow of evening torches surrounding the lovers as they exit to the applause of heaven and earth. This was the only moment in the second half, other than Antony's death itself, where we were allowed a glimpse of the potential power and beauty of this relationship as opposed to its mutual destructiveness.

Before moving to consider Hall's staging of the play's great final scenes, I want to devote some commentary to Michael Bryant's performance of Enobarbus. Bryant is the precise example of the actor who best personifies the virtues and glories of the British repertory system. His many seasons at the National were crowned by his interpretations of Gloucester, Enobarbus, and Prospero as the Hall era came to a close. His Enobarbus was wonderfully matter-of-fact and understated. His reaction to Antony's report of Fulvia's death was delivered with a "Hey, this is *good* news, Boss" tone of voice. He took the monumental description of Antony's meeting with Cleopatra in a slow, easy, conversational tone, augmented by smiles and chuckles as he became caught up in his own evocation and memory of the scene.

Rome and the triple pillars of the world had been represented by three blue upholstered chairs. When the triumvirs left the scene to their chief aids, Enobarbus leaned over the back of Antony's chair for his response to Maecenas's query about Egyptian breakfasts: "This was as a fly by an eagle." He came round and sat confidently in Antony's chair on "I will tell you," used his hands to imitate the silver oars "which to the tune of flutes kept stroke," and threw his right leg over the chair's arm as he launched into "for her own person,/It beggared all description," he leaned forward to become wondrously confidential on "I saw her once/Hop forty paces through the public street," and then slowly leaned back into the chair to savor "but she makes hungry where most she satisfies." A long pause after "the holy priests/Bless her when she is riggish" caught all three men in rapt contemplation of Enobarbus's vision of the Egyptian queen. This created a tone of resignation to Maecenas's attempt to rescue the proposed marriage of Antony to Octavia:

> If beauty, wisdom, modesty can settle
> The heart of Antony, Octavia is
> A blessed lottery to him.
>
> (2.2.240–43)

To which Enobarbus responded with a smile and a knowing laugh, and all three exited shaking their heads with the understanding that the marriage and thus the peace between Antony and Octavius was doomed.

Another performance which drew critical attention was Tim Piggott-Smith's Octavius Caesar, who found unusual ways to soften the portrait of the archetypal boy-Machiavellian chiseled so finely in many of our memories by Corin Redgrave's performance in Trevor Nunn's production for the RSC in 1972. For me, at least, and I suspect for many others in the audience, Piggott-Smith also had to overcome the image of his own definitive creation of Ronald Merrick in *The Jewel in the Crown:* a character whose repressed insecurity and natural envy could easily have been transferable to his Octavius. Instead, actor and director found the seed for their interpretation of Octavius in his relationship with his sister, which here was presented as absolutely loving and tender; in fact, with such a strong emotional subtext that their famous "swan's-down feather" unspoken conversation in 3.2 was almost painful to watch in its intimacy. Alan Dessen provides a detailed account of Piggott-Smith's portrayal concluding, "Caesar can only pick up the pieces at the end, but his closing tribute to the two lovers meant something very different coming from this Octavius (given his emotional bonds to Octavia and Antony in the first half of the play) than from a consistently calculating Machiavel."[25]

I have indicated that the first half of the production found Cleopatra in constant motion with Antony unsuccessfully trying to capture and subdue her supreme gamesmanship, while in the second half we watched, with Cleopatra, Antony's inability to control himself. The peace in union which neither could achieve, did come, of course, with their mutual movements toward death. Antony was only brought to rest (on his knees) and resolve on Mardian's news of Cleopatra's death, and Hopkins took his long unarming at a deliberate pace, pausing to kiss his "bruised pieces" as he passed them on to

Eros. And, then, moments later he kissed and cradled Eros in his arms as he envisioned (paralleled by Cleopatra's similar understanding at 5.2.207–21) his treatment in Rome by the "fortunate" Caesar. After the bungled suicide—nothing ever comes cleanly to Antony—Hopkins still managed a series of rich laughs through his pain on Diomedes's report of Cleopatra's false death.

Cleopatra's monument was revealed as the space above the double doors created by the thrust of the lintel. Antony was hauled up to her in a great net. "Ah ha! Y'are caught" and "com'st thou from the world's great snare uncaught?" were surely the text's images which inspired Hall's staging here. The space on the ledge was cramped and awkward, but fitting as an image of how much the vast world of this play has shrunk and the necessity for them to find space for themselves only in "a new heaven, new earth."

On Antony's death, Judi Dench delivered "The crown o' th' earth does melt" as one great extended cry with the word "earth" stretched out to seeming infinity. After she successfully cons Caesar into believing that she has packed cards with him only in order to buy time to arrange to die "after the high Roman fashion," Dench's Cleopatra becomes the very image of iron determination. From her exchange with Dolabella about her dream of another Antony onward, Dench's performance, heretofore marked by her unpredictable variousness, became "marble constant," and she embodied the series of transformations which mark her final speeches including, most significantly, naming herself wife, "Husband, I come," and shedding the body and sensuality so essential to her power, "I am fire, and air; my other elements/I give to baser life." Dench here gave the same elongated treatment to "air" that she had earlier given to "earth" to underline her transcendence of the physical universe she had so long personified.

As she slumped on her throne, which tilted her crown awry (defect again making perfection), the last brilliant sign of movement emanating from this presence was that of the second asp still wriggling in the clutch of her right hand. Marianne Moore's definition of poetry as "imaginary gardens with real toads in them," went winging through my mind as a fitting summary of Peter Hall's achievement in capturing Shakespeare's monumental festive tragedy.

I agree with John Peter that we have been living in a golden age of British theater, and nowhere is that more apparent than in the variety of intelligent and illuminating approaches to Shakespeare spawned by Peter Hall and the directors who came to join him at the RSC and their successors. It is a credit to Hall that the world of modern Shakespeare productions he did so much to build proved to be distinguished by its variety rather than its uniformity; by its inclusiveness rather than its exclusiveness, by a fresh response to Shakespeare's text rather than a stale adherence to a particular production style. Hall is in large measure responsible for the Shakespeare revolution in our time, not by articulating abstract theory, but by the daily and arduous task of running large, complex, repertory theaters and by the constant practice of his art and craft.[26]

The chapters which follow deal with the work of younger directors but ones who have flourished in the worlds of the Royal Shakespeare Company and the National Theatre, worlds nourished by the theatrical intelligence and imagination of Peter Hall.

## CHAPTER SEVEN

# Watching the Torches
# Burn Bright: The Diary of
# an RSC Observer

·

THERE is little argument among contemporary interpreters of British theatre that Peter Hall and Peter Brook are the two modern directors who have made the greatest impact on production approaches to classic texts. As I stressed in the previous chapter, Hall's work has evolved within the framework of the large, institutional repertory system he did so much to establish in Stratford and on the South Bank. The focus of his attention has remained riveted upon the text, and even in his work with contemporary plays he has developed close working relationships—some of which have ended explosively—with the playwrights whose work he has produced. I am thinking especially of Harold Pinter, Alan Ayckbourn, and Peter Shaffer.

Peter Brook, however, grew restless in an institutional setting and has spent the last twenty-five years searching out new spaces for performance—from carpets in the Arabian desert to rock quarries in Avignon to abandoned derelict theaters in immigrant working-class districts in Paris and New York. Brook's concentration and experimental interest has been focused more on the actor's body and its relationship to space and storytelling than on detailed attention to classic texts.

This dual Hall-Brook legacy lived on at Stratford after their departure through the company's continuing work with the actor's voice and Shakespeare's text and through its exploration of modern plays in the more intimate and experimental space of The Other Place created by the company in 1973 in a tin shed which had been used as a rehearsal room. The first director of this theater was the talented Buzz Goodbody, whose modern-dress *Hamlet* with Ben Kingsley in 1975 heralded the exciting possibilities of exploring Shakespeare in a space radically different from that of the Memorial Theatre itself. Her tragic suicide four days after the production opened only intensified the RSC's commitment to this new space with Trevor Nunn himself assuming direction for The Other Place in the 1975–76 season. That season featured his production of *Macbeth* with Judi Dench and Ian McKellen, which many hold as the finest Shakespeare work produced by the company during Nunn's distinguished tenure as Hall's successor. In late 1976 Nunn asked Ron Daniels, one of the young directors invited to join the company specifically to direct modern work at The Other Place, to assume leadership for that theater.[1] Between 1975 and 1980 Daniels directed eight productions for The Other Place, only one of which was Shakespeare, *Pericles*, in 1977. In 1980 Daniels agreed, with "some trepidation" according to Sally Beauman, to direct *Romeo and Juliet* as part of the Memorial Theatre's season, his first venture in directing in a space which holds an audience ten times the size of that of The Other Place (1500 v. 150).[2]

From February 4 to April 23, 1980, I had the good fortune to observe Daniels's work with *Romeo and Juliet* from first rehearsal through opening night, which fell neatly on Shakespeare's 416th birthday. Daniels's production of the play was the thirty-second since the founding of a theater at Stratford in 1879; the fourteenth since the opening of the current house in 1932; and the fifth since Peter Hall's formation of the Royal Shakespeare Company in 1960. This production of *Romeo and Juliet* had ninety-three performances at Stratford during the 1980–81 season. It went to Newcastle as part of the RSC's annual winter visit there and then came to the Aldwych, where it had a London run of fifteen performances in October of 1981.

Daniels wanted to accentuate *Romeo and Juliet*'s youthful energy and passion, and his cast was largely made up of actors new to the company. In fact only Brenda Bruce was an associate member of the RSC. The success of Daniels's production revealed Hall's repertory legacy in action as the RSC proved again its ability to keep coming back to these great texts with new ideas and fresh faces. Hall's legacy was also evident in Daniels's repeated advice to his actors: "Trust the text." And while academic critics came in for some good-natured bashing during the rehearsal period, "Trust the text" was surely also the cry of the key modernist Shakespearean critics from T. S. Eliot to Frank Kermode.

The other central precepts of Daniels's approach which echoed through the dingy rehearsal rooms on Floral Street and then at

Stratford once the company moved up from London at the end of March were: be natural, be specific, keep your energy level up, concentrate on telling the rich humanity of your character's story, capture the natural rhythm of Shakespeare's line by being vocally alert to the second and fifth beats, provide a little caesura before central verbs to make them race, and don't stress pronouns.

What follows are a series of entries from the diary notes I surreptitiously scribbled during breaks in the rehearsal period. They capture Daniels's particular success in working with two groups of his players: the younger male members of the cast, particularly Anton Lesser (Romeo), Jonathan Hyde (Mercutio), Chris Hunter (Tybalt), and Allan Hendrick (Benvolio); and Judy Buxton (Juliet) and Brenda Bruce (Nurse). In the first instance, Lesser, Hyde, and crew responded to Daniels's delight in the give and take of rehearsal and his willingness to give them their heads in trying a variety of approaches to capture the physicality of adolescent male behavior, which came to distinguish the production. In the second instance, the rehearsal periods spent on Juliet's scenes with the Nurse developed a special resonance as Brenda Bruce was working her way toward a version of the character both revolutionary and definitive while providing a professional model for Judy Buxton, who was faced with her first experience of playing a major Shakespeare role with the RSC.

The scenes which had a more difficult gestation period and which never fully coalesced centered on the older generation, particularly the Capulets. Most productions, following most criticism, are hard on the Montagues and Capulets, finding them either parents of shallow bourgeois values or brutal capitalist power seekers or both. Daniels started from the premise that the Capulets actually had the best of intentions toward their daughter. He found Capulet's lines to Paris about Juliet's marriage choice "My will is but a part to her consent" a stunning liberal compromise with his daughter, a compromise and bargain he betrays, in Daniels's reading, not as a crass means to solidify power with the prince (Paris being Escalus's nephew) but as a benevolent father trying to provide an antidote to his genuine misunderstanding of his daughter's sorrow. The generosity Daniels wanted to extend to Capulet and his wife proved troublesome for the actors who had to play them, as it took away the rough edge usually given to each as a means of building a characterization.

Daniels's interest in deflecting blame from the older generation also found expression in his emphasis on the paradox of passion which both destroys and creates. He repeatedly pointed to Romeo's early self-assessment, "I have lost myself," as a key expression of passion's ability to transform—a transformation which destroys even as it creates. Daniels also wanted his production to stress the crucial role of accident in the creation of Romeo and Juliet's tragedy.

Another aspect of the production which drew a mixed response was Ralph Koltai's set. Daniels had stressed to Koltai that he wanted the look and feel of an abstract urban environment—not a specific city but the suggestion of street corners, alleyways, walls, and doors which would create the impression of heat, tension, pressure. Here Daniels was after creating a more modern adaptation of Zeffirelli's Italian Renaissance town plaza as the central space for the play's public scenes. Koltai's solution was to create several huge trapezoidal shaped Italian plaster walls, all splotched in whites, yellows, and browns, hinged so that they could be positioned at a variety of angles to give the suggestion of narrow passageways for the street scenes or to create a sun-drenched expanse of wall as a backdrop for Juliet's two scenes awaiting the arrival of her Nurse with news first of marriage and then of murder.

In practice the walls, because of their size, were difficult and dangerous to move and reposition and because the permanent stage constructed for the season was sharply raked, the walls gave the actors the feeling that they were always about to topple over. As Koltai candidly volunteered in his remarks about the production, the walls remained a decoration that the actors moved through to get to the downstage playing area rather than becoming a living part of the action's environment.[3] However, the production's prominent qualities of youth, energy, passion, and life spilling out and overflowing, all counterposed with the secret, hidden, dangerous, thrilling discovery of love and commitment by Romeo and Juliet were brilliantly realized.

It is instructive to recall that as the 1980 company was being assembled in London to begin work on *As You Like It* and *Romeo and Juliet*, the opening productions of the new season, Trevor Nunn and the 1979 company were finishing their Stratford season and had determined to move forward in translating what had been conceived as a company exercise—reading, researching, and dramatizing scenes from Dickens's *Nicholas Nickleby*—into a script for performance. When Ron Daniels and his cast moved out of the cold and drab, and very Dickensian, RSC Floral Street rehearsal rooms, they left them to Nicholas, Smike, and the Crummles come to fashion their own wonderful parody version of *Romeo and Juliet* which closed the first half of their dramatization of the novel.

# Shakespeare Observed

RSC Rehearsal Rooms
Floral Street
Covent Garden

2/4/80   Morning

Ron Daniels on *Romeo and Juliet*. Dream, nightmare, chaos contained within the very formal. Tragic companion to *A Midsummer Night's Dream*. Love both creates and destroys self-identity. Will approach without specific period background. Options will emerge from close analysis of text. Play about secret love, hidden from the world, dangerous. Play shouldn't be tied to recognizable locale. Setting play on West Bank will not solve Arab/Israeli conflict. Wants to avoid easy identification with any specific contemporary social or political context.

Moves immediately to 1.2 from entrance of Benvolio. Using T. J. B. Spencer's Penguin edition as text. Daniels has prepublication copy of the new Arden "The director's crib," he cracks with a smile.

Romeo is Anton Lesser. Small, bright, lively, witty. Looks like an undergraduate. In fact, is only 24 and looks much younger. Allan Hendrick (Benvolio) is slightly larger of build but gives the same impression of youthfulness; shyer and less immediately articulate than Lesser. Daniels expert at reading Hendrick—knows precisely when he is leaving questions unasked and so probes for them.

Daniels emphasizes that the play happens to Romeo. He's caught between male loyalty to his mates and his awakened infatuation with women. His mates are repeatedly trying to uncover his secrets and to lure him back into the fold of male comradeship. This is what Benvolio is trying to uncover in this scene. Daniels asks his actors to imagine the scene being played with lamppost and curb; "or tire and rope" Benvolio responds and Daniels fires back: "Precisely."

2/4/80   Afternoon

Judy Buxton—Juliet—joins the group. She's currently playing Iphigenia in John Barton's monumental nine-hour adaptation of the Troy story: *The Greeks*. She's lithe and angular and serious. No sense of the schoolgirl in her manner. It will be interesting to see how she pairs with Lesser. As they begin to read through Romeo and Juliet's first meeting, I'm amazed that they all seem to come to it so fresh—no remarks about other productions

[ 106 ]

which are certainly whirling through my head. Daniels remarks that he'd like to do the play without the balcony—pause as Lesser and Buxton register disappointment—but won't.

Multiple read through of ball scene moving on to the more famous exchange following. Very quiet. Concentrating on what happens to Juliet because she's already given herself away; she's moved beyond words. Daniels stresses her vulnerability, her insistence on essence, her practicality. She's gone further, faster than Romeo.

One final note. When Daniels distributed the texts this morning he had told the cast that he had done some cutting. "Short evenings make for good theatre," he quipped. He suggested that if he had cut something they wanted to make a case for restoring, that they should propose alternative cuts elsewhere in their part. "Oh, Ron, you can't bargain Shakespeare" was Anton Lesser's smart reply. Peter Hall has infected the actors!

2/5/80

Romeo, Benvolio, and Peter in the morning moving through 1.2 at the table three more times before getting up and moving. Much work on what Daniels calls "structure" and what Anton Lesser calls the "shape" of the scene. Daniels tells them to trust the fourth syllable or second beat when looking for emphasis in the line. They work on Benvolio's feeling Romeo out and Romeo's guilt that he has deserted his mates for love. The two actors are asked to begin across the rehearsal floor from each other to see what happens to the space between them as the cat and mouse exchange develops. Romeo gives his secret away—Rosaline—when he overreacts to reading her name on Peter's invitation list. Then, the first decisive gesture comes when Romeo kicks Benvolio with more than playful ferocity after saying "Your plantain leaf is excellent for that." Lesser's spontaneous action, very much in keeping with the bantering mood which has come to characterize his work with Hendrick, delights Daniels. He encourages more of the physicality—touching, pushing, shoving—which marks the give and take between adolescent boys. The kick alerts everyone to Romeo's temper, and increases Benvolio's wariness of his pal's mood. Monster Love. Love has made Romeo mad. Romeo trying to keep his secret and placate his friend. Benvolio hits the mark on his second stab ("the fair Rosaline") which leads to much fun in comparing her with

Verona's "admired beauties." Daniels works on the way Benvolio parries and withdraws in probing for the source of his friend's odd behavior. Both are relieved that the secret is out: the scene ends on an upbeat challenge as Romeo agrees to prove to Benvolio that his cure won't work. Daniels underlines the play's insistence on love as an infection, a disease, a madness, a transforming power which threatens identity. Benvolio wants to save his friend. "He has lost himself" emerges as a key response to Romeo's condition.

Lesser is very quick—he's a natural mime and wit. I hope he brings some of those qualities to this Romeo to save him from the maudlin. As Lesser and Hendrick work through this scene all the extratextual references are contemporary: pints, pubs, playing games and practical jokes on friends, current movies. I am excited about the way in which the play—through the actors' give and take with it—wheels so effortlessly into our world. Lesser will be off for a week as he's finishing a production in Liverpool and must catch an early afternoon train. No word on who is to be cast as Mercutio.

2/6/80

Brenda Bruce (Nurse) working on the great Lammas Eve speech. Has just come from playing Gertrude in the world tour of Derek Jacobi's *Hamlet*. First western troup to play Beijing. Amazing response.

Nurse's love of life and her girl. Flavor of memory and rich reminiscence.

Daniels has a quiet, intense, but engaging manner with his actors. All his concentration is on them. No idle gossip. No theatrics. His favorite responses are "Right." "Lovely." "Wonderfull." "Ex-act-ly." "Good." Doesn't reveal his ideas except in bits and pieces. Most taken with particularity. "What are you thinking?" "Where have you been?" "What are you doing?" "Be specific."

Afternoon devoted to 2.5 and 3.2 "The clock struck nine" and "Gallop apace": Daniels sees them as one set of a series of mirror scenes in the play. They will be rehearsed repeatedly together. Very strong on getting Judy to return to the text to catch the excitement and impatience of each moment. "Trust the text" is heard again and again in this Verona.

# Watching the Torches Burn Bright

Casting is almost complete. Jonathan Hyde will play Mercutio and Trevor Baxter, Capulet.

Morning given to Romeo, Benvolio, and Mercutio. Hyde makes an excellent addition. He's sharp with a wild wit. Much zanier in his flights of rehearsal fantasies than his counterparts. Lethal. He breaks Hendrick and Lesser up with marvelously improvised dove calls and coos as he tries to conjure Romeo after Capulet's ball. The playful abandon of Romeo's two tipsy pals which emerges from their playing with the text here is already catching at the contrast with Romeo's new seriousness. All this will remain central to the performance and be augmented by Mercutio's playing with a large pink cupid doll with an enormous phallus.

Later in the day Mercutio and Benvolio work on the opening lines of 2.4. Daniels remarks at the end of the session: "That was true RSC style: three hours on thirteen lines."

2/18/80

Peter Woodward leads the lads in a morning of movement exercises and games. He stresses walking from the gut; projecting John Wayne macho; wants them to be cocky, tough young studs. Cautions them to keep their eyes steady, riveted. "Stay calm, the more movement the greater the loss of intensity. You want to convey latent energy and tension."

2/19/80

Sensational afternoon with Anton and Judy doing the balcony scene without texts for the first time. Lesser started out very lyric and love melancholy. Daniels said "Don't do it sob—play with it." We were then treated to the scene as if it were done with Mercutio's manic energy. Eventually the scene will be played with Romeo on the ground propped up on one elbow as he discourses with himself on his new-found infatuation. His sense of the absolute wonder of it all remains central to the scene. He's wrapped up in himself and in his daydream of her. His response to her first sigh "Ay me!" was always rightly received by the audience with a huge laugh—a laugh acknowledging his amazement that she's really up there. This will be compounded when he comes to discover that she shares his daydream and fantasy. Though never discussed in the blocking, their stage positions here come to represent Daniels's formulations about the images each uses to express their love. Romeo's are wide; Juliet's are deep. Here Romeo is horizontally sprawled out on the garden ground and she's perched vertically behind a high abstract wall.

Two bits from the afternoon session. Ron Daniels on *Hamlet:* "The secret of Hamlet is what book is he reading? Machiavelli? Montaigne? Kierkegaard?" Well, Daniels has read Kott. Later on in midst of discussion on Anton's commute to Liverpool.

Anton Lesser: "I'm tired."

Ron Daniels: "Why?"

Anton Lesser: "I've got Brit Rail lag."


2/25/80  Morning

4.5. Trevor Baxter comments that he'd never realized before that they all don't know about Romeo and Juliet until the very end. Why doesn't Juliet try me, he questions. I may very well have agreed. Daniels responds, Why doesn't she? Not a story of two children embattled against a hostile world. No. They are surrounded by appallingly lovely people. The problem lies in an incredible series of mis-matches.

The parents aren't villains. They do what they do for the best possible motives, but like all parents they do lose control and have their own tantrums. This tragedy is more complicated than two silly and headstrong kids destroyed by a bad world.

This response strikes me as indicative of Daniels's way with the play and with his actors. He treats all with the greatest generosity, much like the writer who cannot be brought to stand against any of his creations—even the most vile. Daniels wants to think the best of all the characters in this play. No easy cynicism or structural contrast between older and younger generations with the latter having all the best of it. He repeatedly tells his actors to stress the "rich humanity of their characters." This strikes me as very much in keeping with the production values associated in working at The Other Place, where the intimacy between actor and audience demands a style of playing we might more readily associate with Chekhov's dramatic world than with Shakespeare's.

# Watching the Torches Burn Bright

2/25/80   Afternoon

That afternoon Judy does 4.3 for the first time. She's fighting
a cold but does marvelous work. A dirty mattress is flopped on
an ancient pair of iron springs supported by two benches in the
middle of the cold and dismal upper rehearsal room on Floral
Street. Ceiling fans stand idle, paint peeling everywhere, bare
lights, loudspeakers from special delivery cycles blare up from
the narrow street below. February rain is streaking the dirty windows. A typical London chill permeates the atmosphere. I wrap
my hands around my tea mug for warmth. The contrast between
the condition of the room and the art it contains is astonishing
and paradoxical. One of the greatest repertory companies in the
world is working in the most dismal surroundings, and yet those
surrounds are a perfect emotional landscape for Juliet's speech.
Daniels gets Judy to focus on the key verbs which carry the momentum of her monumental undertaking as well as to concentrate on the crucial second beat of the line so that the following
words emerge as central: thrills, freezes, scene, marriage, married, redeem, stifled, strangled, buried, festering, madly play,
mangled, rage, dash out, Romeo, spit his body, rapier's point. "A
little caesura before the verbs make them live," he reminds her.

2/25/80   Evening

That evening Daniels begins to block Capulet's ball. Wants to
have flowers everywhere. It's a wonderful, homemade, fancy-
dress party. The arrival of the masquers should be thrilling—
they bring the party to life. Wants their masque to convey a
young male fascination with and fear of sexuality.

The meeting of Romeo and Juliet must be absolutely accidental. "They are not meant for one another."

The party celebrates the most wonderful man in the world—
Capulet. All the women will dance about him in delight. I won-
der how this will work? A bit too much like Mr. Pickwick at
Dingley Dell?

2/26/80

Back to work on 1.3. Daniels makes several suggestions to
Judy. "Can you get the sense of Juliet as a daydreamer who
spends lots of time alone. Juliet is very still, quiet, no sense of
trouble or nervousness about her. She is the surface of a nice
clear lake. She comes to life with Romeo."

[ 111 ]

# Shakespeare Observed

2/27/80

Afternoon attention to 2.4. Nursey and the lads. Brenda has imagined her Nurse with a fan from the beginning, now it comes into creative play as she instinctively uses it as a weapon to fend off Mercutio and his bawdy innuendos.[4] Hyde's inventiveness is precisely the sort which invites one to retaliate with a swat or a slap. The banter between Mercutio and Benvolio and Romeo which precedes the Nurse's entrance builds to a giddy climax here with the Nurse hitting Mercutio in the crotch under Romeo's arm as he intrudes himself between them. Mercutio collapses and rolls on the floor, feigning deep injury. This is a brilliant anticipation for 3.1.

2/29/80  Morning

An entire series of gestures have emerged to mark the relationships between a variety of father/son, man/boy moments in the play. When Tybalt angrily interrupts the ball scene to reveal Romeo's presence, Capulet takes him by the ear and marches him downstage out of the swing of the party. When the dance ends, Capulet insists with a prodding elbow in the ribs that Tybalt join him in applauding the dancers. Montague gives Benvolio an open-hand clip to the side of the head as he tries to learn "who set this ancient quarrel new abroach?" When Romeo enters in 2.3. he playfully puts his hands over Friar Lawrence's eyes; in 3.3. it is the Friar who attempts to rub away the stain of a tear from Romeo's cheek to make him presentable to the world again after his attempt at suicide.

2/29/80  Afternoon

A long go at 3.3. Daniels sees this scene as moving along the lines of a rational debate. Imagines that Friar Lawrence and Romeo have spent hours pouring over Aristotle and Aquinas. Wants Anton to capture the passion and pride of intellectual argument. Not to be played as one long laceration. Everything explodes on "Hang up philosophy!"—which becomes Romeo's rejection of adversity's sweet milk; his rejection of his tutor and of the power of the intellect to contain and restrain emotion. Ron encourages Anton to sulk against the rear wall as he rejects the Friar's arguments. This fits with other boyish postures which have emerged. Anton is clearly uncomfortable with this retreat into a passive sulk—wants something bigger to express his frustration with the Friar's "words."

# Watching the Torches Burn Bright

3/3/80

Tybalt and Capulet at the ball. Chris Hunter (Tybalt) is having trouble finding the right tone—he's locked himself into a series of robot-like moves and gestures and deliveries. Daniels is trying to loosen him up. Gets Chris to say the lines without working at them as Daniels snaps his fingers to the beat. Wants him to be more spontaneous, less epic. "You're giving me too much process, relax, say the lines without thinking about them."

As his suggestions take root, Daniels responds to Hunter's delivery of "Now, by the stock and honour of my kin," by commenting: "pluck that word 'honour' out and enjoy it."

Daniels apropos of some lost moment: "As Terry Hands says, an English question is usually a statement."

Random observations as the party scene gets its first thorough blocking. Prelude to entire scene will be Peter tripping and spilling a bowl of fruit as he puts Anthony and Potpan through their paces. This to set up the accidental quality of the party and the world of the play. Romeo and Juliet *not* meant for one another. Their meeting is an accident.

Party to be filled with color, flowers, heaping banquet tables. Capulet famous for his festive parties. The action to be swirled around three dances: Mercutio's impromptu masque, centered on cupid; a reel or folk dance where partners travel so that Juliet and Romeo can have their accidental meeting; and a final one to celebrate Capulet. Kids love coming to his parties.

Tybalt and Nurse will be dance partners to establish their friendship and to give background to Nurse's later lament: "Oh Tybalt. The best friend I ever had."

3/6/80   Morning

Mantua a washed out, barren landscape for Daniels. Should be imagined as a ghost town, tumbleweeds and newspapers blowing through the streets. High noon. It is the landscape of exile and death. A place where one can buy anything.

Anton does several miraculous turns on "Thus I defy you, stars." One version is prefaced by a scream, another done in an intense whisper, yet another building from a quiet "is it e'en so" through a muffled cry for "I defy" exploding out into an elongated howl on "youuuu starrrrrs." Too much? A fourth version emerges with "is it e'en so" delivered with the tone of "so that's the way the game's played" followed by both arms being raised slowly to the heavens on "Thus I defy you—long pause—stars."

Daniels works with Anton on the way in which Romeo begins to yield to the sewer world of the apothecary's shop. Encourages him to see "I defy you stars" as an outstanding dare—and not to let his anger release the pain. By the end of the scene Romeo has become extremely callous—he's broken the sound barrier—he's on the other side of experience. Defying the stars, he's broken all norms.

3/6/80   Afternoon

Work on 2.4. Mercutio and Benvolio leaning against wall. Daniels continues to delight in postures, gestures, poses which capture teenagers kicking about town. Theme again is male concern for Romeo's obsession with love—already dangerous, now mounted to a direct threat in the person of Tybalt. The wit exchange on Romeo's entry becomes a means of trying to lure him back into the world of "mates." Daniels suggests that the wit exchange is a game which they drop into automatically. Lesser and Hyde and Hendrick pick up on this immediately and begin to punctuate their retorts by a clap of the hands and a point of the finger at the questioner who has been "put down." This snapping, scoring points device immediately picks up the tempo of the scene and becomes infectious and spills over into the Nurse's entrance and leads to the smacking and bashing of her fan. This rollicking scene is the happiest moment in the play for Daniels: "the sun is actually shining."

3/11/80   Morning

Daniels back from Newcastle where the current (1979) company has moved for its annual six-week season. He's come loaded with more observed examples of teenage boys hanging about and bothering one another.

He reminds the cast that they will be playing in a 1500-seat theater—they must project without losing the humanity of what they are doing. "In this theatre your last word must be as vital as your first."

Much work on the fight scene. Lads will have sword sticks. Fight begins with sticks. The crowd urges Mercutio and Tybalt on by making the staccato cheer of fans at downhill skiing competitions. Establishes the sport/game rhythm to these standoffs which escalates to swords when Tybalt makes a triumphant gesture ("We've won") in response to Romeo's plea that this "good Capulet" should be "satisfied."

3/11/80 Afternoon

Mab scene. Fourth time through. Romeo's preoccupation, his unwillingness to join in the camaraderie of the masque. Mercutio is offended by Romeo's dreaminess, his sense of being lost in love, his lack of pleasure in the former pleasures of being with the gang as they prepare to crash the party. Hyde wants his Mercutio to value intelligence over emotion; control over passion; reason over love. Wants Romeo to abandon his abandon. Does not want to do Mab as an exercise in which all of Mercutio's insecurities come pouring out.

Mab speech is being seen more and more specifically as Mercutio's attempt to "cure" Romeo of his infatuation. When Romeo responds that Mercutio talks of nothing, Hyde fires back with a handclap for emphasis: "True." Pause. "I talk of dreams . . ." With the implication that he talks of the devastating power of dreams; powers which threaten to radically alter his friend and companion.

In working through Mercutio's fabulous conceits Daniels provides the following advice to Hyde. "The most exciting Shakespearean inflection is the most natural one. Long sentences yes, but make them natural."

3/18/80

Juliet flanked by Lady Capulet and the Nurse. Again Daniels stresses Juliet's calmness as she is exposed to the pressures of her mother (social) and the pleasures of her Nurse (sexual). Daniels encourages Barbara Kinghorn (Lady Capulet) to take the presentation of Paris very carefully: "It's a magnificent present, unwrap it slowly."

Then a move to 3.5 from Lady Capulet's entrance "Ho, daughter! Are you up?" Judy Buxton remarks that the Capulet's do much "Ho-ing," and we are treated to a series of wonderful Ho-calls by Judy and Barbara and Brenda before settling back down to the business at hand.

Judy wonders how Juliet is to react to her mother's news of the marriage with Paris. "Does she think that Mum has put Dad up to this and that Juliet can deal with Dad by turning on the waterworks?"

Daniels reminds them that Capulet has made a most liberal bargain with his daughter, a contract in which "my will to her consent is but a part." He has now betrayed that bargain and his daughter, but for what he believes to be the most benign reasons. When Trevor Baxter (Capulet) joins the scene, he adds several crucial insights into this vision of Capulet. "When a nice person goes nasty it's even worse, as his sense of guilt multiplies his outrage." Capulet's frightening tantrum reveals to Baxter that "we see how he made his money—he's ruthless when crossed."

The bed remains onstage for this scene and becomes a powerful symbolic landscape. It is Juliet's: and more importantly, the site of her marriage's consummation. Now it is usurped first by her mother who sits on it to console her daughter and to announce the news of the marriage with Paris. Then it becomes a battlefield as Capulet slaps Juliet to the floor then pulls her up and flings her back on the bed during the course of his tirade. The Nurse then begins to reappropriate it as she busies herself with tidying it up as she gives her fatal advice to forget Romeo and to marry with the "lovely County." She's reestablished her routine after this frightening family row. Juliet takes final possession of this potent territory as she climbs back on her bed and dismisses the Nurse with "Go, counsellor! Thou and my bosom henceforth shall be twain."

3/22/80

Nightingale and lark. Daniels does not want Judy and Anton to be naked. "Nudity is old-fashioned. Anyway it's not a scene about getting dressed. But I do want lots of arms and legs; you can afford lots of sensual panache in the playing of the scene."

•

AT THE END of March the company broke camp in London and moved to Stratford. For ten days rehearsal periods were sporadic and brief as all attention was focused on opening the first show of the season, Terry Hands's production of *As You Like It*. Once it had opened to preview audiences, concentrated attention returned to *Romeo and Juliet*. In his Saturday morning discussion of the play at The Other Place, Daniels revealed some of the difficulties of being the second production to open when all workshop attention is devoted to getting the first play mounted.[5]

•

4/7/80 Afternoon

Steven Oliver, who has composed the music for the production, objects to Daniels's textual adoption for the end of Juliet's "I have a faint cold fear thrills through my veins." Judy has been using the text of the disputed Q1: "Romeo I come. This do I drink to thee." Oliver argues that the text is corrupt as well as being too rhetorical. The second argument has greater appeal to Daniels. Judy, however, resists the change, so a compromise is struck, and we get the Buxton/Daniels conflation of Q1 and Q2-4: "Romeo I come. Here's drink! I drink to thee!"

4/7/80 Evening

First complete run-through. Daniels makes several remarks to the company by way of a preface. "This is an epic stage. It thrusts you right out at the audience. We need to resist that epic thrust and just concentrate on telling the warm humanity of our story, of your character's story. Let this marvelous text resonate in and through you. You must be excited about it or it will go dead. Be specific. The play is about sacrifice and healing but even more about the obsession and madness of love and passion. You must risk the vulnerability of doing it straight and honest. Strive for clarity, for telling the story without rhetoric. It is the play's humanity rather than its epic spectacle you want to capture. Thrill to the language of the play."

•

BY INCLUDING this diary I have attempted to provide an example of another kind of observing in which one gains a glimpse of the process through which a director and group of highly skilled actors work at shaping and reshaping a performance text. I often felt a bit like the documentary filmmaker, Frederick Wiseman, poking my camera into private, intimate spaces not meant to be recorded even by a single pair of alien eyes. This experience led me to a clearer understanding of the artist's natural resentment for those of us who spend our lives tracing patterns in the carpets they weave. It is at least a fairer game when we have access only to the finished work and are not privy to the endless hours of trial and error which go into mastering the illusionist's craft.

Rather than using my privileged perspective to construct a reading of the production I want to place my rehearsal observations in the context of those professional newspaper critics who came to the performance with relatively fresh eyes. Theirs is yet another kind of observing—that of the professional spectator who takes a quick snapshot and renders a terse judgment packed into 700 words or less and moves on to the next assignment. Productions of *Romeo and Juliet* are often anticipated with a huge yawn by veteran reviewers, who do not quicken to its adolescent passion or its general popularity.

Daniels's production managed to break through those potential dangers, and many of its key dynamics and rhythms were grasped and highlighted by the reviewers. The following excerpts were typical of the production's reception: "Not since the legendary Zeffirelli version have I seen a production which so powerfully transmits the sense of awakening adolescence" (Irving Wardle, *Times*); "Mr. Daniels . . . has created a hot-tempered hectic southern hemisphere society in which impulse is king. And not since Zeffirelli's Old Vic production have I seen a Romeo and Juliet who so convinced me that they were prey to cupid" (Michael Billington, *Guardian*); "The production grips both as comment on the play and as a piece of storytelling" (Robert Cushman, *Observer*); "Every so often, an actor comes along who turns our accepted idea of a Shakespearean character upside down. It happened in 1935 when a young actor threw out the idea of Romeo as a pallid romantic lover spouting beautiful poetry and instead substituted a swarthy Italian who fractured the verse to portray a Renaissance teenager. His name was Laurence Olivier. Now I don't want to build up Anton Lesser disproportionately. But last night he gave us certainly the most unorthodox Romeo I have ever seen." (Felix Barker, *Evening News*); "The best reason for visiting Stratford this summer is undoubtedly Ron Daniels' new staging of *Romeo and Juliet*. . . . this is Daniels' first RSC main stage production and he brings to it all the virtues of textual clarity and fidelity which we have come to associate with the RSC at the Warehouse or The Other Place in their more experimental and less immediately commercial work" (Sheridan Morley, *International Herald Tribune*).

As these exerpts indicate, Daniels's production called forth comparison with the two legendary London productions of *Romeo and Juliet* in the past fifty years: the famous Gielgud-Olivier version of

1935 and Zeffirelli's passionate staging with Judi Dench and John
Stride at the Old Vic in 1960, made even more lasting through its
translation into the most commercially successful Shakespeare film
ever made.[6]

Morley picked up on issues related to "textual clarity and fidelity"
associated with the company's work in the smaller confines of The
Other Place even as he and his colleagues were responding to the
vivid pace and atmosphere of the production. The attention Daniels
had given to the scenes with Romeo and his mates and the unconventional physicality of this humor struck a chord: "Anton Lesser's
Romeo [is] for once a fit companion for the rest of the gang. If not
exactly in the Hells Angels class he is impish and witty, and when he
goes into his verbal tennis game with Mercutio, each hit [is] registered
with a pistol shot hand clap by the group. It is no directorial extrav-
agance when they all wind up with their arms round each others'
necks or writhing in exhausted mirth on the ground" (Wardle); "This
Romeo is both funny and heroic, a blend of the obviously modern
with the historical . . . [while] Chris Hunter's Tybalt and Jonathan
Hyde's Mercutio belong without question to the world of punk and
rock. They set the pace for the street life of the play. . . ." (James
Fenton, *Sunday Times*); "Anton Lesser's Romeo is an intemperate, fe-
rocious adolescent poleaxed by love; he lies back on the ground and
hugs himself in ecstacy at the sound of Juliet's voice . . . this is young
love as it really is: wild, frenetic, and careless of dignity" (Billington).

The pace and energy of the production evoked Zeffirelli, and
Lesser's unconventional Romeo sent some memories scuttling as far
back as 1935 and Olivier's plain-spoken Romeo in startling and intentional contrast to Gielgud's lyricism as the two actors traded the
parts of Romeo and Mercutio. Reviewers reach for comparison with
past productions with the same ease and readiness that academic
Shakespeareans reach for bits and pieces of a critical argument or theory to bolster response. Watching Anton Lesser's performance gradually grow through rehearsals caused me to forget what a radical
rethinking of the part he was approaching, and it was certainly his
performance which most startled the reviewers and came to stand for
the production's bright, daring values.

Daniels's desire not to set the play in a specific period or against a
recognizable landscape also came through as reviewers scrambled to
place locale and costumes. References ranged from punks, to mods
and rockers, to West Side Story, to the Hells Angels in an attempt to
define the teenage culture evoked by the production. Stabs at locale

and atmosphere ranged from South America to the Palio and Cup Final to the futuristic gang warfare film *The Warriors*. Design and costume provoked thought and the reach for modern parallels without finding a specific context precisely as Daniels had intended in his very first remarks to the cast.

If Daniels encouraged and received unconventional exuberance from the young males who set so much of the tone of Shakespeare's Verona, he was clearly after something more still and quiet from Juliet and something less fussy and broadly comic than is typical from her Nurse. As the scenes with Judy Buxton and Brenda Bruce were given the same detailed rehearsal attention as those with the lads, so their performances, too, were uniquely noted. Wardle was taken with the aura of innocence projected by Judy Buxton's Juliet: "When we first see her she is still a child; the Nurse can go up and handle her as unceremoniously as an infant, and when we reach the balcony scene and see her arm involuntarily reaching down to touch her lover's fingertips the unpremeditated lyricism of the gesture is overwhelming." Billington found this same image less lyrical and more passionate: "When she reaches down from her rough-hewn balcony to touch Romeo's fingers it is with the careless abandon of someone who will literally risk her neck for love." Daniels's sense that Juliet is the play's still, committed center surrounded by the turbulence of Romeo's more aggressive passion ("her images are deep, his wide") made Buxton's performance harder to read and grasp. She was called "exquisite," "well-bred," "comely and seductive," "beautiful," "anguished"; her performance "an accurate but impersonal sketch" (Cushman), but also "straight, powerful and very good-looking" (Fenton). Perhaps the headline for Cushman's review in the *Observer* best expressed the images this production projected of the lovers: "Juliet and The Wild One."

Brenda Bruce was a "fine, unfussy Nurse who made the advice to marry Paris sound the most logical thing in the world" (Cushman); "a woman with blood still flowing strongly enough to recognize the call of the young's sexual attraction" (Jack Tinker, *Daily Mail*); "there's lots of energy here, even from Brenda Bruce's unusually young and tough Nurse" (Sheridan Morley, *International Herald Tribune*); "A pugnacious menial given to slapping her hand whenever she speaks out of turn" (Wardle) and "Brenda Bruce gives a gorgeous Nurse, younger and brisker than that character is generally played, and capable of holding her own, armed with a lethal fan, against the Montague Spivs" (B. A. Young, *Financial Times*).

## Watching the Torches Burn Bright

One critic noted Edwin Richfield's "ravished and embittered" Friar Lawrence (Billington), while another called attention to "a splendidly icy Lady Capulet from Barbara Kinghorn" (Morley), but in general the older generation was ignored or trenchantly dismissed: "The elders remain uncharacterized elegantly dressed mannequins" (Wardle). While Daniels wanted his production to stress the horrendous impact of the tragedy on the two families only one critic (Wardle) noted that Daniels filled the stage with candlelit mourners who sang Nash's "In Time of Pestilence" to a setting by Stephen Oliver.

It is always difficult for the tragic stasis of the play's final movement to compete with the vividness of the opening scenes, when all the youth of Verona are on fire. Mercutio's death is the pivotal moment in the tragedy, and it forever changes the play's atmosphere and tone. In a production which so marvelously realized its commitment to the play's young, perhaps it was inevitable that the production's images lost some of their vital spark as the world of Romeo's mates collapsed.

Daniels's mainstage debut was auspicious; he went on to have a string of successes during the 1980s particularly with *The Tempest* featuring Derek Jacobi's Prospero and two *Hamlet*s, one with Roger Rees in 1984 and a second with Mark Rylance in 1989. The latter was a stunning and radical treatment of the play, the best I thought of the many *Hamlet*s that were produced in England in the 1980s stretching from Jonathan Pryce's daring performance in Richard Eyre's production at the Royal Court in the spring of 1980, to Timothy Walker's for Cheek by Jowl directed by Declan Donnellon in 1990. Daniels's *Romeo and Juliet* brought new faces and new energies to the company even as it incorporated them within the Hall tradition of detailed attention to the text and its spoken rhythms.

## CHAPTER EIGHT

# Free Style: Adrian Noble's
# *King Lear* and
# *As You Like It*

•

THE EXPERIENCE of observing Ron Daniels's *Romeo and Juliet* in 1980 brought me close not only to that production but to workings of the Royal Shakespeare Company itself. Over several months of casual conversations with actors, directors, members of stage management, and administration, two central issues in the company's work and direction soon became apparent. One was that the company's creation of The Other Place, in 1973, had become as seminal to the nature of the RSC's work as had Peter Hall's decision to open a London front at the Aldwych in 1960. The second was that there had not yet appeared a second generation of exciting and provocative young directors to succeed Hall, Brook, Barton, Nunn, and Hands, who had revolutionized the company's work with Shakespeare and had become so remarkably successful that they were in danger of being devoured by the administrative demands of their own creation.[1]

In this age of gigantic theater monuments from Lincoln Center to the Sidney Opera House to the South Bank's National, it is a fitting irony that the space which has transcended them all should turn out to be a corrugated tin warehouse which had served as a rehearsal room for the RSC before being transformed into The Other Place; a space conceived as a simple black box with two rows of folding chairs arranged on an upper and lower level, seating at most 150.

By 1980, The Other Place had become, rather than a space where the younger and less prominent members of the company could experiment with small-scale Shakespeare and work on new texts, the chosen venue for the company's major actors and directors. Under Ron Daniels's thoughtful leadership, The Other Place had become a

# Free Style

Stratford outpost for exploring non-Shakespearean classics and the work of contemporary playwrights. But from Buzz Goodbody's famed modern-dress production of *Hamlet* with Ben Kingsley as the prince, this new space became coveted as an arena for Shakespeare. By 1980, Trevor Nunn had directed his landmark *Macbeth* with Ian McKellen and Judi Dench and a brilliant *Three Sisters*, making tickets for The Other Place and its London counterpart, the Warehouse, the hottest items in the British theatrical world.

Why was it obvious to me then, in that spring of 1980, that this living testament to Peter Brook's call for an intimate empty space had created a dilemma in the company's work? As professional Shakespeareans on both sides of the curtain are aware, Stratford's Memorial Theatre is not a happy space. The configurations of the stage and auditorium are not auspicious, and both actor and director need to be on fire to find ways to make Shakespeare live effectively in that house. Also, it takes no Kenneth Tynan come from the grave to tell us that Shakespeare is an epic dramatist and that while the company can surely profit from exploring him in a little room to reckon him truly takes a great hall.

I perceived a lack of creative interest in the big theater in my casual discussions with current company members and longtime observers of the Stratford scene. It appeared to exist as a means of attracting huge numbers of tourists—many of whom had come only to take pictures and nap through the performance—to fill the main house, thus supplying the revenue to support The Other Place, where the real work of the company was done and presented to a small, coterie audience of true believers.

The second issue—where were the new directors—was less fundamentally threatening simply because all creative work runs in cycles and different eras make different demands on actors and directors. My colleagues who are still wondering who will succeed Olivier, Gielgud, and Richardson as the great classical actors of our century have already missed too many memorable performances awaiting news that a new king or triumvirate has been crowned. Nevertheless, it was clear in 1980 that no young director had appeared in Stratford with the energy and imagination and stamina to seize the spotlight from Nunn and Hands and Barton. It was also clear that directors, like actors, need new challenges which often lead them away from very successful institutions. Peter Brook's career provides the prime example of this trend, and by early 1980 John Barton was bringing his long-envisioned nine-hour presentation of the Troy story, *The Greeks*, to fruition at the Aldwych just as Trevor Nunn was moving the 1979 Stratford Company down to London and into the Floral Street rehearsal rooms to move *Nicholas Nickleby* from company exercise to finished production. These two epic theater events were watersheds in the careers of both directors. Barton drifted away from the company soon after to try a West End season at the Haymarket, while Trevor Nunn became absorbed in *Cats* and its progeny and since then has only directed three Shakespeare productions *All's Well That Ends Well* (1981), *Henry IV, Parts One* and *Two* (1981) to open the RSC's London home at the Barbican, and a brilliant *Othello* (1989) as the final production in the tin shed before it was torn down to make way for a new and slightly larger facility constructed to meet local fire codes.

This preface is meant to provide a background for an understanding of how great theatrical companies renew themselves. As these two issues—The Other Place as artistic rival to the main house and the future directorial leadership of the company—circulated in Stratford, Adrian Noble was just arriving to join the 1980 season as an assistant director. In his first season, Noble served as an assistant director for Ron Daniels, Terry Hands, and John Barton. In the following year he directed two productions at The Other Place, one of which, *A Doll's House*, attracted enthusiastic critical attention. Noble, however, had not come to the RSC to direct small-scale productions; in his unassuming yet engaging manner he made it known that he was anxious to work in that space others shunned: the main house.

Noble's choice of his first Memorial Theatre production was appropriately daring: *King Lear*. G. Wilson Knight, Jan Kott, Peter Brook, and Grigori Kozintsev had stamped *Lear* as the most potent and powerful Shakespeare drama for the twentieth century. Brook's 1964 RSC production remains fixed in the minds of my contemporaries as the key production in defining a modern approach to Shakespeare.[2] The Brook production virtually eliminated contemporary competitors. *Lear* was produced only three times at the Memorial Theater (twice by Trevor Nunn) in the intervening eighteen years and had never been produced by the National Theatre until the Hare-Hopkins *Lear* in 1986.

It is typical of Noble's work at the RSC to tackle plays which seem to have had definitive productions in the modern era. His *Lear* (1982) challenged Brook's (1964); his *Henry V* (1984) revised Hands's (1975); and his *Macbeth* (1986) rightly inspired intelligent comparison with Nunn's (1976).

# Free Style

In every generation there are "father" productions and performances, just as there are "father" poems in Harold Bloom's creative
understanding of the ways in which great poems talk to one another
over the generations through what he terms "the anxiety of influence." Actors claim particular roles with definitive performances as
Olivier appropriated Henry V, Richard III, and Archie Rice or as
Paul Scofield stamped Lear, Sir Thomas More, and Salieri. Obviously, the same is true for productions. The Brook-Scofield *King Lear*
was, perhaps, the single production of the Hall era at the RSC which
best defined the company's unique, modern approach to speaking the
verse and imagining the landscape of a great Shakespearean tragedy.

Scofield's blunt, bullet-headed, growling, deeply internalized Lear
was a stupendous revisionist portrait destroying decades of Lears
imagined as Old Testament prophets striking operatic poses, especially in the storm scene. Scofield's Lear wasn't just terrifying, he
was a terror. The verse was handled by the company in a flat matter-
of-fact tone which helped to establish, particularly, Goneril and
Regan as characters rather than stereotypes. Brook took his lead from
his contemporaries, Beckett and Kott, and created a dull, metallic,
iron-age set which became, in Kenneth Burke's critical language, a
perfect symbolic landscape for the play.

Even though almost twenty years had passed by 1982, Brook's
production and subsequent film still dominated modern thinking
about the play. If Brook's approach found *Lear* to be a brutally modern work, Noble's production went one step further by literally
bringing the play into the twentieth century. Drop cloths were used
to cover Lear's throne when the court was disbanded; searchlights
played against the cyclorama when Edgar was being hunted; the
boots Lear removed in 4.6 were distinctly of the combat variety; a
single, unadorned light bulb hung from the ceiling in what was made
to seem a stable attic where Gloucester led the "three on's are sophisticated" out of the hovel. Noble admits that the production ideas he
created in conjunction with his designer, Bob Crowley, were "very,
very anachronistic. . . . what we tried to do was costume the characters rather than create a period, and I thought we should explore
that rather than pretend it wasn't there."[3]

It is clear that one of Noble's virtues as a director is that he is
an inventive creator of vivid stage emblems. The first sight which hit
the audience when the lights went up was of the Fool and Cordelia
sitting in Lear's throne chair frozen at cross angles: each hung in
string. "And my poor fool is hanged" was thrust to the center of our

consciousness as a trumpet blast signaled Gloucester's and Kent's entrance and the Fool-Cordelia tableau dissolved as they came to life and began to play cat's cradle with the string. With one bold cinematic stroke Noble announced that this was a production to absorb the eye as well as the ear. In this moment he skillfully prefigured the horrid image of the promised end while he also established the crucial link between Cordelia and the Fool as Lear's true progeny. This association was made even more poignant when, at the conclusion of Cordelia's banishment, Antony Sher's Fool hobbled over to her and forlornly pressed into her hand the string which had suggested their playful bond.

Noble's use of the Fool in the spatial context of Lear's throne prior to the entrance of the old king was a lively reworking of Grigori Kozintsev's use of a similar emblem in his great film of the play. This was just one of many examples which revealed the way in which some of Noble's directorial inventions are inspired by film images and techniques. Here, he picked up on Kozintsev's device of having the camera discover the Fool huddled underneath Lear's throne (Lear's submerged, other self) and refashioned it by elevating the Fool onto Lear's throne and linking him with Lear's other, blunt, truth-telling child, Cordelia. The backside of Lear's throne had a small seat at its base to which the Fool retired once the division of the kingdom had begun.

The other immediate impact of this opening sequence was our taking in Noble's and Sher's radical conception of the Fool defined by his red clown's nose, battered bowler, tiny violin, music-hall clown's coat, baggy pants, and gigantic shoes. The production's key conception came from the relationship between Lear and the Fool. The Fool's style dominated, but the two are so inextricably linked together that Lear entered into the Fool's music-hall delivery of one-liners as if they had been doing this routine for ages. In 1.5 the Fool hopped up on Lear's lap with Lear then mouthing the Fool's quips and retorts and manipulating the Fool as if he were his dummy.

Nicholas Shrimpton's description of Sher's conception was typical of the critical response to this daring departure from tradition:

> His Fool was a clown—a Charlie from the late Victorian circus with Dan Leno boots, a Grock violin and a red button nose on a length of elastic. When his lines were not funny he amused his audience by miming, or fooling, or—in extremity—strumming his violin like a tuneless George Formby. The immediate

consequence of this was that we understood, for once, why he was tolerated. However bitter his comments became, his act remained ludicrous. He was, simply, the political artist who uses his skills as an entertainer to win himself a platform.[4]

Sher's brilliant conception was beautifully partnered by Michael Gambon's Lear—the toughest and most bittersweet I have ever seen. He looked like Ernest Hemingway in his tragic final years: bleak and wan with a surprising mixture of power and vulnerability for a patriarch.

In the last decade Gambon has emerged as Britain's most admired stage actor, particularly by his fellow professionals.[5] In 1982, however, his performance as *Lear* came as a great surprise, because I had missed his Galileo and while I admired his work in Ayckbourn's *Norman Conquests* and Grey's *Otherwise Engaged* I had not found that his Roderigo and Benedick at the National gave promise of an ability to tackle a titanic tragic role. It is, once again, a measure of Noble's daring that he should not only choose *King Lear* as his first Memorial Theatre production but also do so with a company of actors who did not boast a single star name. Noble, with typical generosity, credits Gambon with the extraordinary atmosphere which came to define the rehearsal period:

> The *King Lear* was one of the most, if not *the* most, exciting productions I've ever been involved with. The rehearsal period was exciting because of the generosity of Michael Gambon in allowing the other actors space and time and the freedom to explore this monumental text, even though we knew he was the monkey who had to get up and climb the pole.[6]

Richard Findlater's assessment captures some of the essense of Gambon's performance:

> Here was no weary octogenarian, sinking under the weight of royal power, but a vain, menacing, wily, passionate and still vigorous man, not long past his prime. He relishes with a small smile his occasional double act with the Fool, joining him in the pat finale of a vaudeville cliché as they stick out their right legs in unison, or serving as a royal straight man. And his mock-abdication (for he never *means* to surrender essential power) starts as a kind of cruel game by a man who still sees himself as a master of creation, a god playing with flies.[7]

One can see from this description that Gambon's Lear was built in the Scofield tradition but without Scofield's deep internalization of Lear's passion. Scofield's Lear was a loner, an outcast long before Goneril and Regan shut the door against him. Gambon's Lear, from the beginning, had an ally in the Fool; they shared a crisp, harsh, bitter view of the world. It was only when the Fool turned that vision on Lear himself that the old man began to unravel. Noble clearly conceived of Lear and the Fool as sharing a common psyche, which brilliantly explained the two most stunning and unusual moments in the production. The first came in Noble's staging of the storm scene. After a huge electronic reverberation we heard Lear's voice give a mighty bellow to "Blow, winds, and crack your checks. Rage, blow" and then two follow spots located on each side of the stage finally located Lear and the Fool perched on a tiny circular platform raised twenty feet above the stage. The Fool was huddled on his knees with his arms wrapped around Lear's legs literally hanging on for dear life. These two figures, once united in the powerful landscape of Lear's throne, now reveal their mutual vulnerability as they sway suspended above an empty landscape. Now to be above the world is not to be in a position of power but to be exposed to the raw and raging elements. The platform began to descend on the Fool's song "The codpiece that will house" which in its riddles reminds Lear once again of his misplaced values as parent and king and reached the ground on Lear's promise to be "the pattern of all patience." Noble literally put his monkeys up the pole in what may be the most difficult scene in the play to stage given the problems of how much prominence to give the storm. Here the storm's potential destructiveness was captured by where and how Lear and the Fool were positioned rather than by volume of thunder or lighting crash.

The second remarkable moment came as a result of Noble's ingenious stage explanation for the disappearance of the Fool at the end of act 3. Modern criticism has taught us well the thematic explanations for the Fool's disappearance. We know that as Lear's mind shatters into "a hundred thousand flaws" he no longer has need for the Fool's highly rational intelligence. Lear transcends the rational as he moves into madness, and this propels him away from the Fool and toward the companionship of his newly found philosopher, Poor Tom. Tom's powerful gibberish evoking images of darkness, devils, and sexual perversity replaces, in Lear's highly charged imagination, the Fool's quips and riddles. Lear fractures rationality as he makes a commitment to the chaos of his anger and his fierce passion for revenge.

# Free Style

Noble captured brilliantly this division when the Fool and Lear and Tom were led by Gloucester from the hovel to a more hospitable surround. They were brought to the attic of a barn or stable where old furniture is in storage, covered with drop cloths. This is a subtle emblematic reminder of Lear's throne being covered with a similar cloth at the end of 1.5. We were witnessing the court in cold storage—a fitting landscape for Lear's production of the trial of Goneril and Regan. The room also contained a large barrel or dustbin which the Fool climbed into as Lear begins to "anatomize Regan." Poor Tom found an old pillow, from which he began to pull and scatter down stuffing and the pillow quickly became an object for the group's aggressions and a surrogate for the daughters Lear's imagination keeps evoking. Tom hurled the pillow at the Fool who caught it and positioned it at chest level as Lear unsheathed his "biting falchion" and charged across stage to plunge his dagger into the pillow. As Lear swirled and continued his charge upstage we saw the Fool reach underneath the pillow only to have his hand emerge covered in blood as he slowly sank out of sight. Poor Tom covered the barrel with a tarp on "lurk lurk" as Gloucester arrived to lead Lear away to Dover.

I was stunned. This was liberty, surely, but not license. Lear kills the Fool's function when he crosses the border into madness. When he is restored into rationality, it is a restoration achieved by reunion with his "poor fool," Cordelia. Noble here created a startling and moving stage image which captured the symbolic essence of Shakespeare's thematic intentions. When I questioned Noble about the genesis of this dynamic moment, he returned, once again, to laud the way in which such key epiphanies in the production had been discovered by the actors themselves in spontaneous rehearsal moments. Our interview came five years after the event, but the moment was still vivid in Noble's memory:

> I can tell you precisely what happened that morning. We sat around talking as they basically knew the text at that point. We just got as much rubbish from the edges of the rehearsal area, put it on the stage, right? Then we just improvised the scene merely using the words; absolutely on the text and in that one run-through the feathers in an old cushion broke. Tony got into the rubbish can, right; just did it, right? Gambon pulled open the feathers and then they began to throw the cushion about. When the scene finished, I said, okay, let's not talk about it at all. Go back to the point when you are looking for Goneril and

Tony's got the pillow, only Tony don't throw it. That's all I said, and Tony just kept it and Gambon did what he did and what I hoped would happen happened and Tony got killed. That's all I had to do. It's one of those moments in direction that's such a pleasure because all you have to do is make one slight suggestion and the actors' imaginations take over and the whole thing was solved. It's so exciting you see when you don't have to choreograph such moments; when they just happen. It was thrilling.[8]

This moment was so powerful that many critics, including Nicholas Shrimpton, found it the climax of the production:

> The fool and his relationship with his master were the core of the production, and most of its imaginative energy had clearly been poured into their scenes together. This had certain notable disadvantages. After the Fool's death, accidently stabbed by Lear as he cowered in the hovel's dustbin, the sense of coherence was much reduced. *King Lear* the history play (that is, the plots and battles of the later acts) was not performed with much conviction.[9]

It is true that not all the stylistic elements of Noble's World War I-period setting provided a coherent vision, though I admired the suggestion that these final acts were being staged with Lear trapped in a no-man's-land behind the enemy's lines and yet, while it may be true that the *Lear*-as-history-play elements were given small attention, the Gloucester subplot emerged as a strong parallel river, not a mere tributary stream. David Waller's Gloucester was no frail prosaic version of Lear but a man of nobility and stature. Waller, from his Bottom in Brook's *A Midsummer Night's Dream* to this Gloucester, is the RSC's equivalent of the National's Michael Bryant (another recent Gloucester to Anthony Hopkins's Lear), and their mutual careers are one of the chief glories and achievements of the repertory system. Richard Findlater rightly remarks that "this admirable actor has done great service to us all in his eighteen years with the RSC. For those who may have taken his dependable professionalism for granted, this performance—with unforced truth touched by sublimity—should be a revelation."[10] Waller joined Gambon as a second "ruined piece of nature," and I have never seen 4.6 played with such sweet tenderness and concern.

On Lear's "Pull off my boots" both men scooted downstage to a shallow pool of water which ran across the stage at the footlights.

They helped each other off with their boots and slippers and then paddled their feet in the ocean as Lear held Gloucester against his chest as he preached patience to his fellow fool of fortune. Once again, Noble's image of Lear and Gloucester tending and tendering to one another became a momentarily frozen moment, like a freeze-frame, before Lear's aggression broke loose again and, after a chase which led him into the ocean, he was captured in a giant net like some exotic animal. Noble underlined this sequence in our memories by having Lear's boots remain on stage, downstage left, as an emblem to remain in the frame of our viewing for the final scenes of the play.

When Lear entered for the last time with Cordelia in his arms she still wore the hangman's noose, bringing us full circle with Noble's initial image of the Fool and Cordelia entangled in the cat's cradle in Lear's throne. Lear removed the noose and hurled it across the stage on "I know when one is dead and when one lives;/ She's dead as earth." Noble's production achieved that rare mixture of intelligence and passion so that one's mind and heart were simultaneously engaged. "This production brings me closer to Lear than I have ever been; from now on, I not only know him but can place him in his harsh and unforgiving world."[1] That comment serves well as a summary response to Adrian Noble's *King Lear*. It happens to be twenty-five years old and was the final sentence in Kenneth Tynan's review of Peter Brook's *King Lear*.

Noble's *Lear* was an auspicious debut. Could it be sustained? His next three main stage productions were *The Comedy of Errors, Measure for Measure,* and *Henry V.* The first was regarded by many as another exploration of clowning loaded with energy but also heavy with slapstick farce; the second an admired attempt to confront perhaps the most puzzling Shakespearean text for a modern audience; and the third was, much like *King Lear,* a major revisionist production. Noble's willingness to tackle *Henry V* on the main stage as the first production to rival Terry Hands's acclaimed 1975 production was in keeping with his ability to be challenged and dared by legendary productions. Of course, Olivier's film flickers behind both productions, and now Kenneth Branagh's film reveals its indebtedness to both Olivier and Noble. Noble was rightfully wise to walk the interpretive tightrope in his approach to the play. The production was heralded as a modern understanding of the nature of civil commitment and loss. Noble transformed Olivier's grand technicolor battlefield into a quagmire, when on the night before Agincourt, Henry's band of brothers huddled together in a downpour under a makeshift tarpaulin, creating a lasting image of their forlorn condition. Bob Crowley's design image here made its own creative play with Farrah's famous tarp in Hands's version, which served as barren ground cover for the meager English but when raised became the ceiling for the Dauphin's tent emblazoned with the emblems of his nobles.[12]

Adrian Noble's *Henry V* was his passage between *King Lear* and *As You Like It*. When Noble turned his attention toward Shakespeare's mature festive comedy he exhibited the same central directorial characteristics as he had when dealing with Shakespeare's tragic and historical material. I found his *As You Like It* a companion piece to his *King Lear* and in keeping with modern criticism's understanding of the linkages between Shakespeare's comedies and tragedies. Examining Adrian Noble's *As You Like It* in close conjunction with his *King Lear* is a productive way of seeing a protean director seize on elements in these plays which link them to a modern sensibility.

I have mentioned that his *Lear* was set in a no-man's-land of World War I; his *As You Like It* was placed in the post-war period captured by Oliver's Oxbridge sport coat (with the collar turned up) and silver cigarette case and Charles's double-breasted, pin-striped suit with a camel's hair topcoat luxuriously hanging loosely from his shoulders. When Rosalind and Celia first appeared they were wearing evening dresses which could have been appropriate for Coward's *Private Lives*. The crowning glory of costume design was Nicky Henson's Touchstone displaying his full plumage in top hat and tails, identifying Touchstone with a modern tradition of sophisticated clowning combining the wit of Noel Coward with the elegance and grace of Fred Astaire. Henson's Touchstone was the flipside of Antony Sher's Fool—Henson stepped out of *Top Hat*, while Sher shuffled out of the solitary follow-spot of the musical hall. Sher's Fool married Chaplin's Tramp with the caustic political humor of a Mort Sahl, while Henson's Touchstone could have circulated comfortably at one of Gatsby's lavish parties. As Shakespeare drew on folk and court traditions in creating his great clowns, so Noble has found rich ways to draw upon modern versions of clowning in reimagining Shakespeare's fools for a contemporary audience.

As I have indicated, Noble concluded the opening section of *King Lear* by having servants cover Lear's throne with a drop cloth. Later, in the hovel, this image was repeated by setting the scene in an attic where furniture had been stored—again covered by drop cloths. Now, in his *As You Like It*, Noble returned to this image and extended it into the heart of his interpretation of the play. The move from

Frederick's court to Duke Senior's, the move from society to Arden, was accomplished by having one great billowing parachute-like drop cloth brought in through a large oval frame which stood at the rear of center stage. This drop cloth was used to cover the furniture of Frederick's court and thus Arden was reimagined as a deserted grand summer house made temporary quarters by those lords in exile trying to escape winter's icy fang and churlish winds. Again, Noble and his designer, Bob Crowley, found an inventive stage incorporation of important ideas in contemporary critical thinking about Shakespeare's comedies.

Modern criticism has had to resist the simplistic tendency to equate Northrup Frye's "green world" with a bucolic setting. The green world is an imaginative landscape not a representation of nature by Constable or Watteau or Monet. Arden is the quality of Rosalind's creative inspiration not a spot on the map which automatically transforms its visitors or inhabitants. Irving Wardle, describing the production as it moved from Stratford to London, captured the essence of Noble's intentions: "wisely the set has been revised towards greater abstraction, leaving open the possibilities of an actual journey while maintaining the image of imaginative escape. The effect is at once ethereal and robustly theatrical."[3] Likewise Nicholas de Jongh in the *Guardian* saw that Noble's production "attempts to reintrepret the idea of Elizabethan pastoral in contemporary psychological terms. . . . the overall effect thrills and challenges."[4] It should be noted that both Wardle and de Jongh were more receptive to the production when it transferred to the Barbican seven months after opening in Stratford. I think their revised attitudes owe much to the ways in which Noble's productions improve with age and make one think about great texts in a fresh manner.

Arden is, like the Boar's Head tavern, a playground most open to those who have the imagination to respond to its liberating possibilities. For a Rosalind or a Hal, such spaces allow them the freedom to release possible versions of self inconceivable in the court world. Noble's staging translated a critical idea into a resonant visual metaphor. Literal-minded purists, missing the trees, failed to see the forest. Noble's fine Rosalind, Juliet Stevenson, articulates the Arden qualities the production sought to capture:

> This production is in modern dress, and it's a rather surreal
> Arden. There are no trees, it's not a forest, it seems to be the
> realm in which you make of life what you want to make of it; it's

a realm where you can dress up and change your gender, change your way of life. It's wild, living wild, living in the realms of imagination—anything is possible in Arden. . . . The set is mostly to do with colors, and space, and different moons. These moons get larger and larger as you get deeper into the forest. It's rather dreamlike, it reminds me of films by Kurosawa, long strips of color and strange landscape, created by Bob Crowley.[15]

Here Stevenson touches on the gender issues raised by recent feminist approaches to the play and responds to Noble's use of space and color and design by thinking of film analogies with a filmmaker long noted for his attraction to Shakespeare and Shakespearean themes. Noble's production ideas not only reflected his canny assimilation of critical formulations about the comedies by Barber and Frye and their followers but also—through the use of a trio of stage devices—brought Shakespeare's play into subtle relationship with several twentieth-century English comic fantasies about growth and transformation in alien landscapes: *Alice in Wonderland* and *Peter Pan*.

I have already made mention of the large oval frame at the rear of the set which became the portal into and out of Arden and which was nicknamed the "moonhole" by the cast. In Noble's original Stratford staging three other devices served as significant metaphors: a large mirror and grandfather clock all in black positioned upstage right and left and, after the interval, a pool of water running parallel with the apron. (These were discarded when the production moved to London.) Also, after the interval the side curtains, previously black, became green as did the mirror and clock (with its face now covered "there's no clock in the forest"). Wardle is quite right to credit Noble and his designer Bob Crowley for streamlining the production. The single oval frame is first used for Rosalind's and Celia's exit on "Now go we in content/To liberty and not to banishment." Their two heads, along with Touchstone's, peered back through the frame at the beginning of 2.4 before they came up through it pulling the white silk floor cloth behind them to create a wintery Arden.

In 1.2 Rosalind rushed in alone, in black evening dress, as though escaping from a dinner party. With her back to the audience she took a long, silent look at the room whose furniture was already partially covered with dust sheets before moving downstage and undraping two objects which are discovered to be large steamer trunks. She knelt and opened the smaller one and removed a picture which captured her melancholy attention. Her pensiveness was underlined by her alienation from the off-stage sounds of a party, and Noble and his Rosalind (Juliet Stevenson) effectively created a resonant image for Rosalind's situation and established a melancholy atmosphere for Celia to try to dispel: "I pray thee, Rosalind, my sweet coz, be merry." Noble was so successful in absorbing our attention with Rosalind that we did not notice Celia's entrance, so that her opening line, delivered as a comic threat, created a laugh which broke the reverent mood.

This moment captured the way in which Shakespeare here uses the play of wit and the laughter of response to dispel more somber and sober preoccupations. Rosalind's natural lament for her father's banishment and its concomitant invitation to self-pity are displaced by Celia's insistence on making merry. To engage in witty banter is a release from self-preoccupation, forcing the mind to be quick and nimble rather than lethargic and morose. Rosalind's natural predisposition to be absorbed by her father's exile is overridden by Celia's desire to reengage her friend with the world. In this initial instance the trunk represented Rosalind's past (her father) which had been banished and remained only in mementos to be stored away.

As Celia began to lure Rosalind out of her memories she was seated on the larger trunk, while Rosalind put the picture away, closed the lid, and stretched out on top of her trunk. When they began the fortune/nature debate Rosalind crossed and sat next to Celia. As they reached the climax of their exchange a knock was heard from within the trunk and both jumped off as its lid opened to reveal Touchstone popping up like a Jack-in-the-box. He was dressed in black tie and tails with one red and one green glove, with his face painted clown white, and with one red tear coming down from his right eye. Here the trunk served not just as a storage for family memories and mementos but also as the theatrical trunk of imaginative possibilities. Touchstone brings professional fooling to the service of Rosalind's melancholy and introduces the possiblity of imaginative transformation of experience. The playful bond between this trio was quickly sealed as all three climbed back into the trunk on "the little foolery wise men have makes a great show" and closed the lid as Le Beau entered to summon them to the wrestling.

Noble moved us toward Arden by opening with a black box set and a black box prop, both of which had their lids lifted to reveal passageways to other landscapes. The interval came at the conclusion of act 2 and Jaques's seven-ages speech. Most reviewers—even those with praise for the production—took exception to Alan Rickman's

Jaques, who suffered not just from a healthy cynicism but from a numbing excess of ennui. I admired the performance as an eccentric theatrical tour de force, and as an appropriate dispirited antithesis to Arden's (and love's) potentialities. If Jaques is too charming (as was Brian Bedford's in the great Robin Phillips-Maggie Smith *As You Like It* at Stratford, Ontario, in 1977–78) his version of the world earns a place in the story it does not deserve. Shakespeare allows Jaques (and thus melancholy anti-romanticism) to be dismissed by both Orlando and Rosalind prior to their two great wooing scenes and credits him with the self-awareness to dismiss himself from the final harmony.

To digress briefly, the idiosyncracies of Rickman's performance tell us something important about Adrian Noble's attractiveness to actors. Most are reluctant to work with directors who have the reputations of being puppet masters. Noble clearly enjoys and respects actors, especially ones with imaginations ready to seize on new possibilities. Young directors, full of ideas, often wish to avoid working with established stars, fearing tension and the clash of strong opinions. Noble's career reveals the opposite tendency. Before he was thirty-two he had directed Helen Mirren, Ben Kingsley, Bob Hoskins, Alan Howard, and Michael Gambon. As he has stated:

> People with imagination—Alan Howard and Michael Gambon—are highly creative, very special, sensitive. My job is to provide them with the framework of a production in which they can work . . . to dig at certain pressure points important to the character [so that] the artist can discover a sort of journey for himself. I like to stick'em out on a bird table with nothing but the words and their bodies, and like that you've got to be bloody good to thrill 1500 people for three hours.[16]

Antony Sher, in his fascinating diary account of the development of his Richard III for the RSC in 1984, captures well Adrian Noble's qualities of energy, imagination, and good spirits which actors respond to so positively:

*Wednesday 18 April*
KING'S HEAD PUB, BARBICAN  It's my first proper talk with Adrian since *King Lear.* Brings back the exhilaration of working with him. Reams of ideas tumble out, his talent almost made visible, along with the twitches, spasms of eye-rubbing, the tuggings at his collar as if he can't breathe. A man possessed.

# Free Style

Almost as if there is an excess of talent and he's having to get rid of the overflow. When he communicates ideas they are so lucid—the gift of a good director.

We talk about *Richard III* and I mention my worry about the humour in the play—I'm finding it increasingly funny each time I read it—in terms of it being a tragedy. Adrian doesn't see this as a problem, in fact the reverse, points to what we did in *King Lear*, but says, 'Richard can only have a tragic dimension if you can find the potential for good in him.'

At last he says, 'Well, what did you think of Nicky's play [Nicholas Wright's *The Desert Air*]?' I tell him about my reservations. When I say that I find the style of the play confusing and inconsistent I touch on a tender spot for Adrian. He says, 'I don't understand this worry people always have about style. What's great about theatre is that you can do anything.' Of course, Adrian's signature as a director is freedom of style.[17]

Let us return to *As You Like It*. After the interval, Orlando entered prior to Phoebe and Silvius's exchange in 3.1 and exhibited the release of his own strong emotions by racing around the box pulling green side and rear curtains to replace the first half's black ones. He then pulled another cord, and the white floor cloth sprang up to make a wigwam on which he pinned his poems. He exited as Phoebe and Silvius entered from the wigwam. The transformation of the opening scene's black box was now complete. However, Noble had the two trunks (now green) remain and put them to use in the first wooing scene, which reinforced their association with magic and play and the world of imagination.

When Jaques and Orlando entered in 3.2 Rosalind and Celia crouched behind the open lid of the trunk upstage left. Rosalind released an ecstatic moan in response to Orlando's "Just as high as my heart," and Orlando and Jaques turned to look in the direction of the sound just as Celia yanked her companion down behind the trunk, and we got our first laugh of their richly comic courtship: a laugh which simultaneously acknowledged the strength and giddiness of Rosalind's infatuation. Stratford opening-night critics felt that Juliet Stevenson's Rosalind was too cool and remote. When I saw the production the following December at the Barbican she gave no such impression. In 3.2 Hilton McRae's Orlando gave her a solid manly thump on the back (which doubled her over) on "where dwell you, pretty youth"; after regaining her composure and her voice she returned with a series of solid pokes to his chest on "Then your hose should be ungartered" which backed him to the edge of the apron as she continued her definition of the overwrought lover. He tottered as if to fall over backward and she caught him in a saving embrace, which she momentarily gave herself to before recovering her persona, pulling away on "You are no such man." In embarrassed glee she ran a three-quarter circle around the stage and leapt up onto the trunk catching Celia's eye with a wicked grin. Orlando, caught by her energy and enthusiasm, bounded up to join her. Again the trunk was the central symbolic suggestion for the Arden landscape Rosalind had created. At this moment her theatrical imagination (however precarious because of her genuine feelings for Orlando) was on fire. She was in the process of discovering and releasing the trunk's potential. As Orlando became too eager, Rosalind crossed to the white silk wigwam and wrapped it around her for "Love is merely a madness," suggesting both her own condition (momentarily redraped as a woman) as well as the objective white-coated medical clinician who knows how to "cure" love's disease. Again this was stunning use of the theatrical imagination by both actress and director to illuminate and extend the text.

A similar blocking pattern was employed in 4.1. When Rosalind arrived in the forest she was wearing a brown fedora, sport coat, white, high waisted, baggy trousers with yellow braces and a scarf—the perfect crossdressing for a stylish member of the Bloomsbury group. The inner confidence to fully assume the role the clothes imply was, however, lacking. Her infatuation with Orlando had continued the process begun by Celia of leading her out of her melancholy. "Is all of this for your father?" "No, some of it is for my child's father." She began her true journey into the essence of her "masculine usurp'd attire" in the initial bargaining with Corin over the purchase of the sheep farm. Stevenson did a wonderful double take in response to Corin's quick spit in his right hand which was then smartly proffered to Ganymede to seal the deal. When we next saw her, she had shed hat, coat, and scarf but had picked up a swell swagger and discovered the pleasure of thrusting her hands into her pants pockets for emphasis; a gesture one might associate with Katharine Hepburn in *Bringing Up Baby* as she badgers Cary Grant.

By 4.1 Rosalind had moved from swagger to panache as she slipped off her braces and declared, "Now I will be your Rosalind in a more coming on fashion," and literally pounced on him. They rolled over on the floor with Rosalind emerging on top as Celia hid her face in a book. Her confident aggressiveness reached its apex as she rolled off Orlando and faced him on her knees for "Why then can you desire too much of a good thing?" This was spirited comedy at its height, where word, gesture, action, and timing was in perfect festive harmony. Fiona Shaw's Celia, initially the more forward of the pair, was astonished and shocked by her mate's cheeky performance and beat a hasty retreat as Rosalind came after her and dragged her downstage center to enlist her services in the mock marriage ceremony where Celia's book (*A Room of One's Own?*) now is used as a Bible.

The magnificent exchange which follows the ceremony: "How long would you have her?" "Forever and a day" "No, Orlando. Say the day without the ever . . ." was set as a dance which Orlando initiated as a romantic sweeping waltz and which Rosalind accelerated into a tango on "but the sky changes when they are wives," and she ended the dance by playfully stamping on Orlando's foot on "I will laugh like a hyen, and that when thou art inclined to sleep." Again the use of the romantic waltz and the jarring tango became a perfect physical expression of the intellectual motion of Rosalind's stunning awareness, in the midst of the realization of her most intense romantic longings, that life is not always lived, or to be lived, at such heights of rapture: "the sky changes when they are wives." Noble's inventive staging here found the perfect accompaniment for Rosalind's remarkable wit.

When Orlando took his leave by planting a gentle kiss on her forehead "With no less religion than if thou wert indeed my Rosalind," Celia had to pull Rosalind back down to the ground to deliver her stinging, but laughing, rebuke of what "the bird has done to its own nest." This scene moved to conclusion, as did 3.2, as Rosalind expressed her emotional commitment ("O coz, coz, coz, my pretty little coz, that thou didst know how many fathom deep I am in love") by leaping up on the trunk from which her performance had issued.

The final use of the "moonhole" was for the entrance of Rosalind and Celia in their wedding gowns and for the arrival of Jaques de Boys, appropriately recalling all back through the window into the transformed and reconciled court world.

As I have argued earlier, Noble's conception and Crowley's design shared certain stimulating resonances with their earlier *King Lear*. An approximate period, an imaginative use of landscape as symbolic action, a concept of a world turned sterile and placed in cold storage, the understanding that Lear's journey to the barren heath and Rosalind's travel to Arden are most significantly internal voyages of the mind, a refashioning of Shakespeare's clowns and fools in a contemporary context, and an ability to nurture in Gambon and Sher and Stevenson and Shaw and Henson performances of unusual clarity and intelligence.

If one could see the influence of Broadway and Hollywood musicals in Trevor Nunn's work long before his move to the world of *Cats*, *Les Misérables*, and *Porgy and Bess*—his *Comedy of Errors* and *Once in a Lifetime* spring immediately to mind as examples—so one's mind flashes naturally to film analogies when watching Noble's work. In fact, Noble's style can be distinguished among this generation of RSC directors by its affinities with film. Noble has an open, engaging, eclectic mind which reaches out and absorbs diverse aspects of contemporary culture which stimulate his work with Shakespeare's text. We have already explored film influences on his *Macbeth* and seen Juliet Stevenson's association of his *As You Like It* landscape with images from Kurosawa. Michael Billington, in his review of *King Lear*, makes reference to Eisenstein as a way of describing Gambon's bearing in the opening scene of the play, and Noble himself has talked about the influence of film on his work as a stage director, particularly in his conception of the Fool as a camera who focuses our response to King Lear:

> When you start to do a scene, point of view is so interesting. What are we to look at? What does Shakespeare want us to look at? The director's great interpretive power is simply editorial power. It's what you get us to look at. It's what print you use. All this in caps, or double caps. The Fool is the editor in the scenes he's on with Lear. He's the one who actually gives you the focus. He tells you what's important and what isn't important. He is the camera. Jaques is a bit of that in *As You Like It*. But he's too self-obsessed. He can't believe art.[18]

Another interesting use of a cinematic subtext, in a very different context, was evident in the way in which Bruce Alexander's Oliver delivered his account of Orlando's rescue from snake and lioness to Celia and Rosalind. All three faced the front of the house and as Oliver's tale unfolded it became obvious that the two women were following his descriptive narrative as though they were watching a film. When Oliver momentarily broke away from the narrative to respond to the fact that Celia had begun to clutch his arm as one might in watching a thriller, Rosalind remained transfixed on the imaginary screen and violently tugged on Oliver's other sleeve to restart the projector—to get the narrative flowing once again. The prompt book in the Shakespeare Centre archives has a marginal note for this moment which reads: "Call Me Spielberg."

These brief examples, along with my remarks about the cinematic qualities of Noble's *Macbeth* in the opening chapter devoted to Polanski's film of the play, serve to illustrate why Adrian Noble has emerged in the decade of the 1980s as the most original of the new generation of RSC directors. Raised in a movie culture, educated in drama at Bristol, blessed with an inventive theatrical imagination, and possessed of a rehearsal manner which considers the actor's imagination as paramount, Adrian Noble has reinvigorated the RSC's main-stage work with Shakespeare and become the heir to the Hall-Brook-Barton-Nunn-Hands legacy at Stratford. It is a signal of his energy and vision, as he assumes artistic direction of the company in 1991, that Noble should express himself in epic terms: "We have to give audiences really big, big experiences, mighty plays, mighty performances, poetry."[9] The era of The Other Place has ended.

## CHAPTER NINE

# Minding Giddy Business:
# Michael Bogdanov's
## *The Wars of the Roses*

•

THE EXHAUSTED but exhilarated cast members of the English Shakespeare Company were taking their calls in Toronto late on a Saturday evening in June after almost ten hours of performing *Henry IV, Parts One* and *Two* and *Henry V*. The particular bond—a mixture of appreciation and affection for having survived such an epic event together—which develops between audience and actor in these marathon theatrical events was sweeping through the old Royal Alexandra Theater when cast and audience alike were given a comic *coup de théâtre* as a figure lurched out from the wings complete with hump and the Olivier-made-familiar black banged wig and long hooked nose. The cast collapsed in laughter at this giddy portent of what lay in store not only for Shakespeare's England but for the English Shakespeare Company as well. The figure limping its way through this tired but happy band was, of course, Richard III, and the face behind the mask belonged to the production's director, Michael Bogdanov.

We live in an age distinguished by an infinite variety of epic theatrical productions: John Barton's *The Greeks*, Trevor Nunn's *Nicholas Nickleby*, Peter Brook's *La Mahabharata*, Ariane Mnouchkine's *Roi du Cambodge*; Peter Hall's *Oresteia*, and now Bogdanov's *The Wars of the Roses*—Shakespeare's two tetralogies trimmed into seven plays with a running time of twenty-two hours.

The grandfather of these recent epic productions was the Hall-Barton *Wars of the Roses* which put Peter Hall's stamp on the company he created when he assumed artistic direction at Stratford in 1960. The Hall-Barton work was limited originally to the first tetralogy. The company was later to add productions of the *Richard II-Henry V* cycle as well, though they were never all performed as a continuous single cycle. Terry Hands directed productions of all six Henry plays in the mid-1970s, but they were never performed by a single cast. He added productions of *Richard II* and *Richard III* in 1980, but they were stand-alones never connected to the tetralogies they begin and end. Hands's discovery that audiences would not only sit still for nine-hour single-day marathon performances but eagerly seek them out surely stimulated the imaginations of Hall, Brook, Barton, Nunn, and Noble—all of whom would follow with their own epics in the next decade.

In fact one of the overlooked rewards of this fertile period in English theatrical history is the way in which these directors have been inspired and challenged by each other's work.[1] While current history stresses what Hall's innovations at Stratford accomplished for actors—extended contracts, an ensemble approach to performing classic texts, a unified theory and method (largely Cicely Berry's achievement) for speaking Shakespeare's blank verse—it may well develop that his most important contribution was in building, with Peter Brook, a tradition of directors who imaginatively seized upon the virtues of working with a relatively stable company of actors as opposed to an annual import of several stars grafted on to a quasi-permanent group of "seconds."

It is intriguing to see Hall-Brook as the center of an ever-widening circle of directors which their example and practice served to encourage, expanding first to include Barton and then Nunn and then Buzz Goodbody and Terry Hands and then Ron Daniels, Bill Alexander, and Michael Bogdanov and finally Adrian Noble and Deborah Warner. These are the directors whose careers have been shaped and anchored by company work as opposed to a series of free-lance assignments, though Bogdanov is surely the most iconoclastic of the group. If Hall's approach to the text has developed to be the most restrained of the generation he has spawned, Bogdanov's is surely the most free-spirited. Because Bogdanov's Shakespeare work is so markedly stamped as risk-taking and distinctly modern, it came as a surprise to me that his reputation has been so clearly etched by just two main stage productions over the past ten seasons at the RSC: *The Taming of the Shrew* in 1978 and *Romeo and Juliet* in 1986.[2]

However, those two productions found strong resonance with the leaders of the latest revolution in British Shakespeare criticism, cultural materialism. An interesting interview with Bogdanov by Christopher McCullough is included in Graham Holderness's *The*

*Shakespeare Myth*, a volume which builds upon the essays published in *Political Shakespeare* and *Alternative Shakespeare*—the collections which define the cultural materialist approach. Though it is in the very nature of such an aesthetic to be skeptical of work emanating from large institutions like the Royal Shakespeare Company or the National Theatre, McCullough makes it clear that Bogdanov's work is an exception.[3] Although Shakespeare observers in the post-Guthrie era are quite accustomed to modern-dress productions, Bogdanov's versions still manage to jolt and startle precisely because he is unafraid to use his style to underline what he sees as contemporary parallels with the world Shakespeare has created. His productions aren't intended to make a neat fit with another era the way Bill Alexander's justly popular *Merry Wives of Windsor* settled comfortably into the 1950s or Trevor Nunn's *All's Well That Ends Well* found interesting resonance with the Edwardian world. Bogdanov's theatrical imagination, when working with Shakespeare, is relentlessly contemporary. He feels more at home with Shakespeare's jagged edges than do any of his fellow directors, and his approach to Shakespeare has far more parallels with postmodern critical analysis than the work of any other major British director of Shakespeare. Bogdanov is firmly in Kott's camp when he insists that "these plays are living documents, they are not history, they are malleable pieces of performance which exist only at the moment of performance."[4] However, the productions themselves raise disquieting and subversive questions about text and tradition that have become the hallmark of postmodern criticism as diverse as deconstructionism and cultural materialism.[5]

Nowhere is this kinship more apparent than in Bogdanov's reimagining of Shakespeare's epic account of British history suspended between the deaths of two Gloucesters: Thomas in 1397 and Richard in 1485. Bogdanov and his co-director of the English Shakespeare Company, Michael Pennington, have created a company style and production design which allows them to place Shakespeare's dramatic action against a background of England, Europe and America in the nineteenth and twentieth centuries. Bogdanov is also keen to seize upon the potentialities in this material which allow it to be envisioned as domestic quarrel and folk epic as well as lessons in statecraft and power politics. Bogdanov has a quick and inventive imagination. The great virtue of his Shakespeare productions, and this is particularly true of *The Wars of the Roses*, is the way in which they are built on a brilliant series of details. If Noble's genius is in creating vivid emblems and images, Bogdanov's is in building a tapestry, a grand design, from countless precise choices made by actor and director in the use of the "things"—props, costumes, music, set—which come to define the world being created by the production.

I have often marveled at Shakespeare's fortuitous choice to tell the latter part of his historical tale first: expending his neophyte dramatic energies on the lesser material provided by the reign of Henry VI and thus coming to Hal's story as he hits the full stride of his powers as a dramatist. He (and we) must work our way through the chaos and the crucible of Hal's legacy before imagining his personal triumph and political achievement. To draw a contemporary parallel, this compares to a modern writer being drawn to depict the American national agony and disaster of Vietnam before writing an account of the life and death of John Fitzgerald Kennedy, who has always seemed to me to be the twentieth-century political leader whose personal myth has the strongest ties with Shakespeare's treatment of the Hal legend. I mention this only as preface to Bogdanov's approach to these plays, which reverses Shakespeare's. The first productions to be mounted by the English Shakespeare Company were *1* and *2 Henry IV* and *Henry V*, and their success is what led Bogdanov to extend his conception to include the full cycle of the two tetralogies. For this reason I want to examine the company's approach to these three core plays before widening this analysis to the other plays which came to surround them in the second season of the company's existence: *Richard II*, the three parts of *Henry VI* condensed into two and retitled *The House of Lancaster* and *The House of York*, and *Richard III*.[6]

Chris Dyer's basic set was a black box whose sides consisted of two black metal scaffolds, one mounted on rollers, each with three levels and a cat walk which could be lowered from the flies to bridge them. The rear wall was a black scrim mounted on a frame consisting of a grid of twenty squares. The center panels of the grid could slide open and were almost exclusively used for royal exits and entrances. So the skeleton set said: machine modern. However, in the tavern scenes of *1* and *2 Henry IV* the scaffolds were draped with red and orange rugs and bedspreads—the Boar's Head airing its linen—which added warmth and color and the suggestion of an ancient galleried coaching inn overlaid on the modern frame. The rugs and bedspreads gave way to a giant British flag at Hal's coronation and his final confrontation with Falstaff.

At the opening of *1 Henry IV* the playing space contained within the box was crammed with the props, furniture, two clothes racks, and other artifacts which would come to be the company's resources.

Here they existed rather as found objects which the company explored—pausing to pick an appropriate coat or shirt or apron from the clothes rack—before gathering stage center before a large standup microphone associated with the early days of radio.[7] They then launched into singing "The Ballad of Henry Le Roi" with its refrain of:

> Oh list to the Ballad of Henry Le Roi
> The King who was mighty but wild as a boy.

Michael Pennington—Hal—lingered on the edge of the group dressed in T-shirt and faded jeans and jacket and we could see immediately that his Hal would have more the touch of a James Dean than a Richard Burton; more Jonathan Pryce than Alan Howard. The interpolated song signaled Bogdanov's approach much as his famous reworking of the Sly prologue had done in his 1978 *Shrew*. The song emphasized the communal nature of the production, the folk spirit to be invoked—perhaps in response to Empson's pioneering analysis of the play which saw it as a version of the happy people/tragic king pastoral tradition—and the risks Bogdanov was willing to take with a series of plays which are as close to the heart of English culture as any works in the rich history of its literature. When one tampers with Hal and Henry V one is tampering with the very source of England's national myth.[8]

At the conclusion of the song's final rousing refrain the cast cleared the stage except for the solitary microphone, which Henry IV approached wearing a black morning coat which could have come from Stanley Baldwin's or Neville Chamberlain's wardrobe and began to address the nation: "So shaken as we are, so wan with care . . ."

The mere mention of Hal's jeans and his father's frock coat suggest the context of Bogdanov's conception. An entire essay could be devoted to Stephanie Howard's costuming of the cycle—which would, I'm sure, also provide a succinct history of military dress in the past five hundred years. The basic movement in costume design ranged from the court of Richard II dressed in nineteenth century Regency style to Richard III's Thatcherite world of double-breasted pinstripes. The key prop in the setting of Richard II's court was an easel and a painting which the king—clearly the artist—proudly displayed; in contrast, Richard III's desk sported a computer. The plays' combatants were dressed in uniforms which ranged from traditional chain mail and tunics for Hal and Hotspur at Shrewsbury and full medieval suits of armor for the ultimate clash between Richmond and

Richard at Bosworth Field to the green and brown camouflage outfits associated with Vietnam or the Falklands.

The great majority of military dress, however, moved between Waterloo and World War II. While the costuming movement of the entire cycle became progressively more modern, Bogdanov mixed styles in each, so that while the Duke of York—befitting his centrist politics—remained firmly in nineteenth-century dress, Bolingbroke was banished wearing a uniform out of Wellington's army and returned to claim his inheritance in a World War I greatcoat with his men bearing rifles and munition boxes.[9] If Chris Dyer's black box with side scaffolds and rear grid gave one the sense of being trapped inside the machine of history—Kott's nightmare version of Shakespeare's vision—the period variety and play of colors in Howard's costumes complicated and enriched our response to what, in fact, came to fill that skeletal space.

Let me use one aspect of Hal's wardrobe in *1 Henry IV* as example. He was defined by a series of jackets: the faded jean jacket I have already mentioned, the camouflage coats he and Poins both disguised themselves in at Gadshill, a wonderfully seedy eighteenth-century (knee-length, tucked waist, large sleeves) coat he wore in 2.4, a hip-length brown leather coat he wore in his exit from the second tavern scene to head to war, the bright red Household Guards jacket—"glittering in golden coats like images/As full of spirit as the month of May"—he sported in his encounter with Falstaff on the road to Shrewsbury, and finally his traditional battle dress mentioned earlier. No other character in the play—not even protean Falstaff—was as changeable. Hal's movement between and among his many coats spoke not only to his prodigal nature but to his growing mastery of role playing. The king may have *many* marching in his coats on this day, but his most potent threat and ally is *one* who marches in many coats.

Pennington's performance meshed with these costume details. His Hal was an interesting mixture of confidence and vulnerability, of reserve and emotion. He was at his most expansive in the great tavern scene, where his eighteenth-century coat was clearly a prop, something lifted from the rack of those used-clothing stores where youth do their shopping when considering something other than leather or jeans. Pennington made us see his Hal as giddy with the triumph over Falstaff at Gad's Hill, even as he pushed himself into a gaiety that often seemed forced, even a bit desperate. He wore his party coat as his own contribution to the punk dress of the Boar's Head regulars who, distinguished by Bardolph's wonderful trombone with its mournful rendition of "Silver Threads among the Gold," owed as much to Bourbon Street as to Eastcheap. Pennington's delivery of the rich mock of Hotspur "Fie upon this quiet life, I want work," here was both a knowing put-down of his rival and an expression of his own desire to move beyond holiday.

The most stunning contrast of dress came in 3.3 where Hal in his faded jeans and jacket confronted his weary father in formal black morning coat and gray trousers. Hal "dressed-up" for this encounter by wearing a kerchief tied rakishly around his neck—the same kerchief he would later use as the "favour" to hide Hotspur's mangled face.[10] Henry IV's administration was never associated with a throne but rather with a large black Edwardian table which now separated father and son. Pennington had a way of making himself seem smaller in his father's presence. In these moments Pennington found and expressed true vulnerability beneath the swagger of his outfit. All of Pennington's body language—slumped shoulders, slightly buckled knees, a way of twisting his upper torso to show discomfort and turmoil—displayed during the great speech reassuring Henry that "I am your son" brought emotional intensity to language that might appear to assert perfect confidence.[11] Pennington made us remember that this was a rebellious son speaking to a stern and distant father rather than one playful equal reassuring his somber partner that he would show up on time for the main event.

The unresolved nature of Hal's emotions in this scene was underlined when Henry moved to embrace his son on "an hundred thousand rebels die in this!" only to have Hal awkwardly slip from his embrace. The age-old father-and-son battle between affection and respect, between warmth and judgment, between love and power was here made manifest by the warm-blooded son's inability (or refusal) to reach out as the cold father begins to melt. Hal was aware, of course, that to accept his father's embrace was also to accept his place in history and to be folded into a world of time and death, parricide and regicide. Pennington expressed Hal's competing impulses through a physical gesture as he lingered on stage after his father's exit and then gave the desk-throne a violent, exasperated kick, releasing anger as much with himself, as at his father. This extended example is meant to serve as an indication of the way in which acting, direction, and design often fused in these productions to enrich and illuminate Shakespeare's text. Bogdanov's inventive use of costume detail was not intended to save money, as Louis Marder would have it, or to reduce the text by ticking off simplistic modern parallels and moving on to the next clever design image, but was meant to take us back into these works by reminding us that they have remained familiar and fresh because they speak vitally to audiences in every age.[12]

Pennington's monumental performance as Richard II, Hal, and Henry V was the glue which bound the first four plays in the sequence. If Pennington's emotionalism in 3.3 and, even more crucially, in 2 *Henry IV*—in the famed encounter with his father in the Jerusalem chamber—was too strong for some readers of the character, here it was critically justified by the way in which Pennington drew upon his portrayal of Richard II and prepared for his Henry V in these scenes.

In fact, this rare example of an actor building a Hal and a Henry V out of his portrayal of Richard II is an interesting contribution to a postmodern approach to these great plays. Formalist criticism insisted on seeing each of Shakespeare's plays as an organic unity to be read more in the manner of a lyric poem by Donne than an epic by Homer or novel by Dickens, thus ignoring the rich possibilities for seeing and making meaning out of the margins and odd juxtapositions and interconnections between and among the plays and the culture which gave them life.

Perhaps the modern theoretician whose ideas spring most rapidly to mind in response to Bogdanov's overall conception of Shakespeare's cycle is Mikhail Bakhtin. Bakhtin's notion of "responsive understanding" seems to me to be at the heart of Bogdanov's approach to these plays. Bakhtin's definition of carnival and the carnivalesque, which he developed in his works on Rabelais and Dostoevsky, have a resonance with Bogdanov's spatial imagination of the Hal-Falstaff-Henry IV triangle. Bakhtin's emphasis on the social significance of carnival and its release of a popular and comic culture has strong parallels with C. L. Barber's pioneering understanding of the importance of carnival to the Saturnalia pattern he found central to Shakespeare's use of the festive, especially in his creation of the Falstaff comedy in *1* and *2 Henry IV*. Bogdanov's creation of the contrasting production images of court and tavern (and the swirl of life and action in each) might have found their subtext and inspiration in Bakhtin's contrast between official and popular culture:

It can be said, with some restrictions to be sure, that medieval man in a way led two lives: one official, monolithically serious and somber; beholden to strict hierarchical order; filled with fear, dogmatism, devotion, and piety; the other, of carnival and the public place, free; full of ambivalent laughter, sacrileges, profanations of all things sacred, disparagement and unseemly behavior, familiar contact with everybody and everything.[13]

If Bogdanov's cycle often resonates with Bakhtin's ideas, Pennington's creation of Hal owed an important debt to the work of Barber and Ernest Kris (whose seminal essay on Hal's development stands behind Barber's more complex work), who also find crucial links between Hal and Richard II. Kris reminds us that the historical Hal was linked with Richard by being with the king on his Irish campaign when Bolingbroke returned from banishment to claim his inheritance.[14] Shakespeare's Bolingbroke reminds us of the negative connections he perceives between his wayward, riotous son and Richard, whom he dismisses as "the skipping king." Pennington found in his version of Richard what Falstaff discovered in his version of Hal: a warm-blooded, quick-witted gamesman. Pennington built his Richard from a precocious and effete dandy who dabbled in art, defined by the canvas he proudly displayed in the opening scene and the sketch pad he busied himself with while being lectured by John of Gaunt, and delighted in his own sophomoric theatrics particularly at the lists at Coventry, where Pennington's performance and vocal shifts of intonation seemed a wicked parody of Ian McKellen's worst mannerisms.

Richard's transformation from manic clown to tragic king was first evidenced in Pennington's playing of Richard's wild swings of mood on return from Ireland. He played the entire scene quietly and reflectively with none of the arch mannerisms which had distinguished the Richard of acts 1 and 2. Pennington was almost motionless, first seated on a steamer trunk and then kneeling beside it as he absorbed and comprehended the practical political realities of Bolingbroke's advance and power. If Pennington's performance from the outset was a gloss on Richard's own eventual self-assessment: "Thus play I in one person, many people,/And none contented," he found his most powerful and commanding personal role in the very moment, in the very act and language, of relinquishing his public power and persona.

There was no trace of Richard the dandy in the great deposition scene. Bolingbroke's somber, sober, businesslike court—defined by the black table-desk and council arranged in two symmetrical rows on either side all dressed in black morning coats—was a vivid contrast to Richard's emotional power and charged language.[15] He seized the center of the stage and toyed with his deposer—getting the intended laughs both in his use of the crown as a prop ("Here cousin, seize the crown" only to pull it back once he has Bolingbroke hooked to its other side) and in his response to Bolingbroke's attempt to humor him by momentarily entering into a rhetorical exchange ("The shadow of your sorrow hath destroyed/The shadow of your face")—and gave full voice to his anger with his former court, now Bolingbroke's council, with:

> Nay, all of you that stand and look upon,
> Whilst that my wretchedness doth bait myself
> Though some of you with Pilate wash your hands
> Showing an outward pity; yet you Pilates
> Have here delivered me to my sour cross,
> And water cannot wash away your sins.
>
> (4.1.237–42)

Pennington here captured Richard's most blazing moment in the play as he also switched into another key for Richard's most painful in 5.2. Here, in Richard's solitary cell at Pomfret Castle, the key prop was a galvanized metal pail. The scene opened with Richard curled on the floor, and we watched as he slowly lifted one bare foot and reached out with it to make contact with the cold side of the pail. This chilling image reflected Richard's fall, his isolation, his vulnerability, his desperate but unsuccessful attempt to find consolation through self-knowledge, his newly discovered affection for things once beneath him (roan Barbary), and his own view of himself as a bucket down a deep well full of tears. This image also pointed to the iron age which lies ahead for England.

Pennington's Hal found his emotional life, his imagination, his sense of play, and his attraction for subversive friends in Richard II. He found his politics, his sense of calculation and timing, his ability to be cold-blooded when faced with ultimately threatening situations (Hotspur at Shrewsbury; Falstaff at the coronation parade) in his father. Pennington repeatedly allowed us to see that these two sides made an uneasy and unhappy mix in *1* and *2 Henry IV*, but as John Peter observed "power brings maturity; and Pennington creates a portrait of Henry V which combines Machiavellian statecraft with insistent humanity."[16]

Two interesting moments stood out in Pennington's fashioning of Hal which revealed the unorthodox nature of his characterization but which relate to the cumulative nature of this production and his performance. The first came at Shrewsbury and its immediate aftermath. As I mentioned at the outset, as we moved toward Shrewsbury, Bogdanov presented us with an increasingly eclectic sampling of battle dress from the nineteenth century to the present. When we met Falstaff on the road to war in the scene with Hal and Westmoreland, he was dressed in a bright red jacket and blue trousers similar to Hal's and was seated in his red tavern chair mounted on a munitions cart pulled about by Bardolph. When we saw him at Shrewsbury he was still mounted on Bardolph's cart but now outfitted in World War II helmet and olive drab camouflage jacket looking like photographs of Hemingway in his jeep headed into the Place Vendôme to liberate the Ritz Hotel. Bogdanov, however, dressed Hal and Hotspur in the age of chivalry's traditional chain mail covering blue and red tunics thus initially signaling a heroic stance to their encounter. But he and Pennington undercut this image with a playing of the fight with an emotional subtext more resonant of the Actor's Studio than RADA. After several minutes of fierce exchange, Hotspur disarmed Hal. Pennington cowered on his knees wrapped in a fetal embrace convulsively awaiting the fatal blow. The playing of this moment was powerful and puzzling.

Even productions I have seen which cast a decidedly anti-heroic eye on the play did not complicate Hal's heroics in his clash with Hotspur, but again the key to Pennington's playing of this moment had its seeds in his creation of the emotionally quixotic Richard. Pennington wanted us to see that Hal's flight to Falstaff, the Boar's Head, and the carnivalesque was a flight from the history his father has created for him by his usurpation. To enter that history, to fulfill his claim to "redeem time" and his pledge of "I am your son," was to move from the timelessness of the tavern into the time-bound legacy as his father's heir and thus into the world of history and death, parricide and regicide.

As Pennington's Hal shivered in his naked vulnerability, Hotspur slid him his sword rather than moving in on a defenseless opponent. In the next series of blows it was Hal who wounded and disabled Hotspur and who then made several almost orgiastic plunges of the sword into his victim as he cradled him in his arms. With the death of Hotspur, Hal entered into history, and the moment was shattering.[17]

It is made even more traumatic by Bogdanov's reversal of the last two scenes of the play. This allowed him to close *Part One* not with

Hal's generous pardon of Douglas and the union of king and son in action against Glendower but with Falstaff's appropriation of Percy, a neat payback, he believed, for his loss of purse to Hal at Gadshill. The scene was staged with the king and Westmoreland still present, an idea Bogdanov relates he lifted from Orson Welles's *Chimes at Midnight*, a film he greatly admires.[18] After Falstaff's tale they both looked at Hal and exited while sadly shaking their heads as though doubting his claim to have killed Hotspur. Pennington delivered "For my part, if a lie may do thee grace,/I'll gild it with the happiest terms I have" quite against the grain by angrily spitting out each word as though suffering a genuine embarrassment at Falstaff's prank. This allowed Bogdanov to end *Part One* on an open-ended note with Hal and his father still estranged and Hal still unresolved in his own development.

Bogdanov allowed Hal to remain on stage for a moment after Falstaff exited. Slowly he reached down to the floor, picked up two swords, and exited through the rear panels with the swords crossed above his head. This posture was one associated with Douglas during the Shrewsbury battle and was used here to underline Hal's painful commitment to Douglas's world and his move away from Falstaff's. By this simple switch of scenes, Bogdanov and Pennington projected a Hal into *2 Henry IV* who was still in process and not one who had slain all his demons and must passively resign himself to a position of psychological limbo until his father dies. It is also yet another example of the creative dialogue between film and stage productions that I have attempted to trace.

The second crucial extended moment in Pennington's portrayal comes in 4.5 of *Part Two*. In this second famed encounter with his father, Hal was dressed in white baggy pants, a red shirt, and tennis shoes; a move in dress from rebellious to casual, and a move in colors toward those of St. George, whose banner always hung at the center of the rear stage for the English Council Chamber scenes. Again, Pennington's body language indicated both Hal's uncertainty and his feelings of reduced stature when in his father's presence. The crown itself helped to underline this atmosphere, for when Hal tried it on, "Lo, here it sits," it sat about his ears, too big for his head. When Hal returned after his father awakes, the crown was effectively used as a symbol of tension and apprehension between the two men. In Bogdanov's staging, Henry IV had never appeared in royal regalia, and the crown, as crucial symbol and prop, had been absent since the moment it passed from Richard II to Bolingbroke. Now the same two actors negotiate its power and its meaning. Now it is Henry's to relinquish; now it is Hal who must seize it even as he denies such a desire.

Hal placed the crown between them as he knelt on his father's bed in a manner reminiscent of the position he curled himself into on the battlefield at Shrewsbury when Hotspur had the upper hand. Now his subservience, his yielding to the powerful but dying father, was a clear indication of his desire to be embraced, to be forgiven, to be folded into his destiny. The moment was played as a release of emotion rather than as an instance of restraint and self-control. The wonderful irony of Bogdanov's staging is that precisely at the moment when Hal submits himself to his father and unashamedly releases his repressed emotions, Henry dies and slumps into his son's arms.

As I mentioned earlier, Henry IV's reign was marked by an absence of court regalia. Henry was envisioned more as prime minister than king. This is, of course, a fine way to establish a contrast with Richard's world and to underline Henry IV's exclusive focus on secular power and politics. Hal's marriage of Richard's understanding of ceremony and his father's understanding of politics was immediately made manifest in his coronation parade and his decisive confrontation with Falstaff. The set scaffolding had been draped with holiday bunting and a huge Union Jack. Falstaff, Pistol, Shallow, and Silence entered equipped with noisemakers and waving tiny flags. Falstaff wore a cheap felt bowler decorated with Union Jacks straight from a Leicester Square souvenir shop. Hal entered in full coronation regalia, and the contrast between holiday and everyday, tavern and court, was perfectly captured by the iconography of the scene. After the king delivered his devastating rejection and his party exited, Falstaff slowly rose from his knees and made his heavy way over a stage floor now littered with the strings of flags which had once bedecked the scaffolding but which were ripped down by Pistol in response to the king's stern sentence, to an exit through the center panel of the back grid, swallowed by history. Falstaff's exit paralleled and reversed Hal's at the conclusion of *Part One*—a movement which signaled Hal's entrance into history and his inevitable rejection of Falstaff.

If I have said little about Falstaff's role in Bogdanov's conception of this material it is simply because, of the many key casting changes between the company's first and second seasons, I found the change of Falstaffs from John Woodvine to Barry Stanton the most crucial. Woodvine, quite simply and surprisingly, was the best Falstaff I've encountered; Stanton was appropriately jovial but lacked Woodvine's bite and command. In person, Woodvine does not appear a natural comedian—especially not a natural Falstaff. He is tall and thin with a long, expressionless face which announces sobriety and seriousness. I had seen him play the four roles at the Royal Shakespeare Company which led him to this Falstaff: Subtle in *The Alchemist* (1977), Falstaff in *The Merry Wives of Windsor* (1979), Malvolio in *Twelfth Night* (1979) and Ralph Nickleby in *Nicholas Nickleby* (1980). His Falstaff was remarkable and unsettling because he managed to be both funny and vicious. Woodvine found just the right Jonsonian edge to give definition to Shakespeare's often sentimentalized creation.

Woodvine's voice is his most remarkable feature: a sharp baritone with a rasping nasal quality capable of throwing a dagger through certain words and projecting them to the back of the house without seeming to turn up the volume. The basic conception of Falstaff as a seedy clubman down on his heels—a distant cousin of John le Carré's Rick Pym especially as realized by the late Ray McAnnally—remained constant in the two actors's performances, but Woodvine's Falstaff was lethal, while Stanton's was simply genial. Woodvine let us see the old pike in Falstaff, while Stanton was content to give us the chewet. Woodvine gave his Falstaff a little nasal "haw haw haw" in imitation of an aristocratic affectation. His last brilliant use of the device came in response to Henry V's admonition that "the grave does gape/For thee thrice wider than for other men" only to have this attempt to re-establish the old rules of verbal combat dashed: "Reply not to me with a fool-born jest."

Besides his use of voice, Woodvine's other great physical contribution to his portrayal was his use of his eyes: sharp and beady eyes ever on the prowl; eyes which one might more naturally associate with the world of Subtle and Face than with Falstaff and Bardolph. He used them most prominently in his reconstruction of the Gad's Hill robbery as he searched for confirmation from the tavern crowd on the one hand and for Hal's response on the other. As Roger Warren has observed about Woodvine's performance: "his swivelling eyes communicated the rapid movement of his mind."[9] The comic climax of Falstaff's lively eyes came as Hal and Poins zeroed in on their fat prey. As Hal backed Falstaff into a corner on "what trick, what device, what starting-hole, canst thou now find out to hide thee from this open and apparent shame?" Woodvine's eyes darted from Hal to Poins and back again . . . pause . . . then the by now familiar "haw haw haw" . . . pause . . . big smile slowly began to spread across his face . . . pause . . . "By the lord (haw haw haw), I knew ye as well as he that made ye." This exquisite sense of timing was missing from Stanton's performance and with it the sense of calculation, and thus threat, Woodvine found in the character.

This sense of timing and vocal comedy can be illustrated by a bit of business which was used by both actors in the Shrewsbury battle scene. As I have already indicated, Falstaff went off to the wars seated in his red tavern chair mounted on a munitions cart pulled by Bardolph. When we first saw them, in the scene with Hal and Westminster, Falstaff was decked out in a fancy red and blue dress uniform with an elaborate hat—no linen on every hedge for him. When we saw him during the battle itself he was dressed in World War II olive drab and helmet. When he rose to a sitting position on "Embowelled!"—a word which Woodvine made ring about the theater as if it had six syllables—he took us through his disquisition on counterfeiting. Stanton took it all at one swift burst, while Woodvine savored every clever turn of Falstaff's nimble mind, building to a solid laugh on "The better part of valour is discretion" . . . pause for the laugh to subside . . . then a reach inside his coat to pull out a large dented No Entry sign he had fortuitously used as a breastplate. Huge laugh which he allowed to swell before completing Falstaff's sentence: "in which better part I have saved my life." Another roar and applause. Woodvine's timing and vocal inflection was perfect. He found the means to release the complicated tension the action had built in the Hal-Hotspur combat through our laughter at his ability to survive such danger with his flesh and wit intact. Stanton said the same words and used the same device but failed to build carefully to the moment when the brilliant prop is revealed.

One other observation on the Woodvine-Stanton contrast as a means of making the transition to *Henry V.* Stanton has the natural physique for Falstaff; Woodvine does not. This worked somewhat to Woodvine's disadvantage in the *Henry IV* plays, where he manufactured some unnatural body humor through his repeated struggle to lower himself comfortably into his tavern chair or to rise from it gracefully but which paid extraordinary dividends when he appeared in blue blazer, pink and blue rep tie, and gray slacks as the Chorus in *Henry V.* He reminded Gerald Berkowitz of Alistair Cooke, but I thought his manner and expression less cozy and civil and more clipped in the manner of John Humphrey, the BBC news reader.[20] What was astonishing was to have Falstaff re-emerge transformed into a svelte official spokesman for the new regime, having traded his red overstuffed tavern chair for a black leather and steel swivel chair of the modern broadcaster—the very chair which would be wheeled over to become Henry V's executive perch in 1.2.

The notion of Falstaff as Chorus was one of the wonderful benefits of having a single company produce these plays in one sweeping cycle. When Terry Hands directed *1* and *2 Henry IV* and *Henry V* at the RSC in 1975, he cast Emrys James, who played Henry IV in the early plays, as the Chorus. I thought then that Hands had created an interesting effect by having the father become the official champion of the son's reign. But I think Bogdanov's casting of the other father was even more imaginative. Falstaff provided a choric function—however subversive—in the Henry IV plays, he was Hal's cheerleader at Shrewsbury, and he was a formidable storyteller. While he had longed to have the laws of England at his command, in fact, his ideal role in his protege's administration would have been as minister of (mis)information. If Woodvine's Falstaff was created with a repertory of vocal tricks and inflections his Chorus was all sober business, all Ralph Nickleby: crisp, clipped, contained.

When we first met Woodvine's Falstaff in *Part Two* his recent triumph was exhibited by his new blue with pink pin stripes double-breasted suit; his jaunty swagger; the tilt of his gray fedora, the size of the cigar he amiably puffed; and—most obviously—the huge medal he proudly displayed on his breast pocket: the Hotspur ribbon. I mention this by way of contrast with the Hal we first met in *Henry V* who was distinguished by the absence of medals on his red dress military jacket in the opening scene and throughout the play. The absence of medals immediately signaled that Pennington's Henry V had achieved the self-confidence that the text reveals about Hal after Shrewsbury where—in my understanding—he magnanimously and graciously allows Falstaff his moment of triumph. Pennington achieved the integrity of his Henry through the rite of passage of his encounter with Hotspur and the emotional embrace with his dying father as he slumps into his son's arms.

When I asked my mentor, C. L. Barber, what he thought of the Hands-Howard *Henry V* (a production I greatly admired) his immediate response was: "Were you convinced by all that suffering?" He was referring to Alan Howard's very tentative approach to Henry's militarism so that the line "May I with right and conscience make this claim?" was delivered as an unsteady emotional outburst, and the threats before Harfleur were delivered with such a queasiness that each distasteful word seemed to stick in Howard's throat. When the mayor capitulated, Howard's anxiety quite literally came up in his mouth. Pennington, on the other hand, played the opening scene as an efficient chief executive who took a set of briefing papers on the Salique Law from the archbishop of Canterbury, scanned them quickly and plopped them down on his desk as he delivered "May I with right and conscience make this claim?"—followed by a knowing smile as he surveyed his advisers.

The Harfleur scene was once again defined by Henry's business-like approach to this enterprise. Rather than being set before the town walls, the governor was brought to Henry's headquarters and the scene was played with Henry seated at his desk as he made the monstrous threats which led to the town's capitulation. Pennington gave a very calculated tick of his tongue to round off his "what say you?" as though such exchanges were all in a mighty executive's day's work. He gave further evidence of his use of theatrics here by sharing a large "whew" of relief to the audience when the governor yielded the town.

What we saw at work in Pennington's performance and Bogdanov's staging was the way in which this Henry V incorporated his father's sense of political efficiency and theory with Falstaff's sense of dramatics and play. However, when Pennington's Henry V arrived at his great moment on the night before Agincourt, which reached its climax in the soliloquy on ceremony, Richard II's rich emotional understanding of the cares of the crown was added to the equation. Pennington delivered the speech with an emotional and vocal intensity which directly issued from his portrayal of Richard II. Watching Pennington's creation of Henry V allowed us to see how the actor's keen critical intelligence was building his portrait from his rivals' virtues: Hotspur's courage, Falstaff's imagination, Henry IV's politics, and—most originally—Richard II's ability to reach through self-pity and pathos to self-awareness and understanding.

These elements came best into focus and harmony in the production, as they do in the play, in Henry's wooing of Katherine in the play's final scene. Here politics and play, statecraft and affection, power and humor are united. Appropriately, Henry the Conqueror of France was dressed in the same plain red-and-blue dress uniform he wore in the play's opening scene. No medals, no ostentatious ribbons or sashes, no braids or epaulettes were necessary to define his achievement. But what did remain—his legacy from his practical father—was the plain black table-desk which defined the inescapable political reality of this moment of private charm: the politics of wooing and wedding. And, as a final imperial touch, the desk displayed the crown; its first appearance since Hal's coronation. As I have outlined earlier, the crown appeared most crucially as a central symbol in Richard's deposition scene, in the final confrontation and reconciliation between Henry IV and Hal, and now it reappeared as an object of negotiation in the extension of the Lancastrian empire.

It was appropriate that when that negotiation was sealed by Henry and Kate's kiss—"Now, welcome, Kate: and bear me witness all,/ That here I kiss her as my sovereign queen"—that the headstrong and impulsive Dauphin should overturn several chairs in disgust and stomp out, appropriate because the actor who plays the Dauphin, Andrew Jarvis, emerged in the next cycle of plays as Richard III— the man who would become the ultimate agent of the destruction of the world sealed by Henry and Kate's kiss. So the final image in what Barbara Hodgdon has called—writing of Bogdanov's production— Henry's "imperialist strategy" is not one of harmony but of impending disruption and chaos.[21] As Pennington's performances were the common thread in the first four plays, so Jarvis's came to be in the final three in the cycle.[22]

A feature of Bogdanov's staging and design in *Henry V* which troubled several critics, I found in perfect keeping with his critical strategy in the cycle.[23] I refer to his handling of the Boar's Head Tavern crew as the spotlight shifted from Falstaff to Pistol. From the moment Pistol arrived at Shallow's wearing a black leather jacket with Hal's Angels emblazoned on the back to announce Hal's elevation to the throne, many felt the production overreached in its willingness to catch at easy modern parallels. But Shakespeare's Pistol is a loose cannon who does go off in crass and vulgar directions meant to embarrass an audience no longer given an attractive comic rival to Hal.

Bogdanov's inventive imagining of Pistol, Bardolph, and Nym's departure for France in 2.3 as though they were English football louts on their way to a drunken revel on the continent was a masterful contemporary understanding of Pistol's explicit cry: "Let us to France; like horse-leeches, my boys,/To suck, to suck, the very blood to suck!" The football fan's paraphernalia, the deafening air horns, the obnoxious banner: "Fuck the Frogs," all made a fit with Shakespeare's clear intention to give us an ironic underside to the Chorus's official version of the invasion: "Now all the youth of England are on fire." I am also sure that this rowdy send-off to Pistol and company created the first ever show-stopping laugh on the French king's opening lines of the next scene: "Thus come the English . . ."

If *Henry V* displays the triumph of the politics of empire, displays the son's achievements of the father's advice "to busy giddy minds with foreign quarrels," then the first tetralogy displays the collapse of that empire and the internal destruction wrought by giddy minds operating in a power vacuum. Bogdanov, following the Hall-Barton example, condensed the three parts of *Henry VI* into two, which he retitled *House of Lancaster* and *House of York*. *York* I found much the more successful of the two as, quite naturally, Cade's rebellion and Richard of Gloucester's rise found an immediate resonance with Bogdanov's approach, while Talbot and Joan of Arc, particularly in Bogdanov's sanitized revision of her character, were more difficult to capture. I did admire the staging of Talbot's death when, after valiant hand-to-hand combat with many, he was suddenly alone and then cut down by a machine-gun-blast from the wings. Joan, on the other hand, had a tire placed around her neck and a can of gas sprinkled on her body and was torched. Talbot, the last of the great warriors brought down by petty politicians and bureaucrats, died a death distinguished by the new age of anonymous warfare. However, I'm not sure what the connection was between the South African "necklace" torture and Joan's death other than an inventive director's failure on this occasion to strike a meaningful contemporary parallel.

Bogdanov's staging of the Temple Garden scene was the finest moment in his *House of Lancaster*. Everyone was dressed in black tuxedos, and as the two factions were created each man plucked the appropriate red or white rose from an elaborate trellis—center stage—and affixed it to his lapel. The use of the boutonniere as the sign of allegiance to York or Lancaster remained a vivid sign of division within the ruling family whenever they gathered—in government or society. The two roses were finally united in Richmond's lapel—and mirrored by all his attendant staff—as he addressed the nation at the end of *Richard III*.

Bogdanov's staging of the Temple Garden scene and other, subsequent, family gatherings—particularly after the loss of France—underlined the petty family bickering at the heart of England's destruction. We were thrust back to the opening scene of *Richard II* where the Bolingbroke-Mowbray dispute was depicted as erupting at a social gathering. Now, once again, Bogdanov envisioned division breaking out in social settings. The climax to this production pattern came at the center of the *House of Lancaster* where the victorious Yorkists, appropriately dressed all in white, were imagined at a family cocktail party to celebrate Edward's coronation. As the seemingly happy family circulated amongst their guests to a modern jazz tune lightly fingered by an onstage pianist playing a white piano, Richard of Gloucester—his bald head gleaming—skipped in three powerful strides through the crowd to downstage center. Nattily attired in a white linen suit, he struck his characteristic lethal pose with his bad left leg bent at the knee and his right leg thrust out at a knifelike angle. As the piano gently picked out a Cole Porter-like society tune, Andrew Jarvis began Richard's first great defining soliloquy in a quiet, cocktail-party conversational tone.

The contrast and context was stunning. Richard is a solo performer; Shakespeare's first great creation to take wing through soliloquy. Throughout the cycle Bogdanov's orchestration of the music, particularly the association of individual instruments with central characters, was an intelligent contribution to his design. Richard II and the violin, Hal and the flute, Falstaff accompanied by Bardolph's trombone, Pistol and the bass guitar, the Andean flute for Joan, the synthesizer for Jack Cade and crew, all came to culmination in the association of the modern jazz piano with Richard III. Richard's cool, ironic, detached, lethal manner found the perfect, chilling, accompaniment in the piano: two complementary timbres insinuating themselves into our confidence. It also called to my mind the great Russian version of *Richard III* by the Rustaveli Company, which came to the Edinburgh Festival in 1979 and then to London the following January. Ramaz Chkhikvadse's Richard III was more bull than vulture, but his wonderfully rambling movements accented by tap plates on his boots were repeatedly accompanied by a small jazz combo playing a jaunty version of "Maybe It's Because I'm an Englishman."

Jarvis gave his Richard an icy stare which often melted into a self-amused gap-toothed smile. He used it to bring the house down in the following sequence: "I'll make my heaven in a lady's lap,/And deck my body in gay ornaments,/And witch sweet ladies with my words and looks" . . . pause . . . icy stare directly at the audience . . . laugh . . . "O miserable thought!" . . . slow smile . . . house in thunderous laughter. The setting and delivery of the entire soliloquy was a perfect illustration of Kenneth Burke's act-scene-agent ratio, where the text's meanings are multiplied and made manifest in the perfect mix of word, actor, gesture, and landscape. From this moment on Jarvis had his audience; perhaps this Chicago audience instinctively recognized him as the ultimate Godfather standing at the head of a family tree which extended to St. Valentine's Day and Al Capone. Certainly it was an audience who came primed for the experience. The words "the first thing we do, let's kill all the lawyers," were only half out of Dick Butcher's mouth before Cade's rebellion was brought to a halt by the audience's roar of assent.

Bogdanov reinforced his desire to see the Yorks as a family as well as a regime by opening *Richard III* with the family gathered around Henry VI's coffin, with everyone being introduced and identified for those just joining the saga.[24] Bogdanov's insistence on always setting this royal family in their private quarters was meant to serve several ends. It underlined that their inability to govern themselves extended to their inability to govern the nation. The only national business conducted in *Richard III* had to do with eliminating rivals and staging coronations. The private setting coupled with everyone except Queen Margaret in the sort of evening dress one associates with the world of *Private Lives* gave a fine modern quality to the essential bitchiness of this family whenever they were brought together. If the Rustaveli *Richard III* gathered its energies from Brecht, I think Bogdanov wickedly found his inspiration for Yorkist decadence in Noel Coward and the England of the 1930s. Even Queen Margaret, dressed in a World War II brown military jacket loaded with ribbons and medals worn over a black dress and topped by a field commander's hat perched precariously on top of her frizzy red hair, could have been a version of Madame Arkadi: one of those mad strangers who often wander into a Coward world which on the surface appears so arch and staid and beneath is so venomous.

Shakespeare repeatedly dramatizes that the sixty years of civil strife which led to the collapse of Hal's empire and England itself comes to focus in the rancor and spite of family quarrel. Margaret's curses sweep the family back over their internecine battle, picking at the wounds which have never healed, refusing to allow history to settle, while her chief antagonist, Richard, is constantly at work unsettling the present. Jarvis's conception of Richard owed more to the vulture than the boar. He was always looming with his bald head poised to strike. He assumed poses in which his body appeared all angles. His chief weapon, first displayed in the murder of Henry VI, was a butterfly shiv, which he came to personify: cold, quick, and double-edged.

His chief accomplice, Buckingham, was transformed into a modern public relations expert by Michael Pennington. Dressed in a three-piece suit with sunglasses and briefcase always at the ready, Pennington created the image of a calm, collected, smooth political operator who might have stepped out of Doug Lucie's *Fashion* or Reagan's White House. The climax of his achievement came at Baynard's Castle, where he and his minion Catesby manipulated the crowd into giving their "amen" to Buckingham's own cry "Long live

King Richard, England's worthy king." If Shakespeare ever created a media event for a sixty-second sound bite on the evening news, this was it. Buckingham was clearly the first great media consultant-press agent in British theatrical history. Pennington enjoyed his underplaying here as much as he had reveled in Cade's excesses. Clearly one of the triumphs of the cycle was the thrill of witnessing this great actor at work in a wonderful range of roles and especially of watching his craft unfold in such a concentrated period.

When Richard III assumed the throne in 4.2, he sat at a modern executive's desk equipped with a computer terminal and printer, and when Buckingham persisted in being "dull" Jarvis spun around in his swivel chair on "I am not in the giving vein today." In the same smooth, matter-of-fact way he organized Richard's ascent, Pennington gave a quiet shrug on "made I him King for this?" put on his sunglasses, and exited as if all in a day's work. When Buckingham was captured at the beginning of act 5 he was not sent offstage to the executioner's block but was shot by pistol at point-blank range.

I mention Buckingham's death because it returned as a part of a series of effective devices Bogdanov employed in staging the dream sequence in Richard's tent on the night before Bosworth. A field camp had been set amid the roaring noise of helicopters overhead, and when Richard returned to his tent the noise evaporated and all was still. Into that stillness, to break Richard's attempt to restore his alacrity of spirit, came each of his victims. In each case Richard was startled into consciousness by the *sound* each made: a sound associated with their deaths at Richard's hand or instructions. Henry VI entered equipped with Richard's butterfly shiv, and the sound of its clicking blades awakened Richard as he dreams he is being stabbed by his former victim. Clarence, drowned in his butt of Malmsey, lifted the wine bottle on Richard's table and slowly poured himself a glass with that sound breaking Richard's sleep. Ann spits at him; Buckingham shoots him in the same manner he was executed. The use of these sounds to trigger Richard's "coward conscience" became a perfect device to focus on his crimes and to signal the final parade of family misery we have watched unfold in the final three plays of the cycle.

Bogdanov staged the battle of Bosworth Field through a series of initial skirmishes which gave way to an empty stage while the sound system provided us with everything from machine gun fire, to strafing bullets, to the release and explosion of surface-to-air missiles: the full sound of modern war. Richard's famous cry for his horse was delivered offstage, and as the sound shifted to the full, deep music of Samuel Barber's *Adagio for Strings* (here Bogdanov received his musical inspiration from Oliver Stone's *Platoon*), two figures emerged in full medieval armor: one in black, the other in gold. When Richmond triumphed, television monitors quickly slid down from the flies, a staff of camera operators and technicians swirled on stage wearing ESC-TV T-shirts, and Richmond reappeared in suit and tie to be given a touch of makeup and a red and white rose for his breast pocket as the cameras adjusted focus and angle. Lights lowered and hand signals gave the countdown. The red light blinked on camera one and over the monitors we received Richmond's address to the nation: "England hath long been mad, and scarred herself;/The brother blindly shed the brother's blood. . . ."

As Richmond's speech continued in its promise to unite the white rose and the red, so Bogdanov's final, brilliant contrast of images served to unite the daring nature of his vision of this vast cycle. The quarrel that began in Richard II's salon and reached out to touch lives lived in London taverns, in Welsh camps, in French courts, in the private quarters of the royal family has now been resolved, and the news reaches out to all of us gathered in front of television sets in living rooms and taverns across the nation. *Richard III* opened with one king displayed inside a glass box—Henry VI in his coffin—and ends with another king framed in the glass tube of a new age. The overlapping ironies of Bogdanov's conception, which reached from Richard II's classical formalism to Richard III's jazz improvization, released and captured the rich Shakespearean energies at work in these plays in their dramatization of an overarching family struggle to mind and mar the nation's business.

As I have noted, British Shakespeare in the past thirty years has been dominated by three institutions: the Royal Shakespeare Company, the National Theatre, and the BBC. It is perhaps fitting as this period of institutional Shakespeare comes to a close that the production which most galvanized audiences throughout England, Europe, Australia, Asia, and North America should be one mounted by a new company devoted less to place than to process, devoted to pitching and breaking camp, bound by no permanent home to contain or restrain. That sense of freedom from place is reflected in the production's daring mixture of styles and images. In many ways Bogdanov's work in his cycle may prove to be as important a development in modern Shakespeare productions as was the Hall-Barton *The Wars of the Roses* almost thirty years ago.

## CHAPTER TEN

# Fathers and Sons:
# Kenneth Branagh's
# *Henry V*

•

A KITCHEN match is struck, illuminating Derek Jacobi's face in close-up. "O for a muse of fire," he confides to us as he moves in the darkness, his boots striking an iron surface. As his language reaches "the brightest heavens of invention," he begins to descend a set of stairs and pauses at the bottom to throw a huge electric switch. A blaze of light, and we see that we are on a sound stage filled not only with the props for a production of *Henry V*—chairs, banners, armor, large standing candlelabras—but also with the film technology necessary for its reproduction: various lamps, huge fans, and a Panaflex 35 camera. As the camera tracks the Chorus through this landscape we see the rear panels—stamped Henry V—of the set flats, bringing us at once backstage as well as behind camera. Jacobi pushes open a heavy, immense set of double doors on "kindly to judge our plaaay" ushering us into the other side, the traditional side, of spectatorship.

This is the auspicious beginning of Kenneth Branagh's film of *Henry V*. All of the film's many admirers, most notably Peter S. Donaldson, have been taken by Branagh's striking inventiveness in this opening and the way in which it echoes and revises Laurence Olivier's famous opening, filmed in a replica of Shakespeare's Globe, to his 1944 film of the play.[1]

Branagh's film, released in the autumn of 1989, ended the fallow period—stretching back to Roman Polanski's *Macbeth* (1971)—in large-scale English-language Shakespearean films. It was also the first Shakespearean film since Zeffirelli's *Romeo and Juliet* (1968) to reach and sustain a substantial audience and to more than recoup its production costs. It was quickly followed by Zeffirelli's *Hamlet* (1990)

[ 165 ]

with Mel Gibson and Glenn Close, raising expectations that we might be approaching another fertile period in the release of Shakespeare films, perhaps one to rival the glories of the 1950s and 1960s.

Branagh's career, as well as his film, reveals another turn in the Shakespeare cycle as British Shakespeare begins to experiment with alternatives to the modes of production associated with the Royal Shakespeare Company and the National Theatre. The Bogdanov-Pennington collaboration in creating the English Shakespeare Company is one manifestation of this trend and Branagh's career represents yet another. At the age of 23 he joined the RSC for a single season, and then he broke away to found his own group, the Renaissance Theatre Company. In its first efforts Branagh directed a *Romeo and Juliet* and *Twelfth Night* and produced a series directed by fellow actors: *Hamlet* (Derek Jacobi), *Much Ado About Nothing* (Judi Dench), and *As You Like It* (Geraldine McEwan). The release and success of the *Henry V* film, his well-publicized marriage to the actress Emma Thompson, and the visit of the Renaissance Theatre Company to Los Angeles and Chicago with productions of *King Lear* and *A Midsummer Night's Dream* all made comparisons with Olivier (and the Oliviers) inevitable. The Olivier parallel is instructive because Branagh's Shakespeare seasons in London with the Renaissance Theatre Company were the first developed, led, and sustained by an actor working outside the confines of the RSC or NT since the days when Olivier, Richardson, and Gielgud organized seasons for Lilian Baylis at the Old Vic or under their own management in the West End. If Peter Hall's success at Stratford and the South Bank had effectively eclipsed the actor-manager tradition last associated with Olivier, it was perhaps fitting that Branagh, born in the year Hall created the RSC, should, twenty-five years later, be the actor to stroll away from a single season with the company to found his own. But he did not leave empty-handed.

The major role Branagh played in the 1984–85 season was *Henry V* in a production directed by Adrian Noble. Reviewers of Branagh's film of the play, such as Peter S. Donaldson, have been quick to see the way it gathers its interpretative energies in competitive contrast with Olivier's film.

This variously nuanced rivalry is part of the film's meaning: the young filmmaker's ambition is paralleled in the French Campaign of the youthful Henry V, and, though Olivier himself does not appear in the film, Paul Scofield, in a magisterial performance as the French King, stands in for him, registering metaphorically the sorrow of an older generation of Shakespearean actors faced with the imperious claims of youth. Like one of Harold Bloom's "Strong poets," Branagh achieves a measure of success in this intertextual rivalry. . . .[2]

Donaldson is also right to see that Branagh's approach is suffused with critical ideas about the play which been articulated in the last twenty years and which distinguish its reading of the play from Olivier's more patriotic spectacle. What Donaldson notes, but does not detail, is the way in which the film grows out of Noble's stage production, many of the film's brilliant details having been expressed first there.

Thus Branagh's film provides an excellent summary example of the issues I have been exploring in the body of this study. His biography provides another example that the Hall era in British Shakespeare is approaching an end and that we are likely to continue to see radical developments in producing Shakespeare shift from the major companies to fringe and alternative groups. His film stands as a marvelous final example of the intertextual dialogue I began to chart in my opening discussion of Polanski's *Macbeth*.

From the first rehearsals of the stage production, Branagh made clear that both he and Adrian Noble "agreed that we should not try to explain this man but rather explore all [his] paradoxes and contradictions."[3] Branagh's account also indicates that his desire to take Henry's doubt and piety seriously rather than cynically was given healthy challenge by his director. The production's unique contribution to our understanding of the play grew from this tension. From the start Branagh saw Henry as "a massively guilty man" haunted by the ghosts of both his father and Richard II, and as the production progressed Bardolph (representing Falstaff and Hal's Boar's Head Tavern past) grew to be included in that equation. Several of our greatest Shakespeare films, Olivier's *Henry V* and Welles's *Chimes at Midnight*, for example, are enhanced by their autobiographical resonances with the careers of their director-stars; Branagh's film can be similarly read. In this case the fathers who haunt him are Olivier and Noble, whom he must, like the character he plays, both acknowledge and transcend and do so through a brazen, youthful gamble. Branagh's journey to Shepperton—against all the odds—parallels Henry's to France, and Branagh is not timid in making the comparison. After the film cast gathered for its single company meeting Branagh reflected, "A disaster it might be, but a singular one. Everyone was glad to be there. We few, we happy few."[4]

As Branagh's boyish, earthy, gritty Henry was built on getting at the man beneath the mask, never flinching from the character's doubt, guilt, anger, rhetorical genius, or sense of humor, so he built his film on his careful study and assimilation of Olivier's film and Noble's stage production. Part of my initial pleasure in watching the film sprang from observing it succeed against the odds and my expectations, much as Branagh's stage performance had done with a part that had come to be associated with two antithetical stereotypes: stirring patriot or cruel jingoist.

Branagh's film grew from a stage production by the most inventive Shakespeare director to emerge in the post-Hall-Nunn-Hands era at the RSC, just as it gathered its interpretative momentum from critical ideas about the play which have come into circulation since Olivier's film. So we have one Shakespeare film speaking to another across an expanse of forty-five years but doing so through a stage production itself perfectly alert to ideas about *Henry V* most cogently presented in Norman Rabkin's famous essay on the play.[5] One final historical element in this linking of film, stage, and critical dialogue should be noted. As I mentioned earlier, Adrian Noble points to Tyrone Guthrie as the godfather of the director's Shakespeare movement. Guthrie, appropriately, directed Olivier as Henry V at the Old Vic in 1937, a season which also featured Olivier's first Hamlet. Both productions provided the basic interpretative strategies for Olivier's approach to each when he directed the plays on film.

Many of the rich details, apart from his own performance, which gives Branagh's film its distinctive character were all central to Noble's production as well: the weather, the intimacy and tension with which Henry confronts Scroop, the death of Bardolph, the metacinematic style, the emphasis on the killing of the boys, the singing of the "Non Nobis" spreading throughout the company, the comic playing of "Here Comes Your Father" in the wooing of Katherine, and Henry V's appropriation of the Queen Isabel's lines about the link between marriage and empire to conclude the play. The stage image which came to define Noble's approach consisted of Henry V's sick and weary troops huddled under tarpaulins as the rain beat down upon them the day before Agincourt. Interestingly, the first conversation Branagh had about the possibility of joining the RSC to play Henry V was with Ron Daniels. Eager with the excitement brought by the prospect of playing such a role at such an age with such a company, Branagh asked him, "What do you see in the play?" Daniels replied, "Mud."[6] My hunch is that Orson Welles's great battle scene in *Chimes at Midnight* was the inspiration for Daniels's remark, and while Branagh gives the exchange a humorous edge, that single image extends from his first conversation about the role and play in 1983 through to the completion and release of the film in 1989, which quickly was christened "Dirty Harry" by Shakespeare followers across England.

A reading of Branagh's account of the stage production's rehearsal period clearly reveals that both director and actor were determined to move beyond the two contrasting stereotypes that had come to define the character: Olivier's stirring patriot and mirror of all Christian kings and Ian Holm's famous anti-heroic revisionist portrait in Peter Hall's 1964 production. Branagh was interested in Henry's psychological complexity, his doubt and guilt, and Noble was searching for a production style that would avoid both jingoistic pageantry and post-Falklands cynicism about giddy minds and foreign quarrels. The latter approach would be, of course, the one taken by Bogdanov and Pennington in their treatment of the play. Noble's solution was, typically, ingenious. The self-referential, metadramatic quality of the play was emphasized by playing it on an open stage frequently foreshortened by Chorus pulling a traverse at the proscenium. Chorus remained on stage throughout, often leaning against the proscenium. In a performance even more startling than Branagh's—and the primary difference between stage and film version—Ian McDiarmid played the character as a deeply conflicted figure. While most accounts of the play read him as providing the official line on Henry—giving us the Palace version—McDiarmid repeatedly provided readings, complete with emotional subtext, loaded with irony and doubt about the powers of theater, imagination, and king. By allowing the frame to provide such a perspective, Noble released Branagh to explore a serious, earthy, and gritty investigation of the responsibilities of political and military leadership.

The betrayal of Henry by Cambridge, Scroop, and Grey and the later death of Bardolph were central to both productions and to Branagh's playing of the king. On stage Scroop fell to his knees in supplication and bent his head backwards as Branagh's Henry pressed his face agonizingly close to that of his bosom friend (who knew the very bottom of his soul) suggesting a tortured depth of intimacy in his delivery of "For this revolt of thine, methinks, is like/ Another fall of man."

In the film Branagh heightens and further intensifies this moment by having Henry grab Scroop violently by the collar and pin him down upon a table. This allows Branagh to shoot Henry's remonstrance in close-up with his face once again positioned intimately just above Scroop's. The close-up allows us to see a mixture of tenderness and revulsion as Henry's hand caresses Scroop's brow even as his words lash out at his betrayal.[7] Henry is, of course, the master of conversion and given the events immediately following his coronation in *Henry IV, Part Two* well understands its personal, emotional price. Noble's decision to stage the death of Bardolph underlined this theme. Bardolph, like Scroop, is on his knees facing the king when Henry pronounces his doom, and then the assembled band of brothers all stare transfixed as Exeter garrots Bardolph, and we quite distinctly hear his neck crack. Branagh singles this moment out as central to his development of Henry and does so in language which is curiously reflective of the unresolved paradoxes Shakespeare places at the heart of Henry's character:

> My recollection . . . of the weeks that led up to the opening night is hazy. There were unforgettable moments, however. The joyous camaraderie of the company led to wonderful revelations, as when we discovered *en masse* the power of having Bardolph executed on the stage in front of the King. The first time we played it in rehearsal was thrilling. For me it shed a whole new light on Henry's loneliness, marking so graphically, as it did, the end of a chapter of events that robbed him of every real friend he had, Falstaff, Scroop, and now, symbolically all who remained to remind him of the Boar's Head life. He was now completely alone with a solitude so painful it must produce 'upon the King'. . .[8]

I am aware that some of this is actor's language—"joyous camaraderie," "wonderful revelation," "thrilling"—but it also reenacts the tensions in the play between the romance and realities of power, and Noble may have created an image and moment not fully comprehended by his leading man: mark silent king the moral of this sport. What Branagh does grasp is the dramatic power of this moment and the earlier ones it connects with, and he capitalizes on them when he reimagines them on film.

Shakespeare sandwiches the Cambridge, Scroop, and Grey scene between those in the Boar's Head dealing with the death of Falstaff. Branagh's film heightens this connection by concluding his version of

2.1 with a pastiche flashback of Hal-Falstaff moments which concludes with the following:

*Falstaff*. But . . . we have heard the chimes at midnight, master
    Harry. Jesus, the days we have seen.
*Hal*. I know thee not, old man.[9]

A similar flashback to memories of Bardolph occurs as Henry prepares to give the orders for Bardolph's execution in the film. Once again Exeter is the executioner, but this time Bardolph is hung from a tree limb and his body is left to dangle, with his boots visible at the top of the frame, through the entire scene with the French messenger, Mountjoy. Christopher Ravenscroft, who also played the part in Noble's stage production, has his Mountjoy cast a very wary eye up at Bardolph, and Derek Jacobi's Chorus makes a similar cold glance—which causes him to pull his great coat closer about his chest—as he enters to allow the pouring dark to fill the wide vessel of the universe. Donaldson's account provides a reading of these moments not likely to be bettered, but while admiring how Branagh has enlarged upon them by seizing on film's ability for close-up and flashback, I wish to stress their source in Noble's staging.

Branagh's justly celebrated battle scene again not only reflects its contrast with Olivier's film and its echoes of Welles but begins and ends with specific details inspired by the stage production. Noble handled the brief battle scenes themselves in a highly stylized manner but did precede them by having Harry's working-day warriors each kneel to kiss the ground as the King tosses the banner to York, who has asked to have "the leading of the vaward." The crucial moment in both productions is the discovery of the killing of the boys. In Noble's staging the bodies of the boys were slumped in a campfire-like circle upstage, and during the singing of the "Non Nobis" several were picked up and carried off stage center. The "Non Nobis" was not as protracted, or swelling, as in the film, but it did last through the opening lines of the Chorus's opening of act 5. The Chorus stood in front of a transparent scrim behind which we still saw the slumped bodies of the dead at Agincourt now illuminated by ten small candles placed among the fallen. This tableau remained visible throughout the scene at the French court which concluded the play.

Branagh does not complicate his final scene with this visual reminder of Agincourt's price, but he does do wonders with the "Non Nobis." Here it is Branagh who picks up the body of one of the boys—clearly Falstaff's page, thus an image linking Agincourt with the other moments of violent rupture and loss in film and play—and begins to carry him out through the scene of carnage. A remarkable tracking shot follows as Branagh moves through the mud and bodies of the battle and the sound track "Non Nobis" swells from a single tenor voice to a full choir as the camera crane elevates to give us a picture of the full field. In a brilliant stroke Branagh has the French women (who in Noble's production placed the candles among the fallen) try to attack the king in outrage for the slaughter of their men. The shot, which fills an incredible four minutes of screen time, ends with Henry—face muddy and bleeding—mounting a cart piled with the bodies of the boys, thus making a circle with the battle's beginning launched by the Saint Crispin's day speech delivered from a similar cart. Of course, this is all a brilliant reversal of Olivier's progress through Agincourt, which also begins with Henry delivering his famous charge and challenge from a cart. In that instance, however, the famous tracking shot follows alongside the beginning charge, accompanied by William Walton's rousing score. Olivier's film sought to celebrate the energy of attack made, as it was, at the very moment the Allied forces were preparing for the invasion of France.

Branagh's film, like Noble's production, was created in the aftermath of Vietnam and the Falklands, where getting home was more essential than going over. Olivier glides through his Agincourt with a stunning grace, while for Branagh's Henry it is a far less glamorous rite of passage. Branagh gives us neither the confident hero nor the anguished tyrant but a worker-king, more bulldog than greyhound, who puts his shoulder and body into the messy scrum of history and emerges, in Donaldson's fine formulation, ritually cleansed, having achieved his final and most miraculous transformation as the film cuts from his battle-stained face at Agincourt to his freshly scrubbed one come wooing to the French court. Earlier Branagh accomplishes another stunning series of transition shots as he slowly dissolves from a close-up of Judi Dench's weeping face after her eulogy of Falstaff and farewell to Pistol to a map of France to a close-up of Paul Scofield's even wearier face as he contemplates the coming of the English. Here Branagh links the play's social stratifications and geography even as he links the threats to Henry's reign. He does so by giving us beautiful, sorrowful images of the actors most closely identified with the early years of the Royal Shakespeare Company.

Donaldson offers the interesting idea that Scofield is a stand-in for Olivier and the older generation of British Shakespearean actors.

He reads the French king's blessing of the marriage of Henry and Katherine as representing a symbolic abdication to the younger generation here represented by Branagh and Emma Thompson. I prefer to see the film itself as a celebration of British Shakespearean actors of the past thirty years, who have been for too long absent from filmed Shakespeare. Scofield, of course, was Brook's growling Lear; Judi Dench and Ian Holm (surely the definitive Fluellen) were Titania and Puck in Hall's earthy *Dream;* Derek Jacobi, Robert Stephens (Pistol), and Geraldine McEwan (Alice) were key members of the repertory company Olivier built during his years at the National; Richard Easton (Constable), Christopher Ravenscroft (Mountjoy), and Brian Blessed (Exeter) played the same roles in Noble's production; Emma Thompson and Richard Briers (Bardolph) were principal members of Branagh's Renaissance Theatre Company; and Michael Maloney (Dauphin) went on to play a brilliantly impish Hal to Robert Stephens's Falstaff (in his first role at the Royal Shakespeare Company) in Adrian Noble's much admired productions of *1* and *2 Henry IV* which inaugurated his directorship of the RSC in 1991–92. Branagh's film is not only a mediation between Olivier's example and Noble's stage solution to the play's central ironies. It is also a work that celebrates the return of filmed Shakespeare after a twenty-year drought.

Branagh's film ends, as did Noble's production, by an interesting textual appropriation. Isabel, the queen of France, appears only in the last scene of the play and speaks but twenty-three lines. Her part is often cut in production, and if her last speech about "God, the maker of all marriages," is maintained, it is often assigned to the king as his blessing to the marriage and political union it represents.[10] Noble and Branagh, however, assign the lines to Henry by simply changing the pronoun from "your" to "our." Henry's French expedition began with the conviction that he inherited his rights there by claiming from the female, and now he completes his multiple mergers by uttering his own dream of union and assimilation; Branagh's Henry and Kate are seen here not only as the makers of manners but as the creators of powerful political symbols as well. These lines cue the reappearance of Chorus, who confides directly to us that the image of union we see over his shoulder will not last, as the great doors slowly close to end the film.

Branagh's achievement is a tribute to his own remarkable imaginary forces, but it is also firmly rooted in the continuing conversation between stage, film, and critical reproduction of Shakespeare's plays which is a distinguishing feature of the Shakespearean dynamic of the past three decades. The revolution Peter Hall began at Stratford in 1960 and continued at the National through the 1980s has produced the richest sustained series of Shakespeare productions in our century. Hall as well as his chief partners and successors from Peter Brook to John Barton to Trevor Nunn to Terry Hands have departed, leaving to Adrian Noble (and Richard Eyre at the National) the challenge of continuing to do bold and innovative work within institutions who are thought to be in danger of being swamped by their own successes. Eyre's *Richard III* (1990) and Noble's *1* and *2 Henry IV* (1991) indicate that the administrative burdens of running such huge cultural enterprises have not dulled either director's creative abilities, but whether they will be able to reinvigorate and sustain, within such large institutions, the close-knit company atmosphere at the heart of the repertory idea remains to be seen. The Bogdanov-Pennington collaboration has survived as the English Shakespeare Company completes its fifth year, at this writing, with productions of *Coriolanus* and *The Winter's Tale*, and Kenneth Branagh's Renaissance Theatre Company builds on the success of its American tour, the positive critical response to *Henry V*, and the popular acclaim for *Dead Again*.

Will smaller-scale companies like Bogdanov's and Branagh's based on touring rather than a fixed house prevail in the future? Will fringe companies like Footsbarn and Cheek by Jowl play a larger role in defining new approaches to producing Shakespeare on stage? Will Shakespeare continue to be an unusual source and inspiration for independent filmmakers as diverse as Gus Van Sant Jr. and Peter Greenaway? Clearly, the end of the BBC's monopoly on producing Shakespeare for television and/or film has already brought immediate positive consequences in the release of Kurosawa's *Ran* (1985), Branagh's *Henry V* (1989), Zeffirelli's *Hamlet* (1990) and video versions of stage productions of Bogdanov's *The Wars of the Roses* (1989), and Trevor Nunn's *Othello* (1990).

As the age of Olivier and Welles gave way in the mid-1960s to the age of Brook and Hall so there resides in our own moment the promise of further interpretative change generated by the collaborative dynamic of stage and screen productions of Shakespeare. Observing Shakespeare in the work of Noble, Branagh, Bogdanov, and Eyre will surely surprise and enlarge both our vision and our reading of the plays as we move toward the new century.

# NOTES

## CHAPTER ONE

1. Steven Mullaney, *The Place of the Stage* (Chicago: University of Chicago Press, 1988).
2. Jack Jorgens, *Shakespeare on Film* (Bloomington: Indiana University Press, 1977) and Richard David, *Shakespeare in the Theatre* (Cambridge: Cambridge University Press, 1978).
3. Harry Berger, Jr., *Imaginary Audition* (Berkeley and Los Angeles: University of California Press, 1989). Berger's imagining of performance possibilities for various moments in *Richard II* would be strengthened by reference to specific productions or, at least, to essays on such productions like Miriam Gilbert's analysis of John Barton's *Richard II* (1973–74) ("*Richard II* at Stratford: Role-Playing as Metaphor," in *Shakespeare: The Theatrical Dimension*, ed. Philip C. McGuire and David A. Samuelson [New York: AMS Press, 1979], pp. 85–102).
4. Orson Welles, *Everybody's Shakespeare* (Woodstock, Ill.: Todd Press, 1934), p. 27.
5. See W. B. Worthen's "Deeper Meanings and Theatrical Technique: The Rhetoric of Performance Criticism," *Shakespeare Quarterly* 40 (1989): 441–55 for several interesting suggestions linking performance practice with critical theory.
6. Anthony Davies, *Filming Shakespeare Plays* (Cambridge: Cambridge University Press, 1988); John Collick, *Shakespeare, Cinema, and Society* (Manchester, England: Manchester University Press, 1989); Peter S. Donaldson, *Shakespearean Films/Shakespearean Directors* (Boston: Unwin Hyman, 1990); Lorne M. Buchman, *Still in Movement* (Oxford: Oxford University Press, 1991); and Barbara Hodgdon, *The End Crowns All* (Princeton: Princeton University Press, 1991).
7. Collick, *Shakespeare, Cinema, and Society*, p. 186.
8. Donaldson, *Shakespearean Films/Shakespearean Directors*, p. xiii.
9. Buchman, *Still in Movement*, p. 3.
10. Philip McGuire, *Speechless Dialect* (Berkeley and Los Angeles University of California Press, 1985).
11. Hodgdon, *The End Crowns All*, p. 17.
12. Ibid.
13. Richard Poirier, *The Performing Self* (Oxford: Oxford University Press, 1972), pp. viii–ix.
14. Here is a vintage Jonathan Miller analogy on the relationship of classic text and production:

Actors and directors working on classic plays remind me of creative breeders. In just the same way that a new iris can be seen to be a florid development of the original wild flower, successive productions cross-pollinate and introduce new varieties that are still visibly related to the original play. Despite certain notable exceptions where it is really very hard to identify the relationship of the performance to the original text, I think that most of the rich variations that have grown up in the last twenty or thirty years are breeders' very elaborate varieties of the original form. One of the exciting things about the theatre in the last thirty years is that this process of selective cross-breeding has become the prevailing form. (*Subsequent Performances* [New York: Viking Penguin Inc., 1986], p. 79.)

15. Stephen Greenblatt, *Shakespearean Negotiations* (Berkeley and Los Angeles: University of California Press, 1988), p. 1.
16. Interestingly, Adrian Noble credits Tyrone Guthrie for being the man "who created the idea of staging as we have received that idea and as we now challenge that idea. He was a man who rewrote the agenda for most theatre directors in this country," thus providing a common source for our respective Shakespearean journeys. See Ralph Berry, *On Directing Shakespeare* (London: Hamish, Hamilton, 1989), p. 162.
17. Alan Lightman and Roberta Brawer, *Origins: The Lives and Worlds of Modern Cosmologists* (Cambridge: Harvard University Press, 1990), p. 262.

## CHAPTER TWO

1. Jack Jorgens, *Shakespeare on Film*, p. 2. An early version of this essay—essentially a Kottian reading of Polanski's film—was published prior to the appearance of Jorgens's pioneering study of Shakespeare films. I was pleased to see that my article anticipated several strands of Jorgens's analysis, and I want to record my debt to his vital analysis of so many Shakespearean films.
2. John Peter, *Sunday Times*, April 12, 1987, p. 6.
3. See Antony Sher, *The Year of the King* (London: Methuen, 1985), p. 97.
4. Jorgens, *Shakespeare on Film*, p. 161.
5. The following list provides a sampling of some of the film's most intelligent critics: William Johnson, *Film Quarterly* 25, no. 3 (Spring 1972); Pauline Kael, *Deeper into the Movies* (Boston: Atlantic, Little, Brown, 1973), pp. 399–401; Robert Knoll, *Western Humanities Review* (Winter 1973); Kenneth Rothwell, *Literature/Film Quarterly* 1, no. 31 (Winter 1973); Norman Berlin, "*Macbeth*: Polanski and Shakespeare," *Literature/Film Quarterly* 1, no. 4 (Fall 1973); E. Pearlman, "*Macbeth* on Film: Politics," *Shakespeare Survey* (Cambridge: Cambridge University Press, 1987), vol. 39.

# Notes

6. Norman Berlin, in *"Macbeth:* Polanski and Shakespeare," has a particularly interesting analysis of this opening scene, primarily concerning Polanski's treatment of the witches. The particular focus of my paper does not invite a detailed examination of Polanski's use of sun imagery—an imagery one does not naturally associate with the nightmare world of *Macbeth.* Polanski manages to link the sun with images of wine and blood which do find expression and interplay in the text. He also uses the sun as an image to show the disassociation of the natural world from Macbeth's evocation of it. For instance, when his Macbeth chooses to open a window and gaze out at the setting sun for the "Come seeling night" speech, the horizon we are shown is both beautiful and benign. The "night's black agents" are instruments of Macbeth's dark imagination and bloody tyranny and not, for Polanski, external elements of nature. The last shot of the sun in the film occurs when Macbeth stares out at Birnum Wood come to Dunsinane. The sun floats over the tops of the trees as Macbeth confesses, "I 'gin to aweary of the sun."

   More recently, Lorne Buchman has noted, in his *Still in Movement*, that Polanski disturbs that first long shot "with a crooked stick that appears, in close-up, from the top right corner of the frame, bisecting the picture and creating the first image of severing in the film" (p. 70).

7. There is no question that Polanski repeatedly flirts with clichés in his treatment of the witches. He has remarked, in an interview about *Chinatown*, that "I love . . . clichés. Practically every film I make starts with one. I just try to update them, give them an acceptable shape. They're extremely valuable. Great artists always use them" (*Newsweek*, July 1, 1974, p. 74).

8. Buchman, *Still in Movement*, p. 73.

9. Ibid, p. 70.

10. The mingling of sex and death, so central to the Macbeths' marriage, is clearly also at work here.

11. See Buchman's interesting linkage of this sequence with other acts of violence in the film, pp. 76–77.

12. Kenneth Rothwell is quite correct in his analysis of the effectiveness of this scene.

13. Michael Mullin in his *"Macbeth* on Film" (*Literature/Film Quarterly* 1, no. 4 [Fall 1973]) states in a footnote (p. 341) that Polanski and Tynan, aware of the youthful nature of Jan Finch's Macbeth, changed the line to read, "My *May* of life . . ."

14. Jan Kott, *Shakespeare Our Contemporary* (Anchor Books: New York, 1966), p. 97.

15. Pearlman, *"Macbeth* on Film: Politics," p. 70.

16. Unpublished interview with Adrian Noble conducted by the author at the Barbican Theatre, December 16, 1987.

17. Michael Billington, *Guardian*, November 13, 1986, p. 11.

18. Ibid.

19. *Times*, November 13, 1986, p. 13.
20. Billington, *Guardian*, p. 11.
21. Noble responded to Ralph Berry's query about this aspect of his work by commenting, "That's the easy bit of directing. . . . The real grind of rehearsals takes place with the actors trying to make a text 400 years old alive with meaning" (*On Directing Shakespeare* [London: Hamish Hamilton, 1989], p. 164.)

CHAPTER THREE

1. Anthony Davies, *Filming Shakespeare's Plays* (Cambridge: Cambridge University Press, 1988), p. 119.
2. Michael Anderegg, *Film Quarterly* 40 (Spring 1987), p. 18.
3. Robert Hapgood, "*Chimes at Midnight* from Stage to Screen: The Art of Adaptation," *Shakespeare Survey*, no. 39 (1987): 52.
4. *The Fortunes of Falstaff* (Cambridge: Cambridge University Press, 1943); *Shakespeare's Festive Comedy* (Princeton: Princeton University Press, 1959); *The Dyer's Hand* (New York: Random House, 1962); "Falstaff as Parodist and Perhaps Holy Fool," *Publications of the Modern Language Association* 90 (January 1975); "Falstaff the Centaur," *Shakespeare Quarterly* 28 (Winter 1977); and "Positioning Psychoanalysis and the Female Reproductive Body," *Shakespeare Quarterly* 40 (Winter 1989).
5. An earlier version of this chapter, published in the *Shakespeare Quarterly*, can be seen as an illustration of the exchange I am attempting to demonstrate between modern criticism and film and stage productions of Shakespeare. Trevor Nunn read my essay as he was preparing to direct the Royal Shakespeare Company's productions of 1 and 2 *Henry IV*, which opened the new Barbican Theatre in London in June of 1982. It is interesting to note that his production featured a Falstaff by Joss Ackland noted for his warmth and humor. While Gerard Murphy gave his Hal a rather sharp-edged and emotionally explosive subtext, his relationship with Falstaff was distinguished by its genial physical humor. Murphy's Hal gave Falstaff a warm bear hug immediately following his mock rejection ("I do. I will."); the two men engaged in hyperbolic horseplay which had them both rolling on the ground and over each other in their meeting on the road to Shrewsbury, where Hal literally tripped over Falstaff, who was preparing for a short nap while Bardolph went in search of sack; and Hal kissed Falstaff as a way of making up after scolding him for his treatment of Doll Tearsheet and Mistress Quickly. These are all instances of a warmth and affection displayed by Hal and Falstaff which my essay had noted were missing in recent stage productions but evident in Welles's film.

Further, several of the opening-night critics responded by stressing that the production placed Falstaff, rather than Hal, at its center. "The

play does not belong to Mr. Murphy. It belongs instead to Falstaff. . . ."
(James Fenton, *Sunday Times*, June 13, 1982); "in performance (largely because Joss Ackland overtops expectation) the tragedy of Falstaff eclipses
the spiritual progress of Hal" (Michael Billington, *Guardian*, June 11,
1982). In Jack Kroll's report for *Newsweek* (June 21, 1982) he adds the
fascinating detail that Ackland revealed he had modeled his characterization "on Orson Welles, as a man who frittered his talent away."

Several critics praised Nunn's staging of the Shrewsbury battle scene
for its chilling and brutal qualities with Billington commenting that
"the fight between Hal and Hotspur . . . has the right sense of two
exhausted heavyweights slugging it out in the fifteenth round," which
only goes to show that newspaper drama critics are also readers of
Shakespeare criticism.

For a full account of Nunn's handling of the Hal-Falstaff relationship
see T. F. Wharton, *Henry IV, Parts* 1 and 2: *Text and Performance* (London:
MacMillan, 1983), pp. 74–79.

6. *The Royal Shakespeare Company's Production of Henry V*, ed. Sally Beauman
(Oxford: Pergamon Press, 1976), p. 53.

7. This was a unique opportunity for Rain because he had played Prince
Hal on the same stage in 1958.

8. Bridget Gellert Lyons, *Chimes at Midnight* (New Brunswick, N.J.: Rut-
gers University Press, 1988).

9. Jack Jorgens, *Shakespeare on Film* (Bloomington and London: Indiana University Press, 1977), and Daniel Seltzer, "Shakespeare's Texts and Modern Productions," in *Reinterpretations of Elizabethan Drama: Selected Papers
from the English Institute*, ed. Norman Rabkin (New York: Columbia University Press, 1969), pp. 89–115.

10. Vincent Canby, *New York Times*, Sunday, March 2, 1975, p. 17.

11. Jorgens, *Shakespeare on Film*, pp. 268–72.

12. Seltzer, "Shakespeare's Texts," pp. 103–4.

13. Ibid., 104–5.

14. Richard France, *The Theater of Orson Welles* (Lewisburg and London: The
Bucknell University Press, 1977), p. 161.

15. Juan Cobos and Miguel Rubio, "Welles and Falstaff," *Sight and Sound* 35
(Autumn 1966), 159.

16. Cobos and Rubio, "Welles and Falstaff," p. 159.

17. Seltzer, "Shakespeare's Texts," p. 105.

18. Cobos and Rubio, "Welles and Falstaff," p. 159. Jack Jorgens enumerates
these farewell moments but does not examine their implications in detail,
being content to allow his listing to conclude with the following sweeping
observation: "Welles portrays people alienated, people driven apart by
death and the forces of history, people betraying each other" (p. 114). I
trust it is no betrayal of Jorgens's fine analysis to insist that more attention needs to be given to the significance of the ways in which Welles's
film says farewell to Falstaff.

19. "Welles on Falstaff," *Cahiers du Cinéma in English*, no. 11 (September 1967): 7.
20. Terry Hands's production for the RSC made another interesting attempt to capture spatially the two-fathers theme. The opening scene was played on a bare platform with only stage right lit by spots; as Henry received the reports of the civil disturbances within the kingdom, the audience gradually became aware of two figures stationed on stage left. One was lying down covered with a blanket. The other stood upstage center equidistant from the busy king and the slumbering body. As the play shifted into its second scene we became aware that the standing figure was Hal who approached the covered body and tried unsuccessfully to rouse it, by a series of buzzing noises. Finally, Hal uncorked a bottle of wine and began to pour it into a huge tankard resting beside the sleeper. The sound of the wine, of course, roused Falstaff into action, and the play had its first laugh before the fat knight had spoken a word.
21. Pauline Kael, *Kiss Kiss Bang Bang* (New York: Bantam Books, 1969), p. 247.
22. Perhaps the finest compliment to Welles's capturing of ignorant armies clashing by day can be illustrated by a personal example. When I first taught this film, my daughter and son (then ages 9 and 7) joined me for one of its screenings. Throughout the unfolding of the Hal-Falstaff relationship prior to the battle scene I was repeatedly bombarded with questions about "who," "what," and "why?" Once the battle sequence began there was a period of long silence, and when my daughter finally offered an observation, she was met with an intense "Shhhhhhhh" from her younger brother, who had become completely engrossed by Welles's surreal landscape.
23. Cobos and Rubio, "Welles and Falstaff," p. 161.
24. Barbara Hodgdon (*The End Crowns All* [Princeton: Princeton University Press, 1991], pp. 164–66) rightly sees that Michael Bogdanov's recent production of the play, contained in his masterful presentation of both tetralogies *The Wars of the Roses*, deliberately quotes Welles's handling of this moment and thus becomes a further example of the exchanges between criticism, film, and stage performance that I am attempting to demonstrate.
25. Hawks made this remark during a television interview with me in April 1976 (televised on WOUB-TV on May 14, 1976). Hawks was in Athens, Ohio to be honored by the Athens International Film Festival and had a seemingly inexhaustible supply of stories which he liberally shared with all.
26. Cobos and Rubio, "Welles and Falstaff," p. 159.
27. Kenneth Tynan, *The Sound of Two Hands Clapping* (New York: Holt, Rinehart and Winston, 1975), p. 170.

# Notes

## Chapter Four

1. Reprinted in Mast and Cohen, eds., *Film Theory and Criticism* (New York: 1974), pp. 338–39.
2. Ihab Hassan, "Pluralism in Postmodern Perspective," *Critical Inquiry* 12 (1986), and "Making Sense: The Trials of Postmodern Discourse," *New Literary History* (1987). I am indebted to my colleague Ray Fitch for calling my attention to Hassan's essays and to his own excellent summary of postmodern literary theory.
3. Hassan, "Making Sense," p. 445.
4. See particularly Michael Bristol, *Carnival and Theater* (London: Routledge, 1985), and Leonard Tennenhouse, *Power on Display* (London: Methuen, 1986).
5. Jack C. Jorgens, *Shakespeare on Film* (Bloomington: Indiana University Press, 1977), pp. 175–90; Anthony Davies, *Filming Shakespeare's Plays* (Cambridge: Cambridge University Press, 1988), pp. 100–18; Peter S. Donaldson, *Shakespearean Films/Shakespearean Directors* (Boston: Unwin Hyman, 1990), pp. 93–126; and Lorne M. Buchman, *Still in Movement* (Oxford: Oxford University Press, 1991), pp. 126–44.
6. Buchman, *Still in Movement*, pp. 142–43.
7. Jorgens, *Shakespeare on Film*, p. 184.
8. Davies, *Filming Shakespeare's Plays*, p. 110.
9. MacLiammoir reveals that Welles had Carpaccio in mind when designing the look and landscape of his production. My examination of several book reprints of Carpaccio's work failed to turn up a painting with a mirror which approximated this one, though Jan van Eyck's "The Marriage of Arnolfini" features a mirror closely resembling Welles's and put to a similar reflective purpose.
10. Donaldson, *Shakespearean Films*, p. 105.
11. Ibid., p. 107.
12. Stanley Cavell, *Disowning Knowledge in Six Plays of Shakespeare* (Cambridge: Harvard University Press, 1987), p. 136.
13. Ibid., p. 137.
14. Michael MacLiammoir, *Put Money in Thy Purse*, 2d ed. (London: Methuen and Erye, 1972), pp. 244–45.
15. MacLiammoir found the dog hateful and repeatedly referred to it as "Ricquette of Mogador."
16. Charles Higham, in his recent biography of Welles, cites several interesting examples of Welles's attention to the film's score provided by Francesco Lavagnino, one of the film score's composers.

> A memorable example of their rapport occurred during the scoring of the steambath scene. . . . Lavagnino had composed somewhat melodramatic music for the sequence but neither he nor Welles was satisfied with it. They sat for a time in silence. They each said

to the other that he had an idea he dared not propose. They agreed they would count to three and then blurt out the concept. They counted to three, then shouted in unison, "Mandolins!" A mandolin accompaniment would be perfect in creating the frenzy of the sequence; in the exuberance of their mutual inspiration, the two men jumped up and embraced, laughing their heads off. And Welles went beyond his inspired composer: he wanted the jangling music to reach a crescendo and then break up with the dissonant sound of the tuning of the instruments. Welles had the score recorded by an orchestra of two hundred but complained that the opening funeral procession dirge sounded like "Tchaikovsky touring in Italy" and had it rescored for harpsichord accompanied by only sixteen instruments and eight voices. (see *Orson Welles: The Rise and Fall of An American Genius* [New York: St. Martin's Press, 1985], p. 268).

17. MacLiammoir, *Put Money in Thy Purse*, p. 28.
18. C. L. Barber and Richard P. Wheeler, *The Whole Journey: Shakespeare's Power of Development* (Berkeley and Los Angeles: University of California Press, 1986), p. 274.
19. Ibid., p. 281.
20. As this book was in press came the good news that Welles's daughter Beatrice had managed to locate the original negative of the film which has been carefully restored by Michael Dawson and Arnie Saks. That version has now been released with strong reviews and perhaps, forty years after winning the top prize at Cannes, it will finally find the audience it deserves.

### CHAPTER FIVE

1. Jack C. Jorgens, *Shakespeare on Film* (Bloomington: Indiana University Press, 1977), pp. 51–78.
2. Jorgens, *Shakespeare on Film*, p. 42.
3. I am indebted to Peter S. Donaldson for the marvelous discovery that the changeling boy was played by the young Kenneth Anger, who became one of the leading underground filmmakers of the 1960s and whose work clearly influenced the style of Derek Jarman's *Tempest*.
4. C. L. Barber, *Shakespeare's Festive Comedy* (Princeton: Princeton University Press, 1959), p. 89.
5. For an interesting view of the film which is less interested in its Shakespearean source than in its Hollywood context, see John Collick's *Shakespeare, Cinema, and Society* (Manchester: Manchester University Press, 1989), pp. 82–93.
6. Janet Dunbar, *J. M. Barrie: The Man behind the Image* (Boston: Houghton Mifflin, 1970), pp. 377–84.

# Notes

7. I am indebted to Andrew Birkin's *J. M. Barrie and the Lost Boys* (New York: Potter, 1979) for its gentle yet thorough documentation of Barrie's lifelong infatuation with little boys.
8. Carolyn Heilbron, *Writing a Woman's Life* (New York: Norton, 1988), p. 93.
9. Stanley Cavell, *Pursuits of Happiness: The Hollywood Comedy of Remarriage* (Cambridge: Harvard University Press, 1981), pp. 142–44.
10. Michael Mullin, "Peter Hall's *Midsummer Night's Dream* on Film," *Educational Theater Journal* (December 1975): pp. 530–31.
11. Quoted in Roger Manvell, *Shakespeare and the Film* (New York: Praeger, 1971), p. 121.
12. Jorgens, *Shakespeare on Film*, p. 59.
13. Jorgens has a particularly effective analysis of this opening scene with the rude mechanicals in contrast to the scene in Theseus's court. See pp. 55–56.
14. Manvell, *Shakespeare and the Film*, p. 123.
15. I should make clear that Hall was well aware that his shooting in a real woods was still highly controlled: "To film Shakespeare out of doors enables me to select what one wants from nature, from actuality. You don't want a total, out-door reality. Selectivity comes through the camera itself, which renders nature in artificial terms to just the right degree." Ibid., p. 122.
16. J. L. Styan, *The Shakespeare Revolution* (Cambridge: Cambridge University Press, 1977), pp. 224–25.
17. For a formalist's response to Jarman's film who found Williams's Prospero the production's only redeeming element, see Frank Kermode's review of *The Tempest* in the *Times Literary Supplement*, May 16, 1980, p. 553.

## CHAPTER SIX

1. Peter Hall, "Shakespeare and the Modern Director," in *Royal Shakespeare Theatre Company: 1960–63*, ed. John Goodwin (London: Max Reinhardt, 1964), p. 42.
2. Hall, "Shakespeare and the Modern Director," p. 41.
3. Hall, *Peter Hall's Diaries: The Story of a Dramatic Battle*, ed. John Goodwin (London: Hamish Hamilton, 1983), p. 223.
4. Kenneth Tynan, *Right and Left* (New York: Atheneum, 1967), p. 3.
5. Michael Billington, "An Interview with Peter Hall," *Plays and Players*, June 1988, p. 9. Hall went on to elaborate:

> I do feel these great works, whether it be Shakespeare or Chekhov or the great masterpieces of the world, are extremely difficult to do. They need going for in their fullness. Therefore you should be very

careful about cutting because that is not just a form of editing, that's
a form of rewriting. . . . If you're doing Shaw, you have to go to the
end of the sentence. If you're doing Shakespeare, you have to
breathe in places which are not natural to modern sense, but they
enable you to play the verse. That's what I mean by classicism. The
form leads you to the truth, not the other way around. . . . No play
speaks for itself; you have to take interpretative decisions and fero-
ciously pursue what you think the man meant.

6. Stanley Wells, *Royal Shakespeare: Four Major Productions at Stratford-Upon-Avon* (Manchester: Manchester University Press, 1977), p. 33.
7. Hall really wanted Finney for *Tamburlaine*—planned as one of six pro-
ductions to open the new building (Hall, *Diaries*, p. 163).
8. Hall, *Diaries*, p. 199.
9. *New York Times*, Sunday July 25, 1976, p. 5.
10. *New York Times*, Sunday December 28, 1976, p. 5.
11. Francis Fergusson, *The Idea of a Theater* (Princeton: Princeton University
Press, 1949), pp. 103–12.
12. Hall's plans to stage both *Tamburlaine* and *The Oresteia* during the National's first seasons on the South Bank underline his epic directorial
mood in the mid-1970s.
13. Judith Cook, *Directors' Theatre* (London: Harrop, 1974), p. 70.
14. Hall's diary entry for October 7, 1975, makes an interesting link between
Hamlet's relationship with Ophelia and his Wittenberg friends:

> Important findings at rehearsal. Hamlet is not so concerned that
> Rosencrantz and Guildenstern are spies; nor is he concerned in the
> Ophelia nunnery scene that he is being overheard. The scenes are
> not about these discoveries; he knows them in a flash. He's con-
> cerned about the honesty of the characters in their replies when he
> charges them with duplicity, and both the scenes show him trying
> to demonstrate his own philosophy, anxiously, vigorously. They are
> a pattern of misunderstandings. (p. 188)

15. Hall, *Diaries*, p. 192.
16. Richard David, *Shakespeare in the Theatre* (Cambridge: Cambridge University Press, 1978), pp. 81–82.
17. Hall, *Diaries*, p. 185.
18. *Sunday Times*, April 12, 1987, p. 55.
19. Michael Levey, *From Giotto to Cezanne* (London: Thames and Hudson,
1962), p. 144.
20. Alison Chitty, "A Pair So Famous," *Plays and Players*, April, 1987, p. 6.
21. Quoted in Jim Hiley, *Theatre at Work* (London: Routledge & Kegan Paul,
1981), p. 8.
22. Hall's intent to link space and psychology in this opening moment was
evident from the first rehearsals as recounted in Tirzah Lowen's *Peter
Hall Directs Antony and Cleopatra* (London: Methuen, 1990), pp. 3–6.

23. Stanley Wells shares my enthusiasm for Dench's performance: "It was Judi Dench, as Cleopatra, who brought greatness to the production in a feat of classical acting by which she extended herself into every aspect of the role, from the sordid to the sublime . . ." *Shakespeare Survey* #41 (Cambridge: Cambridge University Press, 1989), p. 177.

24. Alan C. Dessen and Stanley Wells were also struck by this moment. As Dessen comments, "She [Dench] played the 'past the size of dreaming' sequence in V. ii. with enormous power to a Dolabella standing far downstage [actually on the ramp leading from auditorium to stage] with his back to the audience, so that this invocation of the larger-than-life Antony was directed through him at us (as potential doubters or liars)." "Exploring the Scripts," *Shakespeare Quarterly* 39 (Summer 1988), p. 222. Stanley Wells concludes his description of this scene by observing, "At such moments as these an audience, even in the Olivier Auditorium, can be united in a single emotion." "Shakespeare Performances in London and Stratford, 1986–87," *Shakespeare Survey* #41, p. 178.

25. Dessen, *Shakespeare Quarterly*, p. 222.

26. A measure of Hall's influence and staying power is revealed in the two collections of interviews with leading British directors collected by Judith Cook and published in 1974 and 1989 under the title *Directors' Theatre* (London: Harrop, 1974, and London: Hodder and Stoughton, 1989). Hall is the only director to be included in both volumes, and his influence throughout the 1989 volume is apparent in the remarks of directors as diverse as Adrian Noble, Richard Eyre, Michael Bogdanov, and Alan Ayckbourn.

## CHAPTER SEVEN

1. See Sally Beauman's *The Royal Shakespeare Company: A History of Ten Decades* (Oxford: Oxford University Press, 1982), pp. 319–30 for a full discussion of the founding of The Other Place.

2. Beauman, *Royal Shakespeare*, p. 335.

3. Koltai's remarks came as part of his discussion of the play held in The Other Place on the morning of June 8, 1980. I am indebted to my friend and fellow observer Professor Miriam Gilbert for her notes from Koltai's presentation.

4. Brenda Bruce gives her own fine account of the development of this moment in *Players of Shakespeare*, ed. Philip Brockbank (Cambridge: Cambridge University Press, 1985), pp. 91–101. Brenda's memory is that the fan bashing came after the production opened, but it clearly had its genesis back in February.

5. Saturday, May 17, 1980. Daniels's remarks came as part of a series of Saturday morning discussions of the current season held at The Other Place.

6. For an excellent comparative description of the Olivier-Gielgud and Zeffirelli productions see Jill Levenson's *Shakespeare in Performance: Romeo and Juliet* (Manchester: Manchester University Press, 1987).

## CHAPTER EIGHT

1. In April of 1989 the company announced that Terry Hands would step down as artistic director when his current contract expired in 1991, which means that all the key directors from the Hall-Nunn era have departed from the company. Adrian Noble was appointed the company's new director early in 1990.

2. The production's impact was equally apparent within the company. As Peter Hall has commented, "The Brook-Scofield *Lear* was possibly an even greater revelation inside the company than it was outside" (*Royal Shakespeare Theatre Company: 1960–63* [London: Max Reinhardt, 1964], p. 44). Sally Beauman elaborates: "All of Brook's previous productions at Stratford . . . were the product of his revolutionary theatrical vision, unrelated to other work in the same theatre, pointing the way to new possibilities that were never then explored by other directors. That was not so of *Lear;* in the austerity and simplicity of its staging, in the severity of its costuming, the unsentimentality and rigour of its approach, it chimed with work already being done by the RSC and was afterwards . . . to have a continuing influence on the company's work—an influence detectable immediately the next year in the productions of the *Wars of the Roses.*" (*The Royal Shakespeare Company: A History of Ten Decades* (Oxford: Oxford University Press, 1982), pp. 251–52.

3. From an unpublished interview with the author conducted at the Barbican Theatre on December 16, 1987. Interestingly, the director whose recent debut with the company has been as heralded as Noble's in 1982, Deborah Warner, is distinguished in Joan Dupont's analysis for "productions . . . characterized by bold approaches to stage design and an anachronistic mix of costumes" (*New York Times*, Sunday, April 23, 1989).

4. *Shakespeare Survey* #36 (Cambridge: Cambridge University Press, 1983), p. 152.

5. For Gambon's impact on his fellow actors, see the moving account of their tribute following the opening night performance of *Galileo* recounted in Jim Hiley, *Theatre at Work* (London: Routledge & Kegan Paul, 1981). For a more detailed assessment of his career see Mel Gussow's profile in *New Yorker*, January 28, 1991, pp. 60–77.

6. Interview with Noble, December 16, 1987.

7. Richard Findlater, *Plays and Players*, September 1982, p. 18.

8. Interview with Noble, December 16, 1987.

9. *Shakespeare Survey* #36, p. 152.

10. Findlater, *Plays and Players*, p. 18.

# Notes

11. Kenneth Tynan, *Right and Left* (New York: Atheneum, 1967), p. 131.
12. Noble's association with Bob Crowley follows in the RSC tradition of establishing strong director-designer partnerships, including Peter Hall and John Bury, Trevor Nunn and John Napier, and Terry Hands and Farrah. Robert Brustein has observed, with his usual intelligence, that "Such theater designers are among a director's most cherished colleagues, not just because they help to realize an interpretation of a play, but because they help to formulate it" (*New Republic*, February 1, 1988, p. 28).
13. Irving Wardle, *Times*, December 19, 1985.
14. Nicholas de Jongh, *Guardian*, December 19, 1985.
15. Juliet Stevenson, *Plays and Players*, May 1985, p. 20.
16. Interview with Noble in *Daily Telegraph*, June 6, 1983.
17. Antony Sher, *Year of the King* (London: Methuen, 1985), p. 149.
18. Interview with Noble, December 16, 1987.
19. *New York Times*, November 12, 1990.

## CHAPTER NINE

1. See Barbara Hodgdon, *The End Crowns All* (Princeton: Princeton University Press, 1991) for a detailed comparative discussion of the performance strategies and interpretive angles employed by Hall and Barton, Hands, Bogdanov, and Adrian Noble in their productions of these plays.
2. Bogdanov was an associate director at the National Theatre from 1980–89 but never directed a Shakespeare production there. He accepted in 1988 an appointment as artistic director of the Schauspielhaus in Hamburg.
3. See Christopher McCullough, *The Shakespeare Myth*, ed. Graham Holderness (Manchester: Manchester University Press, 1988), pp. 89–95.
4. Michael Bogdanov, *Plays and Players*, March 1987, p. 11.
5. See Hodgdon, *The End Crowns All*, pp. 88–99, for a more extended discussion of this issue.
6. I saw the initial cycle of three plays (1 and 2 *Henry IV* and *Henry V*) in Toronto in June of 1987 and then the complete cycle of seven plays during the company's month-long residence in Chicago in May of 1988.
7. The microphone was one of many elements which had been edited out of the production between Toronto and Chicago. In this case I thought its removal a mistake, for it would have provided an interesting parallel with the cycle's final moment: Richmond appearing on television to deliver his post-Bosworth Field speech to the nation uniting the white rose with the red.
8. This may explain why critics in America and Australia were more enthusiastic about the productions than their English counterparts.

[ 187 ]

9. Bogdanov confirms that his linkage of stage and costume design was meant to approximate "the eclectic theatre of expediency as practiced by the Elizabethans." His production team's intent was to "free our, and the audiences', imaginations by allowing an eclectic mix of costumes and props, choosing a time and a place that was most appropriate for a character or scene. Modern dress one moment, medieval, Victorian or Elizabethan the next" (Michael Bogdanov and Michael Pennington, *The English Shakespeare Company: The Story of the Wars of the Roses, 1986–1989* [London: Nick Hern Books 1990], pp. 28–29).

10. I owe this observation to my son, who joined me for both productions and whose eye was quicker to catch the details of dress when wayward son meets disapproving father.

11. Pennington literally bawled out "I am your son" rather than delivering it as a cool matter-of-fact statement, which perhaps prepared for the emotional intensity Pennington invested in his response to Falstaff's usurpation of the credit for Hotspur's death at the close of *1 Henry IV.*

12. Louis Marder, *Shakespeare Newsletter* (Spring 1988), p. 10. "Costuming was what the actors could find. Soldiers and officers wore medieval armor, Cromwellian uniforms, full dress (French?) military dress, uniforms of WWI and II, the idea being to save money and to show that war was a universal and ageless activity" (p. 78).

13. See Tzvetan Todorow, *Mikhail Bakhtin: The Dialogical Principle* (Minneapolis: University of Minnesota Press, 1984), p. 78.

14. Ernest Kris, "Prince Hal's Conflict," in *Psychoanalytic Explorations in Art* (New York: International Universities Press, 1952), pp. 273–88.

15. See Harry Berger, Jr., *Imaginary Audition* (Berkeley and Los Angeles: University of California Press, 1989), pp. 47–73, for interesting critical resonances with Pennington's playing of these scenes.

16. John Peter, *Sunday Times*, March 29, 1987.

17. See Macd. P. Jackson, *"The Wars of the Roses:* The English Shakespeare Company on Tour," *Shakespeare Quarterly*, 40, no. 2 (1989), p. 211, for an excellent reading of how this moment parallels Bogdanov's handling of violence throughout the cycle.

18. Bogdanov and Pennington, *The English Shakespeare Company*, pp. 54–55. Bogdanov also acknowledges that his staging of *1 Henry IV* 2.3 with Hotspur shaving was inspired by Welles's filming of the scene with Hotspur bathing.

19. Roger Warren, *Shakespeare Quarterly*, 38, no. 3 (1987), p. 360.

20. Gerald Berkowitz, *Shakespeare Quarterly*, 38, no. 4 (1987), p. 499.

21. Hodgdon, *The End Crowns All*, p. 210.

22. One of the many virtues of Bogdanov's epic undertaking is the series of interesting subtexts created by the necessity for each actor to play many parts. Andrew Jarvis's roles, in particular, are instructive. He moved from playing Richard II's murderer, Exton, to Gadshill (with a wonder-

ful punk, rainbow-colored Mohawk haircut), to Douglas, to the Dauphin, to Richard III: a series of rebels, malcontents, and murderers. When the production entered its fourth and final year Jarvis added Hotspur to his repertoire. As Eric Sams reports: "As Hotspur, even his gait has a Northern accent; as the Dauphin, he struts in French. His Richard of Gloucester, Duke and King, presents the high profile of a killing eagle, with humped shoulders, bald head, and the ominous matching movements of sudden lift and swoop" (*Times Literary Supplement*, February 2–March 2, 1989).

23. Here, for example, is John Peter's reaction: "Some of the comic business is coarse beyond belief. When Henry V sets off for France, thuggish youngsters strut about giving the Nazi salute and a poster reads: Fuck the Frogs! Now Shakespeare was neither a chauvinistic thug nor a left wing pacifist, and this sort of rabble-rousing rubbish distorts and vulgarizes his cool, tough line on power politics" (*Sunday Times*, March 29, 1987). I would agree with Bogdanov that Shakespeare creates Pistol precisely to vulgarize and distort Henry V's cool, tough line on power politics.

24. Bogdanov confirms that the source for this device comes from the opening chapter of Jan Kott's *Shakespeare Our Contemporary*. See Bogdanov and Pennington, *The English Shakespeare Company*, p. 119.

## CHAPTER TEN

1. Peter S. Donaldson, "Taking on Shakespeare: Kenneth Branagh's *Henry V*," *Shakespeare Quarterly*, 42 (Spring 1991), pp. 60–71.
2. Donaldson, "Taking on Shakespeare," p. 61.
3. Kenneth Branagh, *Beginning* (London: Chatto & Windus, 1989), p. 139.
4. Branagh, *Beginning*, p. 222.
5. See Norman Rabkin, *Shakespeare and the Problem of Meaning* (Chicago: University of Chicago Press, 1981), pp. 33–62.
6. Branagh, *Beginning*, p. 133.
7. See Donaldson's "Taking on Shakespeare," pp. 66–68, for an excellent analysis of the entire series of such intimate moments in the film.
8. See Branagh's article on playing Henry V in *Players of Shakespeare* 2, ed. Russell Jackson and Robert Smallwood (Cambridge: Cambridge University Press, 1988), p. 102.
9. Kenneth Branagh, *Henry V: A Screen Adaptation* (London: Chatto & Windus, 1989), pp. 34–35. I find Branagh's fleeting incorporation of Falstaff material from 1 and 2 *Henry IV*, which often strikes me as just a confusing mixture of Falstaff's "greatest hits," the least successful aspect of his film. Donaldson's account almost convinces me that Branagh has truly integrated them into his conception of both film and king.

10. I am indebted to Katherine Eggert for first pointing this textual appropriation out to me, though I have since discovered that Terry Hands's 1975 production with Alan Howard as the king made the same reassignment. See Sally Beauman, ed., *The Royal Shakespeare Company's Production of Henry V* (Oxford: Pergamon Press, 1976), p. 231.

# INDEX

# Index

# Index

# Index

# Index

# A Note about the Author

Samuel Crowl is Professor of English at Ohio University where he has taught since 1970. He has published articles on stage and film productions of Shakespeare in such journals as *Shakespeare Quarterly* and *Shakespeare Survey*. He has delivered papers at the Modern Language Association, the Shakespeare Association of America, the World Shakespeare Congress, and the Ohio Shakespeare Conference, as well as lecturing at several colleges and universities across the country. From 1981–1992 he served as Dean of the University College. He has twice been honored for distinguished teaching and has played an active role in developing and implementing Ohio University's core curriculum which received a Program Excellence Award from the Ohio Board of Regents in 1990. He is a Fellow of the Royal Society for the Arts and held an Observership with the Royal Shakespeare Company in 1980.